Curriculum and Assessment in English 3 to 11

C000148187

Curriculum and Assessment in English 3 to 11: A Better Plan provides an overview of the subject in considerable breadth and depth, and offers a clear, balanced and forceful critique of the current language and literacy curriculum and its assessment arrangements for 3- to 11-year-olds in England, and of developments in the area during the past thirty years.

The book restates fundamental truths about how pupils speak, read and write English with confidence and control. It describes how English can be taught most effectively, calls for an urgent review of some aspects of the current National Curriculum and its associated tests, and – crucially – proposes viable alternatives. This invaluable resource for those working in English, language and literacy education has a wide perspective and takes a principled and informed pedagogical approach.

Based on a series of much-admired booklets released by the UKLA in 2015, this accessible guide to both theory and practice will be of interest to teachers, student teachers, teacher-educators, advisers and policy-makers in the UK and internationally.

John Richmond has a breadth of experience as a classroom English teacher and advisory teacher in London, a local-authority English adviser, an officer on the National Writing Project and the Language in the National Curriculum Project (both in the UK), and a commissioning editor in educational television in the UK and the USA.

Andrew Burn has worked as a teacher of English, media and drama in schools in Cambridgeshire. He is Professor of English, Media and Drama at the UCL Institute of Education, UK.

Peter Dougill has been an English and drama teacher in schools in the south of England, a local-authority English adviser, Chief Inspector in the London Borough of Wandsworth, an HMI and an adviser to the government's education department. He is Senior Visiting Research Fellow at the University of Sussex, and an independent educational consultant in the UK.

Mike Raleigh has been an English teacher in Leicestershire and London, Deputy Warden of the ILEA English Centre, a local-authority English adviser and Deputy County Education Officer in Shropshire, and an HMI. He was Divisional Manager in Ofsted, Regional Director of the National Strategies in England, and an adviser to the Department for Education.

Peter Traves has been an English teacher in London, a local-authority English adviser, headteacher, and Director of Children's Services in Staffordshire. He is an independent educational consultant in the UK.

Curriculum and Assessment in English 3 to 11

A Better Plan

John Richmond
Andrew Burn, Peter Dougill,
Mike Raleigh and Peter Traves

Routledge
Taylor & Francis Group

LONDON AND NEW YORK

First published 2017
by Routledge
2 Park Square, Milton Park, Abingdon, Oxon OX14 4RN

and by Routledge
711 Third Avenue, New York, NY 10017

Routledge is an imprint of the Taylor & Francis Group, an informa business

British Library Cataloguing in Publication Data
A catalogue record for this book is available from the British Library

Library of Congress Cataloging in Publication Data
A catalog record for this book has been requested

ISBN: 978-0-415-78451-1 (hbk)
ISBN: 978-0-415-78452-8 (pbk)
ISBN: 978-1-315-22846-4 (ebk)

Typeset in Helvetica Neue
by Swales & Willis Ltd, Exeter, Devon, UK

Download the eResources from: www.routledge.com/9780415784528

Printed and bound in Great Britain by
TJ International Ltd, Padstow, Cornwall

Contents

Preface

Most of the words in this book have had a former life; some have had two. The book draws on the contents of a series of ten booklets, published in June and September 2015 by the United Kingdom Literacy Association and Owen Education, an independent school-improvement agency. The series was entitled *English, Language and Literacy 3 to 19: Principles and Proposals*. This book, as is clear from its title, is addressed to teachers in Early Years settings and primary schools. It is published simultaneously with a volume addressed to secondary-school and college teachers, entitled *Curriculum and Assessment in English 11 to 19: A Better Plan*.

The idea for the series was brought to me by Peter Dougill and Mike Raleigh, then directors of Owen Education. They saw the need for a restatement of basic principles about the learning of English throughout the years of schooling, for a detailed critique of some aspects of government requirements in England to do with the English curriculum and with testing and examinations in English, and for the putting forward of practical, educationally better alternatives. Eve Bearne and David Reedy then kindly agreed on behalf of UKLA to jointly finance the publication of the booklets with Owen Education. The four people named here have greatly influenced and guided the project at every stage.

Later in 2015, the Centre for Literacy in Primary Education, the National Association of Advisers in English, the National Association for the Teaching of English and the United Kingdom Literacy Association jointly sponsored the online publication on their websites of summaries of some of the material in the ten booklets. These appeared in 2016. Louise Johns-Shepherd at CLPE, John Hickman at NAAE, Barbara Conridge, Paul Clayton and Bethan Marshall at NATE, and Eve Bearne, Andrew Lambirth and David Reedy at UKLA were responsible for this initiative.

I have been the lead author on the series of booklets and the online publications, but three of the booklets – those entitled *Reading 7 to 16*, *Media* and *English 16 to 19* – were written by Peter Traves, Andrew Burn and Angela Goddard respectively. Shorter versions of the first two of those booklets have become Chapters 3 and 8 of this book; their authorship is acknowledged there. Andrew Burn is also responsible for the media element of the alternative curriculum in Chapter 11.

As well as thanking those already named for their invaluable help in bringing the project to fruition, I – on my own behalf and that of my fellow authors – should make some further acknowledgements.

For comments on drafts of one or more of the booklets, thanks to: Myra Barrs, Eve Bearne, Barbara Bleiman, Ronald Carter, Margaret Clark, Henrietta Dombey, Joe Elliott, Deirdre Finan, Rosie Flewitt, Veronica Frankland, Peter Harris, John Hickman, Lesley Lancaster, Bethan Marshall, Myfanwy Marshall, Bronwyn Mellor, Nicholas McGuinn, David Reedy, Helen Savva and Claire Widgery.

I owe long-term debts to Myra Barrs (early writing), Ronald Carter (grammar and knowledge about language), Margaret Clark (early reading and writing), Henrietta Dombey (early reading) and Claire Widgery (drama) for their influence on my understanding in those areas, over and beyond their immediate help with drafts of the text.

Frank Monaghan closely guided all the writing about the needs and achievements of learners of English as an additional language.

Pamela Dix supplied detailed information for the section on libraries in Chapter 3.

Theo Bryer, David Buckingham, James Durran, Craig Morrison, Becky Parry, Anthony Partington, John Potter, Mandy Powell and Mark Reid greatly influenced the ideas which Andrew Burn advances in Chapter 8.

Bronwyn Mellor proofread the text of all ten booklets; her careful work is evident in the text here.

John Hardcastle, first, and Andrew Burn, later, arranged for me to receive a Visiting Research Associateship at the University College London Institute of Education, which gave me access to the Institute's library and its comprehensive collection of books and research papers.

I thank Nicholas McGuinn, whose book *The English Teacher's Drama Handbook* supplied all the information in Chapter 7 on the history of the theory and practice of drama teaching.

I thank the English and Media Centre for permission to quote extensively from *Spotlight on Literacy: Creative Interventions in English and Across the Curriculum*. I thank the Centre for Literacy in Primary Education for permission to quote extensively from *Understanding Spelling* by Olivia O'Sullivan and Anne Thomas; from *The Reader in the Writer* by Myra Barrs and Valerie Cork; and from the Centre's The Power of Reading project. I thank David Wray and Maureen Lewis for permission to quote extensively from their *Extending Literacy: Children Reading and Writing Non-Fiction*, published by Routledge.

My deepest gratitude is to my wife Helen Savva, who has supported and sustained me in every way throughout the project.

John Richmond

Introduction

John Richmond, Peter Dougill and Mike Raleigh

The purpose of this book is easily stated. There should, in the second decade of the twenty-first century, be a professional consensus amongst those who teach English to children and young people, or who teach children and young people *in* English, as to how to help them most effectively gain confidence and competence in the use of English. Although this consensus should exist, in practice it does not. The book aims to describe a desirable, intellectually sound and practically achievable consensus around which those who teach English or teach *in* English could unite.

By 'those who teach English or teach *in* English', we mean, for the purposes of this book, teachers of children aged from 3 to 11 in Early Years settings and primary schools.

There is a particular urgency in our purpose, since all contemporary commentators agree that, whatever progress has been made overall in raising the achievement of learners in English, language and literacy, there is still a large gap between the highest and the lowest achievers. There are still far too many children and young people who are failing to become competent and confident users of English when there is no valid reason, in terms of their potential, why they *should* fail. Those most at risk of failure are learners from socio-economically poorer backgrounds.

Key principles

We believe that the best work on the development of language and literacy draws on seven basic principles.

1 There is no intellectual achievement more intimately connected to a child's and young person's overall sense of worth as an individual and as a social being than the achievement of competence and confidence in the use of her or his language or languages.

2   The achievement of competence in any aspect of language is prior to and more complex than the achievement of the ability to analyse that aspect of language. Learners nonetheless continually engage in acts of reflection on aspects of the language they encounter and use.

3   The achievement of competence in any aspect of language is principally owed to the enjoyable *experience* of that aspect of language. *Instruction* in an aspect of language has a secondary but nonetheless very significant role to play in this achievement.

4   The learner's brain makes dynamic generalisations from enjoyable experiences of language. These generalisations prepare the learner for new encounters with and uses of language.

5   The motivation for any productive or receptive encounter with or use of language is the desire and need to construct meaning. Producers and receivers of language are both engaged in the construction of meaning.

6   Examples of language and literacy in use in English and of potential value and interest to learners are vast in number and diversity. Some of that diversity should be evident in the selection of examples which teachers present to learners.

7   Learners' experience of language in education should both value and confirm their linguistic, cultural and social backgrounds, and introduce them to cultural and social contexts beyond those they are familiar with.

The seven principles are stated here at a level of generality and abstraction which probably seems high-flown and dry. We shall try to invest them with a living practicality later on. In the meantime, it may be asked: What is so remarkable about them? Are they not self-evident, uncontroversial? The answer is: They should be, but they haven't been. The reason why they haven't been has something to do with the history of the contest for control of the teaching of English, language and literacy in our schools over several decades. It also has to do with the fact that worthwhile professional knowledge can sometimes be forgotten or get lost in the welter of new initiatives and changes of direction – often politically driven – affecting the curriculum.

The argument: truths restated

The rest of this book puts detailed flesh onto the bare bones of the seven principles. It makes no great claims to originality. It attempts to restate, sometimes even to exhume, truths about the effective learning of English which, as we have just said, have been forgotten or got lost, have indeed frequently been sidelined, sneered at, buried by those in power. The book represents the realisation that ground gained is not ground won forever; that truths can easily be overturned, ground can easily be taken back by forces of ignorant, retrospective reaction with the power to do so.

The National Curriculum for English

Chapters 1 to 8 also contain detailed critiques of the latest version of the National Curriculum for English at Key Stages 1 and 2, statutory in state schools in England other than academies and free schools as from September 2014 or September 2015 (Department for Education, 2014a). (We return below to the point about academies' and free schools' exemption from the legal force of the National Curriculum.) Here, we offer some general remarks.

The English orders then . . .

In the late 1980s, when the idea of a National Curriculum was proposed, we welcomed the principle that all children and young people in state schools have a common entitlement to a range of knowledge, understanding, competences and skills in the major school subjects.

The first version of the National Curriculum for English (Department of Education and Science and the Welsh Office, 1990), which was statutory as from 1989 and 1990, was over-detailed and contained some absurdities, notably to do with its system of ten attainment levels. But there was also much to praise: the document demonstrated an overall understanding that the learning and use of language by children and young people, both as producers and receivers, are essentially to do with the making of meaning. It disappointed the government of the day, which had seen its introduction as an opportunity to return classroom practice to an imagined golden past in which 'rigour' had prevailed: a time before the spread of sloppy, optimistic notions of 'creativity' which the so-called 'education establishment' was supposed to have smuggled into schools more recently.

. . . and now

We knew then and we know now that dualisms like 'rigour versus creativity', slogans like 'back to basics', bandied about by Secretaries of State for

Education then and since, have no basis in reality. Language, possibly the most advanced and delicate of human inventions, is both profoundly creative *and* profoundly structural. In spite of and in wilful opposition to this simple, central insight, governments of all colours since 1989, in the course of many revisions of the National Curriculum for English, have returned to the site of their disappointment: determined to impose an English curriculum freighted with detailed instructions to do with *method* and drawing its inspiration from the same regretful, simplistic vision of the way things had once been that had motivated the government a generation ago. This vision was and is a fantasy, but a politically advantageous one: 'back to basics' plays well in large sections of the media and burnishes ministers' credentials as tough, no-nonsense defenders of standards, as scourges of 'trendy teachers'.

Some of the most important instructions in the new National Curriculum for English are plainly wrong. As John Richmond argues in detail in Chapter 2, young children do *not* become fluent readers as a result of the exclusive application of *only* one method of teaching reading – the conscious internalisation of long lists of grapho-phonic correspondences. As he argues in detail in Chapter 4, they do *not* become correct spellers by learning dozens of abstract spelling rules from the age of five. Neither, as he argues in both Chapter 4 and Chapter 6, do they acquire grammatical competence in speech and writing by being introduced early to heavy loads of abstract grammatical concepts and terminology.

The government White Paper on education, *Educational Excellence Everywhere*, published in March 2016 (Department for Education, 2016a), proudly asserts, repeatedly and in successive paragraphs:

> *We believe that outcomes matter more than methods, and that there is rarely one, standardised solution that will work in every classroom for government to impose.*
>
> (paragraph 1.17)

> *The elected government should set out the outcomes – what needs to be achieved for the public money invested in education. But we start from the basis that the country's best school leaders know what works, and that good, enthusiastic leaders should be able to use their creativity, innovation, professional expertise and up-to-date evidence to drive up standards.*
>
> (paragraph 1.18)

> *So this government will very rarely dictate how these outcomes should be achieved – it will encourage and support teachers and leaders to develop*

the best possible solutions for their pupils, and will hold them to account for
rigorous, fairly-measured outcomes.

(paragraph 1.19)

Such noble sentiments! We endorse them whole-heartedly! If only they rep-resented the truth. The truth, so far as some key elements of the new English orders are concerned, is the opposite. We have come to the point where teachers of English in primary schools in England are effectively treated as machine operators, given sets of instructions narrowly related to method, and told to follow them. This is a woeful state of affairs.

If there are sins of commission in the new orders, there are also sins of omission or inadequacy. For example, as discussed in Chapter 1, the whole of the spoken English language, from Year 1 to Year 6, is dealt with in an undifferentiated 132 words: an excessive brevity which is ironically welcome, in that it does not at least prevent teachers from teaching well. Meanwhile, as discussed in various chapters, the orders decisively turn their back on the multimodal, digital, electronic world of information, communication and enter-tainment in which almost all children and young people now participate. Media education (see Chapter 8) has been expunged. The references to drama in the orders (see Chapter 7) carry no coherence laterally – to do with the range of dramatic activities which a learner should be encountering at a particular Key Stage – nor any sense of progression chronologically.

An alternative curriculum

This book is not the first critique of the new English orders. But it may be the first to propose, in detail, a different way of doing things. Chapter 11 is an entire alternative curriculum for English 3 to 11: more rigorous, in the proper sense of that word, than the government's effort, and much better balanced. Our alternative English curriculum derives its principles from the work of some of those who have, over many decades, thought most deeply and written most persuasively about how effective language development in English occurs, and whose work is reviewed in Chapters 1 to 8.

The non-National Curriculum

England is currently (2017) in the incongruous position of having a majority of state secondary schools and a growing minority of primary schools – those that are academies and free schools – which have been released from the obligation to follow the National Curriculum at all. Why go to all the trouble of designing a legally enforced National Curriculum and then abandon the principle of general entitlement? This is an incoherent and inequitable position. Either have legal enforcement for all – and the logic of this position, utopian as it may seem, would be to include independent schools within the scope of the legal enforcement – or achieve a broad national consensus on the knowledge, skills and understanding which children and young people are entitled to have gained in each curriculum subject at various stages of their schooling, without the need for legal enforcement.

By the purest of ironies, this was, for a brief moment, exactly the implication of the government's announcement in its March 2016 Budget statement, followed up in detail in the White Paper from which we have already quoted, that all state schools in England must, by law, become academies by 2022. The White Paper said:

> *We will embed a knowledge-based curriculum as the cornerstone of an excellent, academically rigorous education up to the age of 16, establishing the national curriculum as an ambitious benchmark which autonomous academies can use and improve upon.*
>
> (Department for Education, 2016a: paragraph 1.55a)

Two months later, the government changed its mind about requiring all schools to become academies, in the face of hostile opposition from the teaching profession (which it might well have ignored) and its own rebellious back-benchers and Conservative local councillors (whom it could not ignore). But it still sees universal 'academisation' as an 'aspiration'. In these circumstances, the invitation to 'use and improve upon' the National Curriculum is intriguing: Chapter 11 is a detailed proposal for the direction such improvement might take at Key Stages 1 and 2.

Tests and examinations in English

Unfortunately, the eventual liberation being offered to all state schools in England with regard to the content of the curriculum is not being equivalently offered with regard to tests and examinations. As the government undoubtedly understands, legally binding tests and examinations on which schools' effectiveness is judged will constrain teaching much more effectively than will curricular requirements, particularly if those requirements are transmuted to a 'benchmark' to be 'used and improved upon'.

Even more unfortunately, there is a great deal wrong with current and proposed tests and examinations in English across the entire 3-to-11 age range. Here we summarise the main points.

A broadly good assessment instrument for the Early Years – the Early Years Foundation Stage profile – was, until April 2016, in danger of being unnecessarily and unhelpfully elbowed aside by baseline assessment. Fortunately, baseline assessment has, at least for the time being, been abandoned for accountability purposes.

The Year 1 phonics check, with its absurd requirement that children should sound out words that don't exist, fails to appreciate what succeeding readers *can* do, and to detect what failing readers *can't* do, because learning to read is a more complex process than the assignment of regular phonic responses to regular graphic signals, necessary and useful as that part of a reader's equipment is.

The testing arrangements at Year 6 dismember the whole, complex activities of reading and writing by testing grammar, punctuation and spelling separately from them. From the summer of 2016, this incoherence is replicated at Year 2.

No attempt is now made to assess pupils' achievement in the spoken language at Key Stages 1 and 2.

Alternatives in assessment

Critiques of tests and examinations 3 to 11 appear briefly in Chapters 1 to 8. As we equivalently do for the curriculum, we propose a complete set of alternatives for assessment in Chapter 12.

As will be seen, we are not 'anti-testing'; we recognise that a government has a right, indeed a responsibility, to know how well its schools are performing. Our proposals, however, are based on the principle that assessment should *follow* the curriculum, not lead it. Government and professionals should first decide on a curriculum which embodies what we know about effective learning; then design assessment arrangements which discover, as delicately as possible, the extent to which effective learning is taking place. Many of the current and imminent tests and examinations in English operate on the reverse of this principle.

The Early Years

Although the National Curriculum and tests at Key Stages 1 and 2 receive the lion's share of attention in the book, we also discuss in detail curriculum and assessment 3 to 5.

The Early Years Foundation Stage is considered along with Key Stages 1 and 2 in Chapters 1 to 5, 7 and 8. It forms the first part of each of the sections of the alternative curriculum 3 to 11 in Chapter 11. As already mentioned, its assessment arrangements are discussed as part of Chapter 12.

Learners of English as an additional language and speakers of non-standard varieties of English

Similar but not identical things may be said about each of the major elements of English as they apply to learners of English as an additional language (EAL) and to speakers of non-standard varieties of English. To avoid repetition across the other chapters, the needs and achievements of EAL learners and of speakers of non-standard varieties of English have their own chapters: 9 and 10.

A desirable consensus

It should have been possible nearly 30 years ago, and it should be possible now, to achieve a consensus uniting professionals and the government on the question of how children and young people come to learn English most effectively. That, as we said in the first paragraph of this introduction, is the purpose of this book. Its authors share a passionate concern that our children's and young people's schooling should equip them with a confident control of English – whether as first or additional language – and show them the pleasure that is to be had in its use. To have confidence, to exercise control and to take pleasure might be regarded as *the* essential characteristics of successful speakers, readers and writers of English or any language.

No one will disagree with these last remarks. It remains a matter of deep regret, however, and a disservice to our children and young people, that the professional opinions represented in this book are so often at variance with legislation on the curriculum and assessment in English in England. In the book, we express our criticisms of aspects of government policy in terms that

are sometimes robust, but we hope never destructive. Every negative criticism is accompanied by a positive suggestion for an alternative way of doing
things. Whether, in the immediate term, our alternative suggestions have any
effect on the policy of the government in England is a matter of doubt. But
we hope that they will be seen as a constructive contribution to the debate in
the medium and longer term and, for the present, as an encouragement and
a support to those many practitioners – in England, in the United Kingdom as a
whole and in the English-speaking world more widely – who share our passion
and our concern.

1 Talk

John Richmond

Summary of main points

Speech, and attention to speech through listening, are fundamental to learning.

The spoken language is the mode of language from which competence in all the other modes springs. Literacy could not have come into being historically without the prior existence of speech; it cannot take root and flourish in the human competence of every potentially literate person without that prior existence.

The teacher has a crucial role in guiding learners' use of the spoken language and in setting contexts in which learners can practise and extend their competence in spoken language through acts of learning.

To be productive, group talk – in groups of whatever size – needs a clear structure and purpose, which it is the teacher's responsibility to provide. That structure and that purpose may be very simple: one open question and a time limit. Or it may be more complex, involving a series of tasks to be undertaken. Sometimes the teacher will be an active participant in learners' talk, sometimes not.

Group talk may well involve the other modes of language: reading and writing. But it should not become an automatic preliminary to writing. Talk should be regarded as work of equivalent status and seriousness to other kinds of work.

A key aspect of the teacher's skill is in setting tasks for learners which make demands at the edge of but not beyond the reach of their existing state of knowledge or grasp of concepts. When that happens, the value of collaborative talk, in terms of insights gained and difficulties overcome, may most clearly be seen.

Pupil talk should, over time, embrace a range of purposes and take a range of forms, from the more exploratory through to the more presentational, from the more tentative to the more declaratory, from the more collaborative to the more individual.

Some 17 per cent of the UK school population now speak English as an additional language. These speakers range from new arrivals speaking no or very little English to advanced bi- or multilingual speakers who out-perform their monolingual English peers. Support for these learners should take the form of an adapted version of the means by which teachers support the development of monolingual English speakers, not a different kind of pedagogy.

The teacher's approach to learners who have access to a variety or varieties of English other than Standard English must be based on respect for the language of the learner's culture and community.

The government's new legal requirements for the spoken language at Key Stages 1 and 2 are insufficiently detailed. Chapter 11 offers a much fuller alternative curriculum for the spoken language 3 to 11.

Voices from the past

Seven admirers on learning to talk

Linguists, psychologists and educationists compete with each other in expressions of wonderment at the intellectual achievement of almost all children in the first two or three years of life. Here is Roger Brown, the American social psychologist and expert in children's language development, writing in 1968:

> *Most children, by the time they are ready to begin school, know the full contents of an introductory text in transformational grammar. One such text is a bit more than 400 pages long and it covers declaratives and interrogatives, affirmatives and negatives, actives and passives, simple sentences, conjoined sentences and some kinds of embedded sentences. The preschool child knows all this. Not explicitly, of course. He has not formulated his grammatical knowledge and he cannot talk about it in transformational or any other terms. His knowledge is implicit, implicit in the range of sentences he understands and in the range he is able to construct.*
>
> (Brown, 1968: v)

Here is Lev Vygotsky, the Russian psychologist, writing in the early 1930s (but published in English in 1962) and referring to the work of the German psychologist William Stern:

the most important discovery [made by previous investigators about the genetic roots of thought and speech] is that at a certain moment at about the age of two the curves of development of thought and speech, till then separate, meet and join to initiate a new form of behavior. Stern's [1914] account of this momentous event was the first and the best. He showed how the will to conquer language follows the first dim realization of the purpose of speech, when the child 'makes the greatest discovery of his life', that 'each thing has its name'. [We might add that, for the bi- or multilingual child, each thing has more than one name.]

This crucial instant, when speech begins to serve intellect, and thoughts begin to be spoken, is indicated by two unmistakable objective symptoms: (1) the child's sudden, active curiosity about words, his question about every new thing, 'What is this?' and (2) the resulting rapid . . . increases in his vocabulary.

(Vygotsky, 1962: 43)

Here is Korney Chukovsky, the Russian children's poet, in a work published in English in 1963:

To be sure, in order to learn language, the child imitates adults in his word creativity. It would be nonsense to claim that he adds to a language in any way. Without suspecting it himself, he directs all his efforts, by means of analogies, toward assimilating the linguistic riches gradually developed by many generations of adults. But the young child adapts these analogies with such skill, with such sensitivity to the meaning and significance of the elements from which words are formed, that it is impossible not to be enthralled by the power of his understanding, awareness, and memory, so apparent in the very arduous efforts he makes every time he speaks.

(Chukovsky, 1963, quoted in Rosen and Rosen, 1973: 55)

Here is Michael Halliday, the British-born linguist, in his famous 1975 study of his son's language development, *Learning How to Mean*:

It seems sensible to assume that neither the linguistic system itself, nor the learning of it by the child, can be adequately expressed except by reference to some higher level of semiotic organisation [by which Halliday means a system-based resource for meaning] . . . The child's task is to construct the system of meanings that represents his own model of social reality. This process takes place inside his own head; it is a cognitive process. But it takes place in contexts of social interaction, and there is no way it can take place except in these contexts. As well as being a cognitive process, the learning of the mother tongue is also an interactive process. It takes the form of the continued exchange of meanings between self and others. The act of meaning is a social act.

(Halliday, 1975: 139–140)

And here is James Britton, the British educationist, writing in 1970:

It is, everyone agrees, a colossal task that the child accomplishes when he learns to speak, and the fact that he does so in so short a period of time challenges explanation. We can imagine ourselves cast up on a remote island and living with people whose language we did not know, whose alphabet we could not read: in the course of time, in the course of a great deal of activity where action and speech have gone together, we might succeed in resolving the stream of spoken sound into segments with meaning – given of course that we have infinite curiosity and patience and that the people around us have infinite patience and goodwill! But the endless streams of undifferentiated sound represent only one of two problems that face an infant learning his mother tongue. There is for him also the endless stream of undifferentiated experience. This is something we can imagine only imperfectly, for once in any language we have organized experience to form an objectified world we can never reverse the process.

(Britton, 1970: 36–37)

It was Andrew Wilkinson who coined the term 'oracy', and proposed in 1965 that oracy is to speaking and listening what literacy is to writing and reading. Wilkinson extended his definition as follows:

Oracy comes from practice in specific situations, whether these occur naturally in the classroom, or elsewhere, or are created as a specific teaching device. It is helped by unconscious invitation, it is stimulated by the response of others, and speech becomes clear in the necessity of communication. The main job of the teacher is to provide situations which call forth increasing powers of utterance [and, we might add, of comprehension].

(Wilkinson with Davies and Atkinson, 1965: 63)

Our final admirer is one who qualifies her admiration with a warning: it is that we should not be so overwhelmed by this admiration for the preschool child's achievement in learning spoken language that we assume the job is done by the time the child comes to school. The job is very far from done. Katharine Perera, in *Children's Writing and Reading: Analysing Classroom Language* (1984), which despite its title has plenty to say about spoken language too, has a chapter on the acquisition of grammar. This shows, with detailed examples, that development towards mastery of more complex grammatical structures continues throughout the school years. Perera concludes the chapter thus:

> *During the Seventies, it was commonplace for books on language acquisi-*
> *tion to suggest that, apart from vocabulary, children had virtually completed*
> *the learning of their mother tongue by the age of five; for example, Slobin*
> *(1971: 40) wrote: 'a little child . . . masters the exceedingly complex struc-*
> *ture of his native language in the course of a short three or four years' . . .*
>
> *although children have acquired a remarkable amount of language by*
> *the time they start school, the developmental process continues, albeit at*
> *a slower rate, until they are in their teens.* [For the speaker of English as an additional language, we might add, the developmental process may begin at any time during schooling.]
>
> *There are many grammatical constructions that are more likely to occur after*
> *five than before – some, indeed, that are not at all frequent until adolescence.*
>
> (Perera, 1984: 156)

Five points of agreement

Whatever detailed differences there may be between the many thinkers who have studied early language development, there is agreement on at least these five points:

1 'Language' and 'thought' are not two words to describe the same thing, either in a newborn baby's head or at all. However, a moment (or perhaps a series of moments, or perhaps a period) arrives when the two become linked and interpenetrating in the child's conscious and unconscious mental activities. This linkage is immensely significant and an essential gateway to future learning.

2 The learning of spoken language is not merely a continuing act of imita-tion. Imitation is there, to be sure, but far more powerful is the continuing generalising act which young children perform, whereby they infer patterns, tendencies and rules from the raw material of the language they hear, and apply those inferences to the making of utterances whose collections of

words, arranged in certain orders and in some cases varying their form according to context, they have never heard before.

3 The learning of spoken language is essentially social and dialogic. Language awareness and competence grow as a result of a constant process of language exchange and interaction with others.

4 Full meaning precedes full linguistic expression of meaning. When a child says 'Milk!', the adult can interpret that single word as 'I would like some milk', or 'Please give me some milk'. But to the child, the whole meaning (which the adult needs several words to express) is held within one word. As development proceeds, single-word and very short utterances give way to grammatically more complex utterances. At the same time, the child learns the subtleties of phonology, of sound: for example, the differences of intonation between a statement and a question, between mild request and emphatic insistence. For an adult to shout 'Milk!' when he or she wishes someone to pass the milk jug would be regarded as offensive. The child learns that there are various patterns of sound in which to express the wish to get hold of some milk.

5 The sheer scale and complexity of what the preschool and school-age child (whether mono-, bi- or multilingual) learns is testament to the astonishing powers of the learning brain operating in normal and generally happy circumstances.

Two government reports on talking to learn

The Plowden Report

The Plowden Report, *Children and their Primary Schools* (The Plowden Committee, 1967), was a highly significant, influential and wise document. It caught the optimistic spirit of much excellent work going on in primary schools in the 1960s, and set a tone for practice in primary schools in the following years. The report is quoted several times in this book. It is worth saying something more general here about reactions to the report in the years following its publication.

The report's recommendations, indeed its overall stance on learning in the primary school, soon came under attack from voices calling for a return to transmissive rote learning, to 'formal methods', including the teaching of language in artificially graded steps. The report, or – to be more exact – the position that some people believed the report had taken, became a matter of intense professional and political dispute.

It is true that in some primary schools in the years following Plowden, the report's call for an education based on experience, placing the apprehension and construction of meaning at its heart, was misconstrued and traduced, so that aimless freedom was regarded as experiential discovery, and the rigorous balance which Plowden strikes between a recognition of the centrality of the child in the act of learning and the responsibility of the teacher to guide and inform that centrality was abandoned. In these schools, to parody slightly, the curriculum became all child and no teacher. The authors of the report were well aware of the danger:

> *A word which has fairly recently come into use in educational circles is 'discovery'. It includes many of the ideas so far discussed and is a useful shorthand description. It has the disadvantage of comprehensiveness in that it can be loosely interpreted and misunderstood . . . The sense of personal discovery influences the intensity of a child's experience, the vividness of his memory and the probability of effective transfer of learning. At the same time it is true that trivial ideas and inefficient methods may be 'discovered'. Furthermore, time does not allow children to find their way by discovery to all that they have to learn. In this matter, as in all education, the teacher is responsible for encouraging children in enquiries which lead to discovery and for asking leading questions.*
>
> (*ibid.*: paragraph 549)

In the decades since Plowden, the balanced wisdom the report offers, based on diligent scholarship and thorough field research, including the use of inspection reports by Her Majesty's Inspectors on primary schools in England, has not been built on and adapted to changing circumstances and new technologies with sufficient determination and imagination.

This relative failure represents a grave loss of opportunity. Worse, there has been an easy tendency by reactionary voices to dismiss the report as the origin of most of the ills that they perceive, or claim to perceive, or find it politically advantageous to claim to perceive, in primary schools more recently. Over the years, many teachers have felt obliged to abandon the spirit of Plowden under the pressure of demands for narrower, more easily measured definitions of educational success. And few commentators have been prepared to argue publicly that to abandon Plowden because some primary schools misconstrued it was to throw a very large baby out with a rather small quantity of bathwater.

Plowden is clear about the importance of spoken language in learning:

Spoken language plays a central role in learning. Parents in talking to their children help them to find words to express, as much to themselves as to others, their needs, feelings and experiences. Through language children can transform their active questing response to the environment into a more precise form and learn to manipulate it more economically and effectively. The complex perceptual-motor skills of reading and writing are based in their first stages upon speech, and the wealth and variety of experience from which effective language develops. Language originates as a means of expressing feeling, establishing contact with others and bringing about desired responses from them; these remain as fundamental functions of language, even at a more mature level. Language develops through the stages of speech, of repeating the commands and prohibitions of others, to become finally part of the child's internal equipment for thinking. Language increasingly serves as a means of organising and controlling experience and the child's own responses to it.

(*ibid.*: paragraph 54)

Discussion with other children and with adults is one of the principal ways in which children check their concepts against those of others and build up an objective view of reality. There is every justification for the conversation which is a characteristic feature of the contemporary primary school. One of the most important responsibilities of teachers is to help children to see order and pattern in experience, and to extend their ideas by analogies and by the provision of suitable vocabulary.

(*ibid.*: paragraph 535)

The report also puts the point negatively:

A teacher who relies only on instruction, who forestalls children's questions or who answers them too quickly, instead of asking the further questions which will set children on the way to their own solution, will disincline children to learn.

(*ibid.*: paragraph 531)

In sum, Plowden takes on and promotes the idea that children's talk must be built into the normal patterns of learning which the teacher initiates and guides, and into the structures of the primary curriculum.

The Bullock Report

The Bullock Committee was not set up to say anything about talk. It was brought into existence because two educational psychologists had claimed, on the basis of some tests they had done, that children's reading standards were falling. The claims came to the attention of the government, which did what governments tend to do when they are unsure of what else to do: it appointed a committee to look into the matter.

The committee chose not to confine itself to answering the question which it had been set up to answer. It went on to offer a description of the state of language, literacy and English teaching in schools in England and to make recommendations. The Bullock Report, *A Language for Life* (The Bullock Committee, 1975), had a good deal to say about talk, beginning with the early years of schooling:

> *Most nursery and infant teachers recognise that when young children are involved in some activity the talk that accompanies it becomes an important instrument for learning. Talk is a means by which they learn to work and live with one another. It enables them to gather information and build into their own experience the experience of others. Between themselves and with the teacher they 'process' or interpret the information, creating their own links between what is new and what is familiar.*
>
> (*ibid.*: paragraph 5.22)

The report discusses in some detail the challenges facing the teacher as he or she attempts to communicate information or concepts to a class:

> *By its very nature a lesson is a verbal encounter through which the teacher draws information from the class, elaborates and generalises it, and produces a synthesis. His skill is in selecting, prompting, improvising, and generally orchestrating the exchange. But in practice the course of any dialogue in which one person is managing 30 is only partly predictable . . . It has also become clear what difficulties face the teacher if he is to encourage genuine exploration and learning on the part of his pupils, and not simply the game of guessing what he has in mind. What the teacher has in mind may well be the desirable destination of a thinking process; but a learner needs to trace the steps from the familiar to the new, from the fact or idea he possesses to that which he is to acquire. In other words, the learner has to make a journey in thought for himself. The kind of class lesson we have been describing has*

therefore to be supported by others in which the pupils' own exploratory talk has much more scope.

(*ibid*.: paragraph 10.2)

That is the heart of it: not in any sense to take away from the teacher's central role, but to see 'pupils' own exploratory talk' as a bridge by which their new knowledge or grasp of a new concept can be securely connected to knowledge or conceptual understandings they already have.

We could extend the bridge metaphor by referring to a bridge that does not extend. Talk is not *le pont d'Avignon*, which stops in the middle of the Rhône. Teachers do not leave pupils there, peering into the water. Using pupil talk as an aid, they enable pupils to cross the bridge, to make a link between where they were and where the demands of the school want them to be. But if there is no bridge at all, pupils are just gazing at a distant territory with which they have no connection.

The report's list of conclusions and recommendations includes the following:

Children learn as certainly by talking and writing as by listening and reading.

(*ibid*.: 37)

Exploratory talk by the pupils has an important function in the process of learning.

(*ibid*.: 108)

A child's accent should be accepted and attempts should not be made to suppress it. The aim should be to provide him with awareness and flexibility.

(*ibid*.: 109)

Children should be helped to as wide as possible a range of language uses so that they can speak appropriately in different situations and use standard forms when they are needed.

(*ibid*.: 110)

A stimulating classroom environment will not necessarily of itself develop the children's ability to use language as an instrument for learning. The teacher has a vital part to play and his role should be one of planned intervention.

(*ibid*.: 112)

Oral work should take place in both large and small group situations, with an emphasis on the latter.

(*ibid*.: 113)

As part of their professional knowledge teachers should have:

- *an explicit understanding of the processes at work in classroom discourse;*
- *the ability to appraise their pupils' spoken language and to plan the means of extending it.*

(*ibid*.: 118)

To put the bridge metaphor in other terms, if there is no relation between school knowledge and the learner's experience, there is an alienation between the learner and the school. The young person becomes a 'reluctant learner', with only a grudging sense that what the school has to offer her or him is of any interest or value. In some cases, he or she develops an actual antagonism to the school's mission and tries to disrupt it.

Without wishing to deny the authority of the teacher, and while recognising that teachers in many cases do know 'the right answer', or at least 'a right answer', the Plowden and Bullock Reports argue that much contemporary classroom practice was denying learners the opportunity to develop a vital human and intellectual competence: that of the genuine enquirer. They conclude that properly managed pupil talk is one way in which young people can *be* genuine enquirers.

Children who fall behind

Even taking into account Katharine Perera's qualified admiration as to young children's achievement as language learners, the tone of the seven admirers and the two reports quoted is overwhelmingly optimistic. However, this book's introduction includes the statement:

There are still far too many children and young people who are failing to become competent and confident users of their language when there is no valid reason, in terms of their potential, why they should fail. Those most at risk of failure are children and young people from socio-economically poorer backgrounds.

This assertion is confirmed by a recent (April 2014) report by the Office for Standards in Education, *Are You Ready? Good Practice in School Readiness*. The title page of the report describes its purpose:

The aim of this survey was to capture how the most successful Early Years providers ensure disadvantaged and vulnerable children are better prepared to start school. Her Majesty's Inspectors visited children's centres, childminders, pre-schools, primary and infant schools providing for pupils within the Early Years Foundation Stage. The providers were selected because they were successful in achieving good outcomes for children in deprived areas.

(*ibid.*: 1)

The first paragraph of the executive summary runs as follows:

For too many children, especially those living in the most deprived areas, educational failure starts early. Gaps in achievement between the poorest children and their better-off counterparts are clearly established by the age of five. There are strong associations between a child's social background and their readiness for school as measured by their scores on entry into Year 1. Too many children, especially those that are poor, lack a firm grounding in the key skills of communication, language, literacy and mathematics.

(*ibid.*: 4)

This is a sobering counterbalance to optimism. The report does, as promised, take us to Early Years settings which are having some success in overcoming the disadvantages and vulnerabilities of 'children in deprived areas'.

To paraphrase a familiar question in sociology, education can never wholly compensate for society. Societies where inequalities are smaller do better in educational terms than societies where inequalities are greater. A high degree of inequality is, sadly, a fact of life in the United Kingdom. To imagine that, at current levels of funding and even in the best, most committed, most educationally enlightened Early Years settings, the handicap of socio-economic deprivation may be eliminated completely is to delude ourselves. A government policy which significantly reduced overall inequality would be a much more powerful tool to enhance the prospects of tomorrow's preschool children from today's poorer backgrounds. But that is a grand, long-term ideal. The Ofsted Report is right in saying that things can be done now at least to reduce the degree of underachievement by children from poorer backgrounds, and in some cases to transform a child's chances of future educational success.

Here is one example of successful practice, described in the section of the report entitled 'Developing communication skills':

All of the settings made reference to specific actions taken to address developmental delays in children's communication skills. Such actions were a significant factor in helping children to develop their speaking, listening and communication skills.

In response to many children arriving in their reception class speaking only 30 to 40 words, the school expected adults to model activities in their role play area. In the doctor's surgery, for example, teachers played and pretended to be a doctor or nurse, modelling the kinds of questions that encourage children to respond. The school videoed this role play and put it on an interactive white board so children were continually exposed to the language and the type of role play that staff were expecting. Children were able to copy, learn the vocabulary and then extend the role play using their creativity and imagination. Once the children became more confident, they were encouraged to take on the role of an adult, leading activities. The school was training children to use an area and learning environment appropriately to improve their language. Where children did not respond to the model, a member of staff intervened and pointed children to appropriate practice, often using other children as the secondary modelling cue. The school was clear that providing secure modelling significantly accelerated children's readiness for learning.

(*ibid.*: 17–18)

Approaches of this kind have the greatest chance of success in giving children who come less well prepared to education the extra affirmation and boost that they need.

The potential of collaborative talk and of good teaching

'What children can do with the assistance of others'

One of the clearest accounts of the value of collaboration in learning is Lev Vygotsky's 'Interaction between Learning and Development', written in the early 1930s and published in English in 1978. Vygotsky understands a child's mental capacity in terms of its potential rather than its actual achievement. He is writing at a time when the testing of individual children and the assignment to them of a 'mental age' was commonplace, especially in the realm of educational psychology and research. But, he says, this is an inadequate, a static way of describing what a child can do:

> *We give children a battery of tests or a variety of tasks of varying degrees of difficulty, and we judge the extent of their mental development on the basis of how they solve them and at what degree of difficulty. On the other hand, if we offer leading questions or show how the problem is to be solved and the child then solves it, or if the teacher initiates the solution and the child completes it or solves it in collaboration with other children – in short, if the child barely misses an independent solution of the problem – the solution is not regarded as indicative of his mental development. This 'truth' was familiar and reinforced by common sense. Over a decade even the pro-foundest thinkers never questioned the assumption; they never entertained the notion that* what children can do with the assistance of others might in some sense be more indicative of their mental development than what they can do alone.*
>
> (Vygotsky, 1978a: 85, my emphasis)

The zone of potential development

Vygotsky proposes that what children are capable of at any point in their development, but have not yet achieved, be called the 'zone of proximal [or potential] development'.[1]

Good teaching and the use of collaborative learning are both ways in which children's incomplete grasp of an idea or a concept or a piece of knowledge may be helped towards completion, in which the zone of potential develop-ment may be explored. The zone is:

> the distance between the actual developmental level as determined by inde-pendent problem solving and the level of potential development as deter-mined through problem solving under adult guidance or in collaboration with more capable peers.
>
> (*ibid*.: 86, original emphasis)

These insights of Vygotsky's have been quoted many times by writers on talk; and rightly so. It should not be forgotten, however, that Vygotsky attaches equal importance to the role of the teacher in helping children to push at the boundaries of their potential understanding and competence.

A model of the process of learning through talk

Having harvested some of the wisdom of the past, let us attempt to summarise it in terms of a working theory of the role of talk in learning.

The materials for learning

We start with the raw material – the learner. He or she has a certain quantity and kind of pre-existent knowledge and experience, a certain degree of linguistic power, and a certain set of social habits and attitudes which will influence the working relationship with the other learners with whom he or she will be asked to collaborate. To her or his pre-existent knowledge and experience, the teacher brings new material in the form of external knowledge, provided either directly by the teacher or indirectly through resources (for example, books, films, the internet) which he or she makes available to the learner, or shows the learner how to access.

The task

We then move to the task. The skill of the teacher, to return to the slightly extended quotation from Andrew Wilkinson included earlier, is 'to provide situations which call forth increasing powers of utterance [and of comprehension]'. The teacher does this by setting tasks which operate, in Vygotsky's terms, in the learners' zone of potential development. There will always be a degree of approximation in the judgement as to where this zone is, because it will not be exactly the same even for the participants in a discussion involving two people, let alone in a discussion involving the whole class. But judge the teacher must, and the more skilful and experienced he or she is, the likelier it is that the task will be pitched at a level which makes challenging demands on the learners, while maintaining the probability that, through collaboration and mutual support, they will achieve at least a considerable measure of success in finding the answer, solving the problem, discussing the issue, understanding the poem, making the argument: whatever is the nature of the task set.

The outcome

Finally, there is the outcome. The argument on which this chapter's case rests is that, as long as the learners are equipped with or have available adequate sources of knowledge and/or experience to bring to the task (an essential proviso), there is something in the acts of dialogue that occur in the course of doing the oral task which enhances, deepens and earths the new knowledge, skill or understanding that the teacher wishes the learners to acquire, and which reinforces existing but uncertain knowledge, skill or understanding.

Analysis of the outcome

Teachers don't have the time or the need to analyse the outcome of every oral task they set in any detail; but occasionally such analysis could bring a clearer sense of learners' progress in speaking and listening. If we ask of a particular oral task 'What has been gained?', we might be asking what has been gained cognitively, linguistically or socially, or in all of these respects.

Cognitively: what is being learned in the course of the talk, by whom, how does that learning come about, and can we see examples of learning which probably needed to happen in this specific context if they were to happen at all?

Linguistically: what types and degrees of facility with language do the talkers display, and is their facility affected by the topic or the mood of the discussion, or by the role or stance they adopt in it? Is there development or change in any of these areas during the course of the talk?

Socially: who dominates, who follows, who is anxious for consensus, who likes to strike postures of disagreement, how ready – if at all – are individuals to modify or abandon previous positions? Is there development or change in any of these areas during the course of the talk?

Recording development

These questions could be discussed while studying a tape and/or transcript of one particular oral activity. That kind of study is a cut across time. It is equally important to have some means of recording what progress is being made in learners' oral competence *through* time. The categories we might use in such a developing record don't have to be complex. For example, they could be framed in questions as simple as:

- *What are the natural qualities of this talker/listener as seen in class?*
- *How constructive is the part he or she takes in whole-class or large-group activities (for example involving exploration, exposition, argument, presentation, role-play, performance, debate)?*
- *How constructive is the part he or she takes in small-group or paired activities (for example involving exploration, research, examination of evidence, argument, response to and discussion of reading, preparation for writing)?*

- *In a supportive context, can he or she present, maintain, support, develop or modify ideas (and respond to others in doing so)?*
- *How much progress in terms of eloquence, coherence, span of attention, quality of attention, self-discipline in small-group and whole-class work has he or she shown since the last progress report on the pupil's oral work?*

(Adapted from 'Record-keeping:
One model', in Richmond, 2012c: 92)

(These questions draw on part of a record-keeping system which was devised by the English department at Aylwin School in the London Borough of Southwark, whose work is acknowledged with thanks.)

We could express the attempt to describe the process of learning through talk more briefly in the form of a model (Figure 1.1).

A note of warning

While enthusiastically acknowledging the role of talk in learning, I simultaneously acknowledge the practical difficulties which can confront teachers in introducing pupil talk in the classroom.

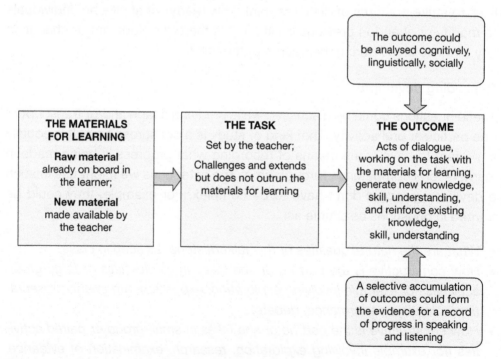

Figure 1.1 The process of learning through talk.

These difficulties may lie in the discouraging attitudes to talk which some teachers communicate to their pupils from an early age. Let us not be dewy-eyed. There are a few teachers in the profession, with plenty of years of service behind them, for whom the continuing and overriding priority in classroom management is that they should retain a monopoly of control over every event in the room. In these classrooms, there is a failure to discriminate between disruptive chatter which slows or halts learning, and constructive talk which advances it. Here, classroom culture and routines have never been established in such a way that learners recognise talk as a valid form of work. The desire to keep a monopoly of control may come from a teacher's fear of what might happen if even a little autonomy in learning were granted to pupils; or the ease with which a lazy pedagogic habit can be repeated lesson after lesson, year after year.

How do teachers who wish to incorporate pupil talk in their teaching deal with this? There is no simple answer. If pupils have come to believe that talking equals messing about and working equals performing written tasks in silence, then their belief, or rather the first half of it, needs to be dismantled gradually and consciously. Talk needs to be admitted as a kind of work with a validity equal to that of written tasks, and one which, apart from its intrinsic value as a means of extending knowledge and of developing language competence and social skill, can also directly benefit pupils' reading and writing.

A teacher should not be expected to make space for talk in the classroom as a solitary pioneer in a school. The most successful schools have broadly agreed policies on the important principles relating language to learning and on the implications of those principles for classroom practice. One such principle must be that, whatever the actual diversity of teaching styles across the staff of a school, the use of properly managed pupil talk is respected and admired, and not regarded as evidence that a teacher cannot control the class. Those in leadership positions in the school have a special responsibility in this respect.

The present situation in England

We come now to the curriculum requirements on talk as they apply to Early Years settings and primary schools (other than academies and free schools) in England.

Spoken language in the Early Years Foundation Stage

The statutory framework for the Early Years Foundation Stage (Department for Education, 2014c) proposes 'seven areas of learning and development'.

'Communication and language' is one of three 'prime areas' within the seven that 'are particularly crucial for igniting children's curiosity and enthusiasm for learning, and for building their capacity to learn, form relationships and thrive'. 'Communication and language' is described thus:

> *Communication and language development involves giving children oppor-tunities to experience a rich language environment; to develop their con-fidence and skills in expressing themselves; and to speak and listen in a range of situations.*

(ibid.: section 1.5)

Quite rightly, the framework says that 'All areas of learning and development are important and inter-connected' (*ibid.*: section 1.3). There are plenty of opportunities for speaking and listening within the other six areas.

Each of the prime areas has its set of early learning goals. Those for communication and language are:

> *Listening and attention: children listen attentively in a range of situations. They listen to stories, accurately anticipating key events and respond to what they hear with relevant comments, questions or actions. They give their attention to what others say and respond appropriately, while engaged in another activity.*
>
> *Understanding: children follow instructions involving several ideas or actions. They answer 'how' and 'why' questions about their experiences and in response to stories or events.*
>
> *Speaking: children express themselves effectively, showing awareness of listeners' needs. They use past, present and future forms accurately when talking about events that have happened or are about to happen in the future. They develop their own narratives and explanations by connecting ideas or events.*

(ibid.: section 1.12)

This is a perfectly acceptable and enabling framework for the development of children's spoken language up to the age of five. It is important to note that the learning goals are just that: ambitions to aim for by the end of the school year in which a child is five. The process by which, for example, a child sorts out 'past, present and future forms' in verbs is a dynamic one, likely to involve uneven steps towards correct usage, and certain to be different, and to advance at different rates, from child to child. The introduction to the framework acknowledges this as one of four overarching principles: 'children develop and learn in different ways and at different rates' (*ibid*.: Introduction, paragraph 6).

On this sound basis (at least as far as spoken language is concerned; there are more critical things to say in other chapters about the framework's requirements with regard to reading and writing), we turn to the requirements for spoken language at Key Stages 1 and 2.

Spoken language in the National Curriculum for English

The way it was

The programme of study for talk in the original National Curriculum for English (Department of Education and Science and the Welsh Office, 1990) was entitled 'Speaking and Listening', and there was much debate at the time about the different connotations of the words 'speak' and 'talk'. Some supporters of talk felt that 'speaking' implied too formal, too presentational an understanding of the spoken language. It does tend in that direction; and this was a tendency the government of the day approved of. However, the title of a programme of study matters less than its contents; and the contents did allow for a diversity of kinds of talk. There was a continuum in the original programmes of study from the more tentative, exploratory and collaborative kinds of talk to the more finished, assertive and individualistic: from discussions to debates, from conversations to oral presentations.

In the years since 1990, many Early Years and primary-school teachers have maintained their belief in the value of talk in learning, and have developed their practical skill in its implementation, through all the revisions and re-revisions that the National Curriculum has seen.

Key Stages 1 and 2 now

We zoom through time and come to the present day, to look at the new curriculum orders for speaking and listening in English at Key Stages 1 and 2, statutory as from September 2014 or September 2015.

Primary-school teachers are burdened in the new orders with the obligation to teach lengthy lists, finely graded year by year, of grapho-phonic correspondences in reading and of spelling patterns and grammatical rules in writing. (See the critiques of these requirements in Chapters 2, 4 and 6.) By contrast, the entire, undifferentiated list of statutory requirements for speaking and listening for Key Stages l and 2 combined consists of 132 words (Department for Education, 2014a):

> *Pupils should be taught to:*
>
> - *listen and respond appropriately to adults and their peers;*
> - *ask relevant questions to extend their understanding and knowledge;*
> - *use relevant strategies to build their vocabulary;*
> - *articulate and justify answers, arguments and opinions;*
> - *give well-structured descriptions, explanations and narratives for different purposes, including for expressing feelings;*
> - *maintain attention and participate actively in collaborative conversations, staying on topic and initiating and responding to comments;*
> - *use spoken language to develop understanding through speculating, hypothesising, imagining and exploring ideas;*
> - *speak audibly and fluently with an increasing command of Standard English;*
> - *participate in discussions, presentations, performances, role play, improvisations and debates;*
> - *gain, maintain and monitor the interest of the listener(s);*
> - *consider and evaluate different viewpoints, attending to and building on the contributions of others;*
> - *select and use appropriate registers for effective communication.*
>
> (*ibid*.: 18)

It is perhaps not surprising that the development of children's spoken language between the ages of 5 and 11 should be dealt with as briefly as it is here, since when those who gave the new orders their statutory status seriously considered leaving out speaking and listening altogether. That said, the Key Stages 1 and 2 orders have virtue. In their brevity, they do not at least prevent primary-school teachers from teaching well. Under the rubric of these orders, it is perfectly possible for teachers to do any or all of the things explicitly or implicitly recommended in this chapter. There is range here, and the more informal, collaborative uses of talk are not squeezed out.

But we can do better than this

The previous paragraph damns with faint praise. Brevity may be a virtue, but the current orders remain an inadequate account of the role which the spoken language should play in pupils' learning in primary schools. Chapter 11 offers an alternative curriculum for the spoken language 3 to 11, containing much more detail at Key Stages 1 and 2.

To conclude . . .

Schools and teachers should see the development of learners' confidence and capability in the use of the spoken language as one of their principal responsibilities.

To allow any measure of autonomy to learners in their use of talk means that a teacher must thereby relinquish complete, detailed control of classroom interactions. This relinquishing brings risk. The way to ensure that risk brings rewards is to structure the talk so that learners are operating within constraints (for example of time, or of purpose, or of format for their talk) which they can handle.

There are no set rules for what the constraints on learners' talk should be, but there is one developmental principle: the better established are the classroom culture and routines allowing for talk, and the more familiar are pupils with the idea that talk is a kind of work with equal validity to other kinds of work, the likelier it is that the constraints can be light, the task more open-ended, without discipline breaking down and the talk degenerating into aimless or destructive chatter.

All forms of, contexts for and groupings for talk have equal potential worth. Forms may range from exploratory discussion to oral performance. Contexts may range from conducting a piece of factual research (where there *are* right answers) to debating a moral issue (where there may not be). Groupings may range from pairs to the whole class.

Development in effectiveness as a speaker and sensitivity and responsiveness as a listener come when the teacher offers learners appropriately engaging and challenging oral tasks.

Despite the widespread agreement on the value of talk for learning which this chapter has summarised, and despite the wonderful work involving the spoken language which many teachers are doing, the achievement of a state of affairs where, in all Early Years settings and primary schools in England, talk is seen as a normal part of the work of an effective and well-disciplined classroom is still some way off.

Note

1 Robin Alexander, in his pamphlet *Towards Dialogic Teaching*, quotes Joan Simon (1987), 'a pioneering translator of the work of Vygotsky', who writes that '"Zone of potential [or next] development" is a more appropriate translation from the Russian than the more usual "proximal"' (Alexander, 2005: 11).

2 Reading 3 to 7

John Richmond

Summary of main points

Successful entry into literacy depends on an existing competence in spoken language. The beginning reader, to be successful, must employ all the resources of her or his retentive memory, generalising brain and propensity to make meaning.

Much of a beginning reader's learning takes place unconsciously, just as does virtually all of a beginning speaker's learning. However, while allowing full play to the powerful forces of children's unconscious literacy learning, the teacher has a vital part to play through appropriately pitched conscious instruction.

Pleasure in reading is an essential prerequisite to success in reading. This principle applies at all levels of encounters with writing, from word recognition up to full-scale comprehension of continuous texts.

Learning to read is learning to infer and construct meaning from writing. To do this effectively, beginning readers need a range of ways of grasping meaning. This range includes the recognition and retention of whole words, to which beginning readers have been introduced by the teacher or other experienced reader. It includes the making of links between the semantic and syntactic patterns and structures of spoken language, of which most beginning readers already have substantial experience, and their equivalents in written language. It includes the recognition of grapho-phonic correspondences in written English in the many contexts where they exist.

Beginning readers need full access to a wide range of books, crucially including books which have been composed using the natural patterns, usages and rhythms of English.

The support of parents and other experienced readers at home is of enormous importance in the development of successful young readers.

Successful teaching of reading does not depend on allegiance to a particular method, but on an overall understanding of what it is that the beginning reader does in successfully encountering a text.

These principles apply with equal force to EAL learners (about one in six children in the age group with which this book is concerned). EAL learners are engaged in the complex process of sorting differences and recognising equivalences between their first and additional language(s). The appropriately pitched conscious instruction by the teacher to which I refer above will have a particular application to EAL learners who have some level of literacy in their first language, where there is likely to be a conscious transfer of knowledge and skill from one written form to another. Appropriate books in the first language and in bilingual editions should be provided, so that the writing systems of English and the other language(s) can be compared.

Current government policy and statutory requirements in the area of early reading are based on a simplistic view of the reading process, which fails to do justice to the diversity of strategies which young children in fact use to become successful readers.

Reading: two camps

Two camps, two schools of thought, have long dominated the reading debate. One, the phonics camp, says that when a child learns to read, he or she relies largely or solely on a system of symbol-to-sound correspondences. Enthusiastic proponents of phonics believe that it is the only means by which children learn to read effectively, and they believe that the system can be taught. There are a number of intellectual sources from which phonics has sprung, of which the most important is probably behaviourist psychology: that school of psychology which says that human behaviour can best be understood as a set of responses to stimuli. In the case of reading, the stimulus is the letter or the group of letters or the word on the page or the wall or the flash card or the computer screen, and the response is the child's attempt to say aloud what that word or word-part 'says'.

The other camp says that reading is a predictive, meaning-making activity in which the young child's brain is engaged at a much deeper and more dynamic level than is required by the simple recognition of grapho-phonic correspondences. Of the various intellectual sources for this position, the most important is a branch of psycholinguistics which is interested in how the learning brain generalises from information about language which it receives. Psycholinguists of this school recognise that we say, write, think and understand things in the course of our lives which go far beyond the mere copying or re-enactment of direct experiences of language we have had. Humans are creative in this area of their activity, as they are in every other area; and this fact has immense implications for readers, including beginning readers.

Another school of thought presenting a strong challenge to phonics is gestalt theory, which says that humans perceive phenomena in the outside world as wholes, not as summations of their parts. When we see a tree, we do not, even unconsciously, say to ourselves, 'Ah, there is a trunk, and some boughs and branches, and many leaves. Now that I have worked all that out, I can see that I must be looking at a tree'. Neither do we recognise a human face only once we have independently taken in the size and shape of its nose and mouth, the colour of its eyes, the shade of its skin. No; we perceive the thing as a whole. If gestalt theory holds water, its relevance to reading is obvious: normally, we perceive written words not as collections of separate contributory letters and (in the case of multi-syllabic words) as collections of separate contributory syllables, but as wholes.

The people in between

So, two camps; and in between these two camps, the teachers. Teachers are the people (though not necessarily the only people) who actually teach children to read. They are the people who make sure that every year hundreds of thousands of children in schools throughout the world perform this remarkable feat. How do teachers do it? I suggest that most professionals are eclectic and pragmatic. They use whatever works. They are suspicious of miracle cures and evangelistic enthusiasts guaranteeing success if the teachers will only use the enthusiasts' method, and if they will only use *only* the enthusiasts' method. And they are right to be sceptical in that way.

Also stationed between the two camps are the children. Children are remarkable survivors. They learn to do things, including learning to read, in all sorts of circumstances, having been exposed to all sorts of teaching methods. Further, a method which a teacher thinks has been the key to success in teaching a child to read may not necessarily deserve that accolade. If one could go back and, as it were, run the secret tape which reveals the truth about what was going on in the child's brain at the crucial period of her or his advance towards confidence and control as a reader, some quite other influence might turn out to have been the key.

The limitations of camps

'The reading wars' is a common phrase used to describe the long-standing disagreement just described. My use of the metaphor 'camps' in the title of this section is perfectly appropriate. There has been an almost military quality to the contest. And huge sums of government money in the English-speaking world have been expended in trying to answer the question: how do children learn to read? In the USA, the two camps have been labelled 'whole language' and 'phonics'. Borrowing the American terminology, I'll start our discussion of this vexed question by disposing of the oppositional model.

(PHONICS VERSUS WHOLE LANGUAGE) = A FALSE ALTERNATIVE

I should say at the outset that this chapter will argue that an exclusive reliance on phonics in introducing young children to reading is wrong, however successful the phonics camp has been in seeing that such an exclusive reliance has become government policy in England. However, I also say immediately that apprehending structures in words, including apprehending grapho-phonic correspondences, is an essential part of how children learn to read.

There is now convincing evidence that effective reading teaching – the kind that gets children to like reading and to do it skilfully – involves attention *both* to meaning (and all the semantic, syntactic and subject knowledge that children bring to the process) *and* to the structures of words. Attention to the structures of words includes attention to grapho-phonic correspondences. I'll quote from some of this evidence later. In the meantime, here is a paragraph from Henrietta Dombey's 'How Phonics Works in English' which succinctly sums up the both/and position taken in this chapter.

> *Drawing an analogy with computers, Rumelhart (1976) has persuasively written of skilled reading as 'simultaneous, interactive multilevel processing'. When presented with a text, the skilled reader proceeds from the top down and the bottom up, simultaneously. Observations at any one level generate hypotheses at other levels. So the reader uses her awareness of the context surrounding the text to create expectations of the kind of discourse it represents, from which she generates hypotheses about its content, while at the same time identifying letters, and making hypotheses about words, sentences and larger meanings which draw on knowledge of spelling patterns, words and syntactic structures – and her overall expectations of the text.*
>
> (Dombey, in Dombey *et al.*, 1998: 10)

So the question for the reader of this chapter is not whether I am for or against phonics. That is the wrong question. The right question is 'Does his understanding of the reading process make sense to me and accord with my own experience of teaching children to read?'

The virtues and limitations of phonics

Let us return to our first camp: to those who believe that phonics holds the sole key to success in learning to read.

There is a common-sense authority underlying their position, based on the fact that our writing system makes use of an alphabet. Alphabets did emerge, it is true, as attempts to match single symbols to single sounds. The Egyptians gave their hieroglyphs to the Phoenicians, who were the first people, so far as we know, to adapt picture symbols in order to construct an alphabet. The Phoenicians had no symbols for vowels. They gave their alphabet to the Greeks, who introduced vowels. One version of the Greek alphabet was the model for the Roman or Latin alphabet, in which, of course, Latin was written. 'The Roman (or Latin) alphabet' is the term still in use in English and in other languages to describe that group of letters (26 in English; slightly different numbers in the case of other languages). The ancient Greek alphabet is the ancestor of the Cyrillic alphabet, which is used today to write Russian and other languages in Eastern Europe and Asia. It is also, in another variation, the ancestor of the modern Greek alphabet.

To return from ancient history to the present day, let us acknowledge without any difficulty that there *are* regular symbol-to-sound correspondences; that there are lots of them. Yes, the cat sat on the mat. Yes, the rain in Spain stays mainly on the plain. Yes, Ned is in his red bed. We certainly should make use of these convenient facts as we help children to learn to read.

However, having acknowledged that phonics has an important contribution to make to the young child's success in learning to read, I challenge with equal conviction the zealotry of some in the phonics camp who claim that identifying symbol-to-sound correspondences is the *only* means by which children learn to read – and furthermore that any other method of teaching is not merely useless but damaging. We will not properly understand the relationship between the written English language and the teaching of reading except by recognising that the relationship is far more complex (and far more interesting) than can be explained by simple symbol-to-sound correspondences.

Theory and method

Too often, debates about the teaching of reading have been reduced to arguments about methods. 'Which method should I use? "Look and say"? Phonics? If so, which kind of phonics? Syllable-building? Or onset and rime, leading to analogy?' To seek a fail-safe single method is to seek the wrong thing. At one particular moment in one particular child's early experience of reading, any one of these methods – or, more likely, a combination of them in harness – might work.

The most important piece of intellectual equipment which a teacher of beginning readers needs is not a *method*, but a *working theory*: an understanding of the processes involved in becoming a reader. The next five sections (four in print and one online) are intended to help towards such an understanding.

Snapshots from the past

In this section, I summarise the findings (as I equivalently did in Chapter 1) of two influential government reports from the now quite distant past, both of which have much to say of continuing relevance to the teaching of reading, and the work of some major thinkers on the topic.

The Plowden Report

The Plowden Report, *Children and their Primary Schools* (The Plowden Committee, 1967), has a clear view of the approach to the early teaching of reading most likely to be successful. Here is a selection from the report's findings.

> *Many children first glimpse the pleasures of reading from listening to stories read to them at school; as teachers' aides are introduced . . . it should be possible for even more children to have the opportunity that others have at home of looking at pictures and text as a picture book is read to them individually or in small groups. Books made by teachers and children about the doings of the class or of individuals in it figure prominently among the books which children enjoy. They help children to see meaning in reading and to appreciate the purpose of written records. Children who show interest in reading but who are not ready to make steady progress on a graduated*

series often profit from using home-made books and picture books. They can get much interest from them, without mastering the whole vocabulary, and they will be protected from feeling that they are failures because they have not passed quickly to a second book in a series.

(*ibid.*: paragraph 583)

As to the systematic teaching that follows this introduction to reading and writing, the most successful infant teachers have refused to follow the wind of fashion and to commit themselves to any one method. They choose methods and books to fit the age, interest and ability of individual pupils. Children are helped to read by memorising the look of words and phrases, often with the help of pictures, by guessing from a context which is likely to bring them success, and by phonics, beginning with initial sounds. They are encouraged to try all the methods available to them and not to depend on only one method. Instead of relying on one reading scheme, many teachers use a range of schemes with different characteristics, selecting carefully for each child: some schemes emphasise sight reading, others phonics; some consist of short books, with a very slow build up of vocabulary, and suit children who need quick success; other schemes help children who are able to advance rapidly and to discard primers. Reading schemes should never determine the practices adopted for all children. A few children are able, with a little help, to teach themselves to read from books of rhymes and stories learnt by heart. Rather more can pass direct from home-made books to simple story books. Many children will not need to go right through a series of books: others will require a great deal of supplementary material.

(*ibid.*: paragraph 584)

We are concerned about the quality and content of many primers and particularly of those used by children who come late to reading from an unbookish background. Too often, the difficult problem of combining interest with a controlled vocabulary is not solved. The middle class world represented by the text and illustrations is often alien to the children, the characters shadowy, the content babyish, the text pedestrian and lacking in rhythm and there is rarely either the action or the humour which can carry children through to the end of the books. We agree with the recommendation made to us by the National Association for the Teaching of English, that research should be instituted into the types of primer and library book which are most effective with children from different backgrounds and of varying levels of ability.

(*ibid.*: paragraph 587)

In sum, Plowden recommends that children should be helped to learn to read using the whole range of cues and clues available to their active, generalising brains and their retentive memories. It supports the use of an eclectic range of methods in the teaching of reading. And it criticises the narrowness and artificiality of 'many primers', the forerunners of today's reading schemes.

The Bullock Report

As mentioned in Chapter 1, the original brief given to the Bullock Committee, whose report was published as *A Language for Life* (The Bullock Committee, 1975), was to investigate claims made in a study by two educational psychologists that standards of reading in schools in England had fallen. In the event, the Committee largely rejected the findings of the study, *The Trend of Reading Standards* by Start and Wells, published in 1972 by the National Foundation for Educational Research.

The committee then went far beyond the narrow definition of its brief, to make a much wider statement about language and learning, including the teaching of reading. The report's conclusions and recommendations about the teaching of early reading include the following:

> There is no one method, medium, approach, device or philosophy that holds the key to the process of learning to read.
>
> (The Bullock Committee, 1975: conclusion 56)

> A detailed understanding of the reading process should inform decisions about the organisation of teaching, the initial and in-service education of teachers, and the use of resources.
>
> (*ibid*.: recommendation 58)

> The learning of sound-symbol correspondences should take place in the context of whole-word recognition and reading for meaning. It is important . . . that children should . . . have had a full range of pre-reading experiences.
>
> (*ibid*.: recommendation 62)

> The most effective teaching of reading is that which gives the pupil the various skills he or she needs to make the fullest possible use of context cues in search for meaning.
>
> (*ibid*.: conclusion 66)

It should be established from the beginning in the mind of the child that reading is primarily a thinking process, not simply an exercise in identifying shapes and sounds.

(ibid.: recommendation 73)

Reading schemes which use contrived and unnatural language prevent children from developing the ability to detect sequential probability in linguistic structure.

(ibid.: conclusion 79)

The difference in [teachers'] effectiveness lies not in their allegiance to any one method but in (a) the quality of their relationships with children, (b) their degree of expert knowledge, and (c) their sensitivity in matching their teaching with each child's current learning needs.

(ibid.: conclusion 83)

There has not been a government document on language, literacy and learning in schools since 1975 to match the Bullock Report in scope, balance and wisdom. This is not to praise it unreservedly. It is of course a political document, albeit one produced in the relatively – only relatively – gentle politics of the mid-1970s, and it hedges its bets on a number of matters, some of which, like the initial teaching alphabet, now look distinctly quaint, and others of which, like phonics and reading schemes, are still very much with us. We might agree that the text of the document is sometimes obliged, in the interests of compromise, to settle for too easy and optimistic an eclecticism of method. Nonetheless, the report's great achievement was to place on official record the complexity of the job that teachers of language do. In the area of early reading, as in other areas, it ought not to have been possible for any responsible person, organisation or government to suggest thereafter that one-dimensional approaches based on transmissive rote learning would be the salvation of any teacher or learner. It ought not to have been possible ever again to escape Bullock's emphasis on the multi-skilled nature of all language learning, and on language learning's central purpose – to take and make meaning in acts of language, spoken and written.

Reading – the search for meaning

So far, I've quoted from two influential government reports. The views expressed in these reports challenged the simplistic notion that reading is nothing more than the decoding of print by the application of learned rules. I'll review now a very small sample of the research into reading in recent decades. This work lays out a theoretical understanding of reading, arrived at on the basis of careful observation of readers and teachers of reading at work in real contexts. The understanding to be gained from the work provides the essential intellectual equipment that teachers need in order to teach reading well.

The principle at the heart of the understanding is simple to state yet complex to grasp. It is referred to in the last sentence of the penultimate paragraph. Reading is above all the search by the reader to construct meaning in and from a text. In this search for meaning, the reader employs – or should employ if he or she is allowed to – a formidable panoply of strategies at different points in an encounter with a text, and at different stages of her or his development as a reader. The majority – not all – of these strategies operate fast and automatically, below the level of conscious awareness. The job of the teacher (and of the parent, in a less specialised, less expert but no less important way) is to create the conditions in which the young reader's strategies as a maker of meaning can operate unhindered and to greatest effect.

Marie Clay

Marie Clay's work on reading has influenced countless teachers across the English-speaking world over more than 40 years. In particular, her *Reading: The Patterning of Complex Behaviour* (1979) and her *Becoming Literate: The Construction of Inner Control* (1991) are superb studies of the learning behaviour of beginning readers. Clay defines reading as follows:

> a message-gaining, problem-solving activity, which increases in power and flexibility the more it is practised. My definition states that within the directional constraints of the printer's code, verbal and perceptual behaviour are purposefully directed in some integrated way to the problem of extracting a sequence of cues from a text to yield a meaningful and specific communication, conveying the author's specific message.

(Clay, 1979: 6)

Both Clay's books show, as a result of detailed, developmental studies of early readers, the complexity and magnificence of what the beginning reader, in good circumstances, does in order to become a successful reader, attending to the diversity of clues and cues, and the interaction of these clues and cues, which provide access to meaning. Clay is critical of 'method' in the narrow sense of the word, by which teachers attempt to impose on the complex behaviour of reading a limited regime of procedures.

> *all readers, from the competent 5-year-old on his first reading book to the efficient adult, use:*
>
> - *the sense;*
> - *the sentence structure;*
> - *the order of ideas, words, letters;*
> - *the size of words or letters;*
> - *special features of sound, shape and layout;*
> - *and special knowledge from past experience.*
>
> *As explanations of what we do when we read, the terms 'look and say', 'sight words' and 'phonics' are nonsense. Reading is more complex than that.*
> *By far the most important challenge for the teacher of reading is to make it easier for the child to operate successfully in getting precise messages from books.*
>
> (ibid.: 244–245)

Clay's later book is an extended second edition of her first, and includes much new material. It reinforces the case she makes, supported by substantial evidence drawn from observing beginning readers, that:

> *Education contributes to reading failure if it allows (or encourages) children to use ineffective strategies for literacy learning at this time [that is, in the early years].*
>
> (Clay, 1991: 323)

By 'ineffective strategies', Clay means over-reliance on narrow method. And she has a profound understanding of the approach which interventions with failing readers should take.

> *If we can reach a better understanding of the complex strategies developed by successful children in reading we have every chance of helping other young children [that is, failing readers] develop those strategies.*
>
> (ibid.: 325)

Clay discusses the relationship between phonological awareness and reading thus:

> *My assumption is that the reader/writer can most easily become articulate about phonological aspects of reading when he is already making use of them, that is once he is reading and writing small stretches of text. One need not teach him phonics in order to be able to read, but could use what he is able to read and write to develop the articulate awareness of phonology and print, on many different levels, which the good reader needs.*

> (*ibid*.: 322)

This elegant summary of the relationship between an activity and a skill, between a prior competence in reading and an 'articulate awareness of phonology and print', is – as we shall see later – utterly at variance with the instructional orthodoxy about early reading being imposed on schools in England at the moment.

Kenneth and Yetta Goodman

Kenneth and Yetta Goodman have, over many years, shown how children's 'incorrect' approximations to an actual text as they read it are powerful evidence of the activity of the learning brain. Famously, the Goodmans have called these approximations 'miscues'. The miscues they have observed and documented while working with beginning readers, or with readers having difficulty, show the young brain operating the big gears of evidence-sifting and unconscious rule-generation. Children reading aloud – and in particular children whose reading aloud in some way departs from the actual text on the page – reveal to the observer insights into what is going on in the reader's head as he or she endeavours to make sense of a text. And the revelation is dramatic: the observer realises that readers are bringing to the text a pre-existent, complex, subtle body of knowledge about how language works, syntactically, semantically and in terms of the relationship between sounds and marks, as long as they have had a normal positive experience of the spoken language and as soon as they have some positive experiences of noticing writing and being told what the writing says.

This is not to idealise the young reader. There is a great deal that he or she does not yet know. The scheme that he or she has so far built for approaching a text and getting meaning from it will need to be adapted in the light of new experience and – we hope – with the aid of good teaching. But an impressive start has been made, and teachers should take advantage of it.

The Goodmans' many publications include Kenneth Goodman's *Reading: A Psycholinguistic Guessing Game* (1967); his *Reading: Process and Programme* (with Olive Niles, 1970); *Reading Strategies: Focus on Comprehension* by Yetta Goodman and Carolyn Burke with Barry Sherman (1980); and the Goodmans' jointly authored 'To Err is Human: Learning about Language Processes by Analyzing Miscues' (2004). In the second of these, Kenneth Goodman states his case thus:

> *Reading is an active process in which the reader selects the fewest cues possible from those available to him and makes the best choices possible. If he is highly proficient, he will have good speed and high comprehension; reading will be a smooth process. If he is less proficient or if he is encountering unusually difficult material . . . reading will be less smooth and will involve considerable cycling back to gather more cues and make better choices.*
>
> *Meaning is the constant goal of the proficient reader and he continually tests his choices against the developing meaning by asking himself if what he is reading makes sense . . .*
>
> *Such traditional terms as word recognition, sounding out and word attack stem from a view of reading as a succession of accurate perceptions or word identifications. Such a view is not consistent with the actual performance of proficient readers.*
>
> (Goodman with Niles, 1970: 19–20)

Earlier in the booklet, Goodman categorises the information used during the reading process under three headings: grapho-phonic information, syntactic information and semantic information (terms which, amongst others, I've already used).

In 'To Err is Human: Learning about Language Processes by Analyzing Miscues', the Goodmans describe the reader as an intuitive grammarian, and show with examples how a reader's unconscious understanding of grammar pounds away at a text to get it to yield its meaning. Grammatical (syntactic) information is one of the kinds of information just mentioned. All the information-giving systems are needed, however, and they interrelate:

> *Readers sample and make judgments about which cues from each system will provide the most useful information that will get them to meaning.*
>
> (Goodman and Goodman, 2004: 631)

Like Clay, the Goodmans propose that the teacher's task is not to identify one and only one particular category of information which will yield success in reading. The teacher's task is to help the reader to gain access to all the sources of information which link groups of black marks, separated by white spaces, with the apprehension of meaning.

One of Clay's and the Goodmans' most significant achievements has been their use of encounters with children having difficulty in reading to generate insights which throw light on the reading process generally. In other words, they have seen difficulty as a means of making visible what is invisible when readers are successful and at ease.

Don Holdaway

Don Holdaway's *The Foundations of Literacy* (1979) is a formidable combination of polemic, detailed theoretical framework, critical review of trends and practices in reading teaching, and close study of classrooms in which early reading and writing are being successfully learned. He begins his book thus:

> *Learning to read and write ought to be one of the most joyful and successful of human undertakings. Notoriously, it is not so. By contrast, most developmental tasks such as learning to walk or to talk are learned almost universally with deep personal satisfaction. What explanation can we give for the continuing difficulties experienced by so many children in learning the tasks of literacy? Are reading and writing intrinsically more difficult even than learning to talk? Are they artificial and unnatural in relationship to other developmental tasks? Are the methods of teaching inefficient even after so many generations of experience and research? Is the school environment unsuited in identifiable ways to the literacy undertaking?*
>
> (*ibid.*: 11)

He then proceeds to answer his own questions.

Near the end of the book, he summarises his conclusions in a series of eight succinct paragraphs. Here is one of them:

> **The dismembering of the literacy processes.** *The traditional attempt to simplify learning by dividing the literacy processes into an ever-increasing*

list of minor skills is self-defeating. Unless they function in concert and are taught largely within meaningful contexts, the so-called 'basic skills' constitute a parody of reading and writing. What in the abstract seems logically *sound – the breaking of complex wholes into parts – turns out to be quite* illogical *in the classroom, especially when the crucial learnings are concerned with the interrelationship of parts within organic functioning.*

(*ibid*.: 190)

What are these authorities telling us?

We can summarise the findings of this small sample of the best that has been written about early reading by scholars since 1967, plus the balanced judgements of the Plowden and Bullock Reports, as follows. Reading is a complex intellectual activity, essentially concerned with the making of meaning in encounters with writing. The young reader should use all the meaning-grasping powers at her or his disposal to make successful sense of written texts. Pleasure in reading is a vitally important driver of developing competence in reading. To talk of teaching 'methods' is to miss the point. To focus on one 'method', whatever it is, is too narrow, too instrumental a way of viewing the activity we are concerned with here. What is needed is an approach that enables the full range of a child's meaning-grasping powers to get to work.

Written English

For reasons of space, this section, which discusses the evolution of written English and some of its characteristics now, is available online at www.routledge.com/9780415784528. The section uses historical and contemporary examples to point out the limitations of an exclusive reliance on the apprehension of grapho-phonic correspondences as the sole means of teaching reading.

The big question

We come now to the big question: how *do* children learn to read, and how can we help them to do so?

Written words are like faces, places and things

The earliest answer, chronologically, has a beguiling simplicity. Children begin to learn to read by being introduced to and then recognising and remembering whole words in contexts that make sense, drawing on their existing understanding of those words in the spoken language. There are about 50,000 words in the sight vocabulary of a person who can read a popular newspaper or magazine, and many more in the sight vocabulary of a more highly educated person. That is impressive. Surely children can't begin to make an assault on these large numbers without being taught some rules in advance? Yes they can, given the enormous power of the learning brain.

By the time a child is three years old, he or she has learned to recognise and distinguish many thousands of faces, places and things. Faces of family and friends; shapes of toys; shapes and behaviour of animals; the difference between a knife and a pencil (both pointed things that you can hold); colours; characters on television; machines of many kinds; different kinds of food, and their names: the hugely varied reality of the world surrounding the child and making an impression on her or him is being sorted and named. It is being named, of course, with the help of the child's developing spoken language.

This complex and varied world, being named, being understood, forming patterns that make sense in the child's mind (the bed is in the bedroom, not the kitchen; mum or dad sound the way they do, not like granny and granddad who come to the house sometimes; cows don't bark and dogs don't moo; pencils of different colours make marks of different colours on paper, and those colours can be named, and can make pictures of things or people that can be named): this world, already coming under the child's comprehension and control, is actually far more complex and varied and, we might even say, challenging to decode than the first written words which the child will encounter in a book or on the wall or on a bus or in a shop or on the front of the fridge. The breakthrough moment for a young reader is when he or she realises that those marks which he or she notices in any of those places actually relate to sounds which he or she already understands as words in speech. Closely connected to this realisation is another: that sounds are temporary but writing is permanent. These realisations are supported by the beginnings of alphabetic knowledge which the child is gaining at school and at home.

The many thousands of faces, places and things which the child has come to recognise are meaningful because they exist in contexts that make sense. When a child comes to read pieces of continuous text, he or she similarly apprehends words in contexts that make sense: in patterns and groups. If that were not the case, if words existed independently of each other, then 50,000 flash cards, physical or electronic, would be the best way to learn 50,000 words. The grouping of the words, the learner's familiarity with what they refer to and the patterning of their relationship with spoken words, combine to ease the reader into meaning.

I also want to emphasise the supreme importance of the development of spoken language, because learning to read might be described as discovering a closely related (but not identical; there are differences) world of meaning – the written language – to set next to and to interact with the world of meaning – the spoken language – with which the child is already familiar.

The situation may be more complex for the EAL learner who has no experience of literacy in her or his first language, and whose first encounter with continuous print is in English. The teacher in this case should be helping the child to draw connections between her or his developing knowledge of spoken English and English in the written form.

Surrounded by, drenched and soaked in meaning

In a moment, I'm going to list the different kinds of support, or clue, that young readers rely on as they encounter texts. But before that, I'll say something which the reader may think too obvious.

To return to my contention that beginning readers learn to read by being introduced to and then recognising and remembering whole words in contexts that make sense, I must add that of course they need to be absolutely surrounded by, drenched and soaked in meaningful and interesting writing. Meaningful and interesting writing can be found in all kinds of places, but let us start with the most obvious place: books. There are books that the teacher reads to the class. There are big books where the children can follow the words as he or she reads. There are books that, once the child has heard and seen being read aloud by the teacher (or any other adult in the room), he or she can read in a group or alone, repeating the experience more independently. There are books accompanied by a CD or DVD so that the child can hear an experienced reader giving voice to the marks on the page. There are books which older children in the school might come into the class once a week to read with the younger ones. There are books in the school library and also down the road at the local public library, available for a class visit once a week or once a fortnight. There are books which go home to be read before bedtime or whenever there is a quarter of an hour to spare. Fortunately, there is no shortage of interesting, entertaining, beautifully illustrated books for beginning readers now. Teachers of reading in primary schools will rightly remark that funds are limited. Even so, it is worth getting hold of as many as the budget will allow. I'll say more about this later, in the section '*What* should beginning readers read?'

Re-reading is terribly important. The adult reader and the older child reader will re-read books from time to time and enjoy the experience. For the beginning reader, however, re-reading is vital. There is something about the revisiting – it may be again and again and again – of words, phrases, sounds and whole texts which seems to earth and reinforce understandings in the beginning reader's brain. We should never be impatient with a beginning reader's desire to return and re-return to a book.

Jessica Horst and her colleagues at Sussex University have recently brought academic support to these assertions. In referring to their research (Horst *et al.*, 2011), Horst writes:

> *This research suggests that it's not the number of books, but the repetition of each book that leads to greater learning. We know that children who watch the same TV programme over and over again do better in comprehension tests afterwards. What we think is happening with reading is that each time a child hears the book they are picking up new information. The first time it might just be the story, the second time they are noticing details of description, and so on . . . I think the message here could be that children don't necessarily need a vast quantity of books, but they do benefit from repeated exposure to those books.*

(Horst, no date)

Apart from books, there are other places where meaningful and interesting writing can be seen: all over the classroom walls; in the corridors; in the school hall; in the course of a half-hour walk outside the school; on the television and computer screen. The young child's learning environment must be saturated with this meaningful and interesting writing, pitched at the range of levels of competence represented by the children in the class. The teacher of reading shouldn't become preoccupied with exact micro-levels of difficulty – there is a great deal of pseudo-science to do with the measurement of difficulty in texts – but use her or his best judgement, and have books and other texts of a range of difficulty which will challenge the most confident readers and support the least confident.

The reason for offering this rather obvious and familiar advice is that, without it, the sections to follow, which are about the clues which readers use to make sense of texts, would be like a series of hooks with nothing to hook on to them. Beginning readers need the raw material on which to get to work. They need to see lots of words in meaningful and interesting groups so that their powerful remembering brains can first, obviously, remember; but next, and equally important, can begin to generalise from the raw material, can apprehend patterns and similarities in words which will lead them to make hypotheses – highly intelligent guesses, which will sometimes be wrong, but are evidence of learning nonetheless – about words they have never seen before, but may have heard read to them, and very probably will already have in the stock of their spoken language.

The reader's clues – semantic

The first of these sets of clues is very directly to do with meaning. The child makes use of *semantic clues* (semantics being the branch of linguistics to do with meaning) to identify words and make sense of text. If we read a sentence which begins: 'I put the dinner in the . . .' and which is followed by a four-letter word beginning with 'o', we know that this word is far more likely to be 'oven' than 'open'. If we turn the sentence round and chop it in two, so it reads: 'I opened the oven. There was my . . .' and we see that the next word has six letters and begins with 'd', we know that this word is far more likely to be 'dinner' than 'digger', although we admit the possibility that a young child might have put a toy digger in the oven when playing in the kitchen.

('But,' the reader might be saying, 'in all this you are presuming that the child has grasped some initial grapho-phonic correspondences. Where has this come from? Not all children appear to work out these correspondences for themselves. Don't we need in some way to help them do this?' The answer is 'Yes, we do, and we are coming to that shortly'. An irony in writing about reading is that I'm obliged to write paragraphs and sections one after the other. The processes which these paragraphs and sections are attempting to describe are normally going on simultaneously, or at least in very rapid succession, in the young reader's mind.)

For another example of a semantic clue available to the beginning reader, let us turn to one of the most popular picture books in use in the early years of primary education, *Rosie's Walk* by Pat Hutchins (Hutchins, 2009). Its first words, as most of us know, are 'Rosie the hen went for a . . . '. What did she go for? Before we find out what she went for, should we explain to the beginning reader that 'a' plus 'l' between two consonants, as in this word, make the sound /ɔː/, as in 'talk' and 'chalk', but not of course as in 'talc' or 'Malcolm' or 'balcony', where they make the sound /æl/? Should we do that? Or should we let the child's existing knowledge of familiar meaningful phrases in spoken English, perhaps combined – we fully agree – with her or his knowledge that 'w' at the beginning of words makes the sound /w/, perhaps further combined with the useful fact that the word is in the title of the book, do the work necessary to bring her or him to the conclusion that the thing that Rosie went for was a walk? I suggest we do the latter.

The reader's clues – syntactic

The second set of clues to support the young reader is *syntactic*: that is, to do with the order in which English arranges words in sentences or other groups. Word order is specific to a language. German often puts verbs at the end of a sentence. Adjectives in French usually but not always follow the noun rather than precede it. English has its own syntactic rules and conventions. Let us return to the two examples I have already used: one that I invented, one from *Rosie's Walk*. We might say, write or read 'I put the dinner in the oven'. We would not say, write or read 'Put I in dinner the oven the'. There is a grammatical order to those words: subject, verb, object, adverbial phrase telling us where I put the dinner.

The beginning reader does not know these technical terms yet, and does not need to. Her or his implicit developing competence in spoken English tells her or him that this is how that group of words should be arranged in order to do its job. In the case of that sentence being introduced to a child who has never seen the words 'put', 'dinner' or 'oven' written down before, and is at the very earliest stages of encountering texts, I accept of course that the child (or the children, if they are being taught as a group or a whole class) will need to be told what those words 'say'. But even in this case, the child's knowledge of how sentences and other groups of words are arranged, as long as he or she has had a normal experience of the spoken language, will help her or him to read that sentence. (We should acknowledge the extra demand facing some children learning to read English as an additional language when the syntax of their first language does not follow the subject-verb-object pattern of English.)

The first use of that example was to do with word order. I will use the example again to make a point about word class: the specific job that a word does in a sentence or other group of words. If we were to read, instead of 'I put the dinner in the oven', 'I put the did in the over', we would be distinctly puzzled. Not because 'did' and 'over' are harder words than 'dinner' or 'oven'; they are not. Our puzzlement would come about because 'did' is a verb and we were expecting a noun in that place, and 'over' is either a preposition or an adverb and we were again expecting a noun in that place. (In fact, 'over' can be a noun too, but only in cricket, so let that pass.) Once again, I hardly need say, the young child's puzzlement will not be expressed in those terms, but the puzzlement will be there. Looking at the thing positively, the child is being helped to read the sentence 'I put the dinner in the oven' correctly because of her or his implicit understanding of the jobs that particular classes of words do in particular places.

And we can do the same thing with Rosie. The child does not read 'Hen the went walk a Rosie for' or 'Rosie the her wet for a what'. Receptive syntactic power is being brought to bear on those words and, as long as the child's future experience of reading is associated with pleasure and achievement rather than mystification and frustration, that receptive syntactic power will continue to be employed as texts get more and more demanding.

The reader's clues – grapho-phonic

There *are* regular symbol-to-sound correspondences in written English; there are lots of them; and we should certainly make use of this convenient fact as we help children to learn to read. So grapho-phonic clues take their place in the whole box of tools, armoury of weapons – whatever metaphor we find helpful – available to the child to make sense of texts.

There is an important qualification to that statement, however. Grapho-phonic clues can often be useful but do not always work. So, to use language appropriate to a child, we might say that words often, but not always, look like other, similar words: 'hate', 'mate', 'date' and 'late' do indeed look like each other. Furthermore, they sound like each other. But 'blood', 'book' and 'boot', though they look like each other, do not in many accents sound like each other. (In adult terms, they do not share a rime; see the next sub-section.) And, to return to the examples used in the online resource 'Written English' (see page 47), 'bear' and 'stairs' and – let us add another one – 'dare' sound like each other but do not look like each other. In adult terms, there are grapho-phonic patterns in written English and in many other (but not all) languages, but they are not simple or 100 per cent reliable, and readers make use of them principally by unconscious association, not by learning them consciously as rules. But by all means let some of these groups of words – the ones that look and sound alike, the ones that look alike but sound different, the ones that sound alike but look different – be displayed on the classroom walls, and let the relationships between them be taught. In such displays, it is most useful when the words occur in the context of meaningful sentences.

Let me also offer another qualification, already mentioned in the online resource: many common words are pronounced differently in different parts of the United Kingdom and across the English-speaking world. I will repeat part of a paragraph from that resource. In a language such as English, with a great diversity of accents, regional, social and as used – variously – by speakers of English as an additional language, the excessive reliance on fixed symbol-to-sound relationships in the teaching of reading will lead to unnecessary difficulties and confusions. It is true that in many parts of the English-speaking world the word 'book' is pronounced with the short 'oo' sound /ʊ/. But in some parts of the north of England it is pronounced with the long 'oo' sound /uː/. Although in the south of England the words 'flood' and 'blood' are pronounced differently from the word 'book' (/ʌ/ versus /ʊ/), in other parts of the north of England the 'oo' sound is pronounced similarly to that in 'book', as /ʊ/. EAL learners, who are acquiring English as spoken with a particular local accent, may have a particular difficulty when confronted with the requirement to pronounce a particular letter in a certain approved but different way.

Onset and rime

Some researchers (Goswami and Bryant, 1990; Wylie and Durrell, 1970) have convincingly argued that, in English words, a much more reliable correspondence between symbol and sound than that between letters and phonemes is to be found in the onset and rime within syllables. In words beginning with a consonant, the onset is the initial part of a syllable, consisting of one or more consonants. The rime is the remaining part of the syllable, consisting of the vowel which follows the onset and any consonant or consonants following that vowel. So, in the word 'beat', 'b' is the onset and 'eat' is the rime. In the word 'walk', 'w' is the onset and 'alk' is the rime. (Words which begin with a vowel have rimes but no onset.) Rimes provide more reliable (though not infallible) guides to pronunciation than do vowels, either singly or in combination. Wylie and Durrell offer a list of 37 rimes that are regular for nearly 500 words (quoted in Dombey *et al.*, 1998: 9).

The grapho-phonic teaching and display recommended in this section should apply equally strongly to onset and rime, and children should be helped to see analogies between groups of words sharing a rime. The reason why 'The cat sat on the mat', 'The rain in Spain stays mainly on the plain' and 'Ned is in his red bed' are stereotypical examples of traditional phonics teaching is that the rimes are all but two of the lexical words in these sentences are identical.

Helping children to attend to word patterns in this way will throw up fewer 'exceptions' than one-to-one symbol-to-phoneme teaching. But even onset and rime are not 100 per cent reliable. Think of 'sow' and 'row'. In these cases, reliability or otherwise is dependent on the meanings of the words (something you do with a seed, a female pig, to propel a boat with oars, an angry disagreement). Think of 'love', 'move' and 'drove'. Think of 'beat' and 'great'. The rimes don't rhyme!

The alphabet

Children should learn the alphabet. They should practise writing the letters, upper case and lower case, and be helped to develop a clear handwriting style. (There is more on this in Chapter 4.) It is when it comes to teaching the sounds of the letters in isolation from actual words that the problem comes. My advice would be: if the teacher has charts on which letter sounds are to be displayed, he or she should make sure, within the bounds of simplicity, that the charts are telling the truth. It is certainly the case that the letter 'a', whose name is /eɪ/, can be pronounced /æ/ as in 'cat'. But, as time goes by, the teacher should introduce children to some of the other sounds that 'a' can say: it can say /eɪ/ (like its name) as in 'hay', or /ɑː/ as in 'father', or /eə/ as in 'hare'. Charts and other teaching aids should give a small number of examples of the different sounds that a letter makes in different simple words. The diversity of sound is greatest with the vowels. But it's important to be truthful about the consonants too, where the diversity is less. And, once again, the words should be offered in the context of meaningful sentences.

Three more kinds of reader's clue

Picture clues are tremendously important to the young reader. Good picture books – I have quoted from one – help children into reading because pictures are the form of mark-making which children usually encounter and apprehend (as readers or as makers of marks) before they encounter and apprehend written words. There are things in the world. Pictures are the representations of things. Words are also the representations of things, which the child may well have represented first in pictures. He or she may well have drawn a house or a car or mummy or daddy or a bear before he or she writes those words. So when it comes to reading, having those prior representations on the page is a tremendous help in connecting the word to the thing.

I'll mention two other kinds of clue which help the young reader. The first I'll call *textual* clues. We know, without especially thinking about it, that there are differences in style and structure between the written language of a fairy-tale, a cookery book, a technical manual explaining how a computer works, and an opinion article in a newspaper. The examination of these differences in linguistics is called discourse analysis. The child, as long as he or she has had a normal experience of the spoken language and as long as he or she has had an enjoyable experience of being read to, will have an unconscious understanding of different kinds of text. At the beginning, the range he or she will encounter may be limited, but will (or should) certainly include stories of various kinds, poems, rhymes and songs, and simple information texts. Expectations of a particular text in terms of its style and structure are another support to the beginning reader. The reader of *Rosie's Walk* would be as puzzled if the text suddenly turned into a manual for the rearing of hens for egg-laying purposes or (heaven forbid) a cookery book containing delicious recipes for roast chicken, as if the text derailed in the semantic and syntactic ways which I have already mentioned.

Finally, there are *bibliographic clues*: clues to do with the physical form of books. A book has a cover, then a title page, and then we come to the contents of the book itself. Books may be arranged in chapters. Because English is written from left to right and from top to bottom, we read a left-hand page before we read a right-hand page, although a book may begin on a right-hand page, and we (usually) start reading at the top and go down the page. (I say 'usually' because some of our best picture books have words scattered over the page in arrangements other than straightforward top to bottom.) Familiarity with the physical form of books is another support to the beginning reader.

The left-to-right and top-to-bottom convention in English writing is just that, of course: a convention. Teachers should point it out as such, particularly if there are children in the class who can read scripts which use other conventions. In this context, as I've said elsewhere, the reading classroom should contain books written in the first languages of EAL learners, and in bilingual editions.

A whole panoply of support

We can see that a whole panoply of support is available to the learning reader, from semantic, syntactic, grapho-phonic, picture, textual and bibliographic clues.

If teachers and other adults, notably parents, help children to make full use of these supports as they show them into books and other places where they encounter written language, beginning readers will have the best chance of becoming skilled and independent readers by the time they are seven, and very often before that. I discuss below the reasons why some children fail to become skilled and independent readers by seven. One major reason is that those children have not been made aware of the whole panoply of support described here.

What should beginning readers read?

In the sub-section above called 'Surrounded by, drenched and soaked in meaning', I mentioned *what* children read, but overall this chapter has been more concerned with *how* they learn to read. I should rectify this imbalance now, because of course the *what* is just as important as the *how*.

A diverse range of authentic texts

Children are best helped to develop their powers of literacy, to become fully competent and enjoying readers and writers, if they are provided with a diverse range of authentic texts to hear and read – texts drawing on the natural patterns and rhythms of English – which will give them pleasure, information and satisfaction as readers, and supply examples of how to write across that range themselves.

The range, from the start, should include: stories of various kinds, traditional and contemporary, realistic, fantastic, mythic, funny, mysterious, sad, touching; songs, rhymes and poems with the same variety of qualities; and simple information texts on an equally wide variety of topics.

Repetition of words and phrases in the best picture books is one of the ways in which readers are helped to become familiar with characteristic patterns in English: characteristic spelling patterns within words; characteristic syntactic relations between words. And I would particularly emphasise the importance of rhyme. Rhymes naturally give pleasure, because they are akin to music. They also subtly teach about patterns within and between words.

I repeat that, in classrooms where there are EAL learners, the range of books available should include some written in the mother tongue(s) of those children, and in bilingual editions.

'Relevance' in books

Much has been written over the years about the importance of 'relevance' in the reading matter offered to children. My only advice would be that teachers should promote 'both/and' rather than 'either/or'. The range of books we offer should both represent and affirm the children as they are, in terms of their gender and their cultural, linguistic, ethnic and social background, and introduce them to worlds beyond those with which they are familiar. The past 50 years have seen a huge increase in the number of children's books representing cultural, ethnic and social diversity, and representing girls in active and initiative-taking roles. This change is wholly to be welcomed. At the same time, books appealing to children's imaginations and fantasies, addressing their unspoken fears, books which may have nothing to do – at least at a superficial and literal level – with the actual reality of their lives, are, always have been and always will be key texts in children's reading development.

Encounters with this range of writing will extend children's receptive capacity as readers, and also give them a flying start as writers; they will see how these things are made. And the writing children encounter in this way should not just be in published books, although these may well constitute the mainstay. It should also include successful writing by other children in the school, perhaps turned into simple booklets; and writing by the teacher. The teacher needs to show that he or she writes too. My experience is that children are particularly impressed when their own teacher writes for them.

Levels of difficulty

Of course, the texts we offer to children should be broadly appropriate to their age group and to their previous experience as readers. But it isn't necessary to introduce children to texts each of which is supposed to be differentiated by small, regular advances in difficulty. Supposedly 'scientific' and precise calculations of difficulty are open to serious question and pale into insignificance by comparison with the importance of the degree of active interest and pleasure which a child has in reading a book.

Why reading schemes?

Why, when a diverse range of authentic texts is available to the beginning reader in a rich country like the United Kingdom, and in many other countries of the English-speaking world, do so many schools rely on reading schemes as the principal reading material to which they introduce young children?

Reading schemes of one kind or another are in use in many of the primary schools in the United Kingdom. There are better and worse schemes. The worst contain a series of artificial texts, divorced from authentic language use, which rehearse isolated and graded language features according to a theory of language and reading development which exists in the writers' heads. Often, these schemes don't even use books, but series of cards each carrying an unnatural piece of writing, whose purpose is not to interest and engage the reader (whatever the accompanying advertising might say) but to introduce her or him to the next feature or level on the ascending scale of difficulty.

A little better are those schemes containing books (not cards), the language of whose texts is 'natural', by which I mean not mutilated to focus only on one language feature, but all of which have been written exclusively for the scheme by one author or a small number of authors. The tendency here is for the texts to be dull and monochrome, although at least they are written in sentences showing a greater diversity of vocabulary and syntactic structure than the texts in the worst schemes.

However, the best resources grouping texts of increasing difficulty are not reading schemes in the narrow sense at all, but collections which recommend or physically bring together authentic books from different publishers, written by authors for the pleasure of writing and not to go into a scheme, where the compiler of the collection has grouped the books as broadly appropriate for a particular age range. These collections, where we might say that someone else has done the hard work of making choices on the teacher's behalf, can be used as centrepieces or starting points for the teacher's wider collection, which will also include her or his own choices.

Schemes can discourage re-reading

I've already referred to the immense value to the young child of re-reading a book. Reading schemes tend relentlessly to drive readers onward and upward to the next level. There is indeed a competitive element in children's characters. Children in that respect bear a remarkable resemblance to human beings. And sometimes the competitiveness can be against oneself as much as against others. However, the 'onward and upward' drive can easily discourage the desire to re-read. I've said that we should never be impatient with a beginning reader's desire to return and re-return to a book; reading schemes can work against what should be a necessary patience.

What is our understanding of development?

In agreeing that not all reading schemes should be tarred with the same brush, I've delayed answering the basic question of a few paragraphs back: why do schools seem to need them and why are they so popular? There may be mundane economic answers to that question, such as that schools believe a scheme is cheaper to buy than is a pile of really good books. But at a deeper level, the answer goes to the heart of the argument which has occupied this chapter. If our understanding of development is flawed, if we mistakenly imagine that development is logical not psychological, linear not multi-dimensional, largely analytical not largely competence-driven, concerned with parts rather than wholes, of course we will prefer resources which offer a logical, linear, analytical, disassembled model of learning. The casualties of this approach will be some of the children.

It's quite understandable that schools which have invested in a reading scheme can't simply throw away the scheme tomorrow and buy lots of wonderful individual books. Decisions about reading material in primary schools have to be taken collectively by the whole staff. But teachers, literacy coordinators and school leaders should ask themselves whether the reading material in use in their classrooms is offering the children an authentic experience of written language, in all its diversity, at a level broadly appropriate to their stage of development in literacy.

Why do some children fail?

Some children experience great difficulty in learning to read, and a few fail completely. I'm not talking principally here about children with the most severe special needs, but about a range of children who for some reason do not manage easily, or at all, what their contemporaries can do. What is going wrong?

In the very last paragraph of *Becoming Literate: The Construction of Inner Control,* Marie Clay writes:

> *My special plea would be that we recognize that some children need extra resources and many more supportive interactions with teachers to get them through the necessary transitions of reading acquisition to the stage where they can pick up most of the different kinds of information in print. As they read familiar texts or are challenged to engage in reading work on novel texts their literacy 'systems' which generate (a) correct responding and (b) effective problem-solving provide them with feedback on the effectiveness of the strategies they used. Success encourages more risk-taking which, in turn, is likely to extend the range of strategies they try.*
>
> (Clay, 1991: 345)

More privileged access

To put Clay's insight into other words, most failing readers don't need exceptional, arcane teaching routines in which elements of language (learned holistically and unconsciously by more successful readers) are first decontextualised and then presented to them as repetitive sets, to be apprehended and learned slowly and painfully in the low gears of conscious learning.

Instead, they need *more privileged access to the same range of experiences of written language as successful readers have had*, in which the high gears are at work, in which the affective, the cognitive and the linguistic areas of the mind are in interactive and mutually supportive operation, engaging with real language and getting the rewards – small to begin with, perhaps, but felt and accumulating – which encounters with real language bring. In practical terms, this means that once a teacher has identified a failing reader, the help that child receives, whether from the teacher or from a teaching assistant or a special needs teacher or a volunteer parent in the class or at home, should be a personalised and intensive version of what the other children are getting, not something completely different.

There is a small group of children whose physical and/or intellectual needs are so specific or unusual that the teacher's approach to their learning must be specialist. But in their actual encounters with written language, these potential readers – however disabled, damaged or unusual they may be – need to gain pleasure, to grasp and make meaning, in and from whole, real written language, just like the rest of us; and the teacher's approach must recognise and meet this need.

Some reasons for failure

The principal reason for a child's failure to learn to read which could be laid at the teacher's door is an over-reliance on only one method, one programme of instruction. For example, failing readers may have been made to jump through, and failed to jump through, the sound-to-symbol correspondence hoop, offered to them, benevolently but misguidedly, as the only way of learning to read. Their failure has led to anxiety and guilt.

Failure may then have been 'technologised' and medicalised. There is a huge literature in which some writers on reading have tried to explain failure in terms of the pathology of the individual child, while apparently ignoring the straightforward possibility that the conditions likely to produce success, repeatedly described in this chapter, may have been absent. The practices recommended by these 'experts' to cure the 'condition' of failing readers often involve exposing them to decontextualised sets or particles of words, or even sets of particles of words, often on flash cards or computer screens, which are the productions of the adult analytical mind, and are far removed from the contextualised experience of the successful reader.

Failing readers may have been fed an exclusive diet of the worst kind of reading schemes; in other words, their experience has been of *reading* books (or cards) rather than reading *books*. How do you feel when you are still stuck on purple and your best friends have bounded up through green and blue to yellow? Failing readers are likely to read fewer and worse books than successful readers.

On the other hand, failure or difficulty may have been brought about by an over-lax attitude to children's encounters with books: by an assumption that all children will automatically become fluent readers as long as they are put into supportive contact with good books. There are children who do indeed learn to read this way; and those of us who are successful readers and have been so from early childhood can often not remember, certainly not in any detail, how we learned to read. But some children will not achieve fluency so easily; they need closer and more deliberate support, the 'more privileged access' described above.

The present situation in England

The triumph of synthetic phonics

Despite everything which has been argued and demonstrated in the past – some of which this chapter has tried to summarise – to do with the complex interaction of intellectual processes by which young children become readers, the promotion of only one 'method' – synthetic phonics – as the near-exclusive way in which children should be taught to read has now triumphed in primary schools and Early Years settings in England, at least so far as government policy is concerned.

The Rose Report

The initiative which has given synthetic phonics its current official status as the quasi-obligatory method of teaching reading is the Rose Report, published in 2006, whose formal title is *Independent Review of the Teaching of Early Reading*.

The review which led to this report was headed by former Her Majesty's Inspectorate Director of Inspection Sir Jim Rose, in response to a recommendation by the House of Commons Education Select Committee that there should be a government enquiry into the teaching of reading. From its first pages, the report takes the excellence of synthetic phonics as a given, and confidently recommends that teachers and trainee teachers should be required to teach synthetic phonics as the principal means of introducing young children to reading. The government of the day accepted the report's recommendation entirely and uncritically.

The report proposes a 'simple view of reading', which divides the process into two parts: 'word recognition' and 'language comprehension'. In doing so, it advises that teachers and policy-makers should abandon a previously recommended model of reading called the 'searchlights model', which had been introduced in 1998 in the context of the National Literacy Strategy (Department for Education and Employment, 1998). The searchlights model had seen the reader as bringing four kinds of knowledge to the encounter with a text: 'knowledge of context', 'phonics (sounds and spelling)', 'grammatical knowledge' and 'word recognition and graphic knowledge'. (It will be seen that the searchlights model, discarded in the Rose Report, is rather closer to this chapter's understanding of reading than is the simple view of reading.)

The report, therefore, has a binary understanding of reading:

Evidence suggests that word recognition processes and language comprehension processes are separable dimensions of reading.

(Rose, 2006: 78)

Actually, no evidence that I've seen suggests any such thing. This view of reading is simplistic rather than simple. The idea that word recognition and language comprehension can be taught and assessed separately is wrong. All successful encounters with texts, large and small, must involve both recognition and comprehension. In support of the simple view of reading, the report quotes the poignant case of Milton's daughters, taught to pronounce but not to understand classical and modern foreign languages so they could 'read' to their blind father. This is false analogy at its clearest: the daughters were 'reading' the words of foreign languages, some long dead, not the language in whose spoken form they had been immersed since childhood.

As we shall see in a moment, the simple view of reading has made its way into the new orders for reading at Key Stage 1.

The Year 1 phonics check

From June 2012, every state school in England teaching pupils at Key Stage 1 has been obliged to conduct a 'Year 1 phonics screening check' on children towards the end of their first year of compulsory schooling. Additionally, from June 2013, pupils in Year 2 who 'failed' the phonics check (gained fewer than a specified number of marks out of 40) the previous year have been required to retake it. In the introduction to the book, we remarked on one of the more bizarre features of the check: that it requires children to learn some non-existent or nonsense words which nonetheless conform to the graphophonic 'rules' which synthetic phonics asserts. The non-existent or nonsense words are included in the test which 5- and 6-year-olds have to undergo, and some schools have been sending children home with lists of these non-words to practise.

This is an extraordinary state of affairs, and it is hard to know where to begin in criticising the phonics check. The situation is beyond irony. We are in *Alice in Wonderland* or perhaps 'Jabberwocky' territory. Let us say nothing about the cost of the thing. The essential criticism of the check is that it utterly fails to represent everything we know about how a successful 5- and 6-year-old reader should be operating. And it utterly fails to detect a failing

5- and 6-year-old reader, because to be able to pronounce isolated, phonically regular words, half of them non-existent, is no guarantee of being able to
read in the sense of being able to make sense of meaningful print.

The Year 1 phonics check is a triumph of ideology over reason. Apart from
its shortcomings as a brief experience of reading for a child on a particular day
in June, its existence has already had a distorting effect on the teaching of
reading in many classrooms in the months leading up to that day. The check
will one day be looked back on with a mixture of mirth, embarrassment and
regret. It should be abolished.

I don't dismiss the idea of a test of reading a year later, at 7, however.
Chapter 12 contains proposals for assessment 3 to 11, and includes a test of
reading at the end of Key Stage 1 whose construction recognises the whole,
complex activity that reading is.

Statutory framework for the Early Years Foundation Stage

The current version of the government's statutory framework for the Early
Years Foundation Stage has this to say about reading:

> *Children read and understand simple sentences. They use phonic know-
> ledge to decode regular words and read them aloud accurately. They also
> read some common irregular words. They demonstrate understanding when
> talking with others about what they have read.*
>
> (Department for Education, 2014c: 11)

This is an interesting paragraph. The only specific approach to reading the
government is prepared to countenance is phonics. Somehow, children also
'read and understand simple sentences'. 'They also read some common irregular words.' And 'They demonstrate understanding'. How they come to do
these things remains unspecified. Not even the briefest attempt is made to
name the other routes into reading which we have detailed in this chapter.

The National Curriculum for English from 2014:
reading at Key Stage 1

In the government's orders for a revised National Curriculum for English for
Key Stages 1 to 4 (Department for Education, 2014a), the requirements for

reading for Key Stage 1 are divided, following the Rose Report's simple view, into 'word reading' and 'comprehension'.

The word reading requirements for Years 1 and 2 fly directly and deliberately in the face of the idea that reading is a meaning-making activity. They are precise and detailed lists of instructions for the teaching of phonic rules. They demonstrate to its fullest extent the government's determination that synthetic phonics is the only means by which young children should be taught to read. This extremism is carried to the point, in the requirements for children at Year 1, of the explicit discouragement of the reading of books containing words which fail to conform to grapho-phonic regularity (in other words, most of the books which 5- and 6-year-old children have been known over the years to enjoy).

> *Pupils should be taught to . . . read books aloud accurately that are consistent with their developing phonic knowledge and that do not require them to use other strategies to work out words.*
>
> (*ibid*.: 21)

Meanwhile, and coming as an unexpected breath of fresh air, the comprehension requirements offer teachers every opportunity to teach well. They begin:

> *Pupils should be taught to . . . develop pleasure in reading, motivation to read, vocabulary and understanding . . .*
>
> (*ibid*.: 22)

The comprehension requirements then list some entirely reasonable means by which these desirable ends may be achieved (though whether it is possible actually to teach pleasure is a deep question which I shall not pursue further).

Thus, the Key Stage 1 orders for reading as they stand are incoherent and contradictory. Broadly enlightened requirements on comprehension, which give teachers all the professional autonomy they need to teach well, sit side by side with requirements at the word reading level so detailed, so micromanaging, that the teacher here is nothing more than a technician following instructions. And the instructions are simply wrong. An obsessive, exclusive focus on synthetic phonics is not the way to produce confident, accurate readers. Pleasure in reading, which in the new orders is confined to comprehension, must apply equally at every level of encounter with texts, including word recognition. This will only occur when beginning readers are encouraged to bring the whole range of their intellectual faculties to bear on the text in order to derive meaning from it, and are not confined to following one narrow and intellectually flawed set of procedures.

In the introduction, we listed three quotations from the government's March 2016 White Paper on education. They were all to do with the government's ambition to grant a degree of professional autonomy to teachers and school leaders. As we noted, these proud boasts are utterly at variance with reality in several areas of the English curriculum, and notably in the area of early reading.

An alternative

In Chapter 11, readers will find a better-balanced approach to the teaching of early reading at ages 3 to 7, exemplifying the principles laid out in this chapter.

To conclude . . .

I pay tribute to the extraordinary resilience, patience and skill of thousands of teachers in Early Years settings and at Key Stage 1 who continue to guide hundreds of thousands of children every year towards confident success as readers by the age of seven. A central feature of this magnificent achievement is that teachers communicate to children that reading is a profoundly useful and pleasurable activity.

Effective teachers know that young children bring to the task of reading a whole range of intellectual strategies based on their existing understanding of the characteristics, patterns and structures of spoken language, drawing on the links they are beginning to make between spoken and written language, and using the formidable tool of their memory. To these strategies the teacher adds explicit teaching about the characteristics, patterns and structures of written language in books and all the other places where meaningful print is encountered.

I have called teachers 'the people in between' the two opposing camps described early in the chapter, and said that they use 'whatever works'. While this last statement may be true (and there is plenty of evidence from HMI reports and elsewhere that it is), it does not represent an ideal situation, because uncritical eclecticism leaves the practitioner exposed to winds of fashion in teaching method and, worse, with no argument to challenge a government's requirement when it is imposed in the way it currently is in the area of early reading.

It is important to make a distinction between eclecticism in the mind of the beginning reader – the healthy habit of using whatever strategy works to derive meaning from a word, group of words, sentence or whole text – and uncritical eclecticism of method on the part of the teacher, which is a more doubtful virtue.

There is another, even more important distinction to be made: that between *theory* and *method*. Having a theory is not the same as, but is a much larger thing than, using a method. Teachers need a theory which is intellectually robust and demonstrably practical. Out of a sound theory will come a relaxed, inclusive but not uncritical regard for method. I hope that the advice offered in this chapter supplies teachers with the basis for the development and sustaining of such a theory, and with the professional strength to withstand and blunt the negative impact of ill-judged government statute.

3 Reading 7 to 11

Peter Traves

Summary of main points

The ability to read well is vital in our society. It brings with it huge benefits in terms of pleasure, personal enrichment, practical value and power.

The demands on and expectations of readers are increasing. These need to be reflected in the absolute priority given to reading as part of the curriculum from 7 to 11 and in the resources allocated to support it.

The teaching of reading requires an understanding of the different purposes for which we read, the complexity of the task of reading and the range of reading skills needed to support learning. The varied purposes and types of text, and the different means through which text is now carried, call for different skills on the part of the reader. These skills need to be taught systematically, but not mechanically.

Effective reading is needed for success in all areas of the curriculum at Key Stage 2. This calls for a coherent whole-school approach to literacy. One feature of this approach is that productive use of the school library is at the heart of the school's life. Another is that teachers and other adults in school show pupils that they read too.

Reading is inextricably linked to the other modes of language: writing, speaking and listening. These links should be recognised in pupils' experiences of reading across the curriculum.

Pleasure in reading is the key. Research confirms a direct link between the commitment to reading for pleasure and wider educational success.

The interests and experiences learners bring to the classroom are one starting point for the encouragement of reading. But teachers have a responsibility to make sure that pupils become ambitious readers, able to take on a wider range of texts outside their own immediate experience and at increasing levels of complexity and demand.

Reading for information is a basic tool across the curriculum and in life. Pupils need frequent, wide and deliberate experience of it and the demonstration, instruction and encouragement to take on ever more challenging tasks and material.

Pupils should be shown how literature and other texts achieve their effects. They also need opportunities to explore how their own perspectives, values and assumptions compare with those in the texts they encounter.

All learners can experience the pleasure and satisfaction that reading can bring. Those who initially fail to gain the benefits or those whose interest in reading has faded need particular help, tailored to their different histories and characteristics. Underachievement in and underuse of reading by boys are by no means inevitable.

All these principles apply with equal force to learners of English as an additional language (about one in six pupils in the age group with which this book is concerned). However, pupils who have begun to read and write in another language and are learning to write in English are additionally engaged in the complex process of making comparisons between writing systems. Appropriate books in the first language and in bilingual editions can help the comparison of the writing systems of English and the other language(s), in addition to the other benefits they bring. More advanced bilingual learners can derive especial benefit from paying attention to the structures and styles of the more academic forms of writing with which their previous reading in English has not made them familiar.

The coverage of reading for pupils aged 7 to 11 in the current National Curriculum for England is uneven. A more coherent alternative is offered in Chapter 11.

Reading – at large and in school

The ability to read and understand instructions and text is a basic requirement of success in all school subjects. The importance of literacy skills does not, however, come to an end when children leave school. Such skills are key to all areas of education and beyond, facilitating participation in the wider context of lifelong learning and contributing to individuals' social integration and personal development.

(European Commission, 2001, quoted in
Kirsch *et al.*, *Reading for Change: Performance and
Engagement Across Countries – Results from PISA 2000*, 2002: 15)

The most important job

If we are to achieve a coherent and systematic approach to the teaching of reading from 7 to 11, we should begin with an attempt to say what it is we are aiming for. We need to establish what we expect readers to be able to do in the world we live in now.

Our society assumes literacy and, as a result, greatly disadvantages those who lack reading skills. The fact that some people succeed despite low levels of literacy is a tribute to their resourcefulness and resilience, but such success stories are the exception rather than the rule. Those with low levels of competence as readers are more likely to be unemployed or insecurely employed and less likely to have good housing and health. Poor reading skills are not the only factors that contribute to these disadvantages, but the link is clear.

What reading is good for

Creating capable and keen readers is the most important job that schools can do. Here is one way of describing the high-value benefits that skilled independent reading can bring:

1 **Pleasure**: the pleasure of reading easy and entertaining material effortlessly, as well as the more strenuous pleasure which comes from understanding difficult material.
2 **Personal enrichment**: as a source of experience and of knowledge, reading extends your horizons, broadens your vision, enlarges your perspective.
3 **Practical value**: being able to put reading to use maximises your chances of benefiting from schooling and enables you to find out things from print, now and in the future.
4 **Power**: reading means access and enables you to find out things about your history and the society you live in which it's harder to discover in other ways; you can also discover things about other histories and societies which may surprise you.

> (Raleigh, 'Independent Reading', in
> *The English Magazine 10*, 1982; reprinted in *Where We've Been:*
> *Articles from The English & Media Magazine*, Simons [ed.], 1996: 118)

The vehicles of text

There is certainly no less demand for reading than in the past; there is probably more, as a 2006 survey of research for the National Literacy Trust remarked:

Adolescents entering the adult world in the 21st century will read and write more than at any other time in human history. They will need advanced levels of literacy to perform their jobs, run their households, act as citizens, and conduct their personal lives.

(*Reading for Pleasure: A Research Overview*,
Clark and Rumbold, 2006: 5)

The vehicles by which text is carried have never been so varied, ubiquitous and powerful.

The digital revolution has sometimes been assumed to be reducing the extent and range of reading and to make reading more a matter of dealing with short and limited snippets of text. In practice, this does not seem to be the case. Instead, the digital carriage of text appears to have stepped up the volume and widened the range of the reading that is done for social, cultural and work purposes. It has increased the availability of previously rare material, factual and otherwise, giving us much easier access to, for example, historical records, old and new literature, and specialist information. It has transformed research as well as communication. It has also affected styles of reading, putting ever more of a premium on processes such as scanning and skimming, finding routes through sets of material, interpreting graphics, understanding and sometimes challenging the reliability of sources. Because so much more material is available to read than before, the skills of locating, digesting and evaluating information and ideas are in greater demand than ever.

What all good readers can do

The following list is an attempt to describe what all good readers – of any age – can do. It draws on a helpful set of materials produced by the English and Media Centre (*Spotlight on Literacy: Creative Interventions in English and Across the Curriculum*, Bleiman *et al.*, 2013: 209) and on guidance from the School Library Association (*SLA Guidelines: Creating Readers: A Reflective Guide for School Librarians and Teachers*, Goodwin, 2013: 10).

Good readers:

- show versatility, reading different kinds of material in different ways (and sometimes the same material in different ways);

- develop and refine their own preferences for what to read while being open to new possibilities;
- find ways to cope with unfamiliar and challenging material;
- identify and follow the plot of a piece of writing (whether fiction or otherwise), inferring what is happening and speculating about where it may go next;
- interpret ideas, themes and patterns and form questions and comments as they go along;
- skim, scan, select and record in order to locate and log what they are after;
- appreciate multiple meanings, ambiguities and other twists and turns of language;
- connect what they read to their prior knowledge and experience;
- cross-refer, combine and compare information from a variety of sources, as well as connecting what they read with their prior knowledge and experience;
- make and articulate considered judgements about texts and how they are written;
- reflect on the ways in which they go about their reading.

Any or all of the abilities listed above can be applied to virtually any kind of text, whether literary or otherwise, long or short, highly imaginative or deeply routine. Neither is there any hierarchy of importance as between these abilities. Development in reading is not a matter of lockstep progress up through any such hierarchy. Younger readers have both the potential and the need to behave like more mature readers, and so can and should use the full range of abilities from the outset.

One last point about what many good readers do: they communicate and collaborate with others. Reading is not necessarily a solitary activity, though the satisfaction of 'getting lost in a book' is well understood. Discussion of reading with others is also a way of making reading come alive.

What teachers of reading can do

Teachers and librarians are key to developing pupils' enthusiasm for reading and for making reading prominent and talked about in the school. There is evidence that too many teachers have limited knowledge of children's literature, factual and imaginative. It has often been inadequately covered in their training, and they are not able confidently to recommend books and authors.

One source of such evidence is the UKLA Teachers as Readers: Building Communities of Readers project, conducted in 2007 and 2008. The core goal of the project was to 'improve teachers' knowledge and use of literature in order to help them increase children's motivation and enthusiasm for reading, especially those less successful in literacy' (Cremin *et al.*, 2008). It did this by working with 40 teachers in five local authorities in England.

Here are the project's central findings:

As teachers in the project enriched their subject knowledge of children's literature and other texts, they took risks in their choices and responded more aesthetically. Many transformed their conceptions of reading and readers and recognised their professional responsibility to sustain their enhanced subject knowledge. Personally and professionally, the teachers took considerably more pleasure in reading.

The teachers' increased subject knowledge, combined with personal reflection and support, enabled them to create a more inclusive reading for pleasure pedagogy. This encompassed marked improvements in reading environments, read aloud programmes, book talk and book recommendations and the provision of quality time for independent reading. As teachers became more confident, autonomous and flexible in using their enriched subject knowledge, they began to articulate an informed and strategic rationale for selecting and using texts to support children's reading for pleasure.

Teachers came to appreciate the significance of the wider range of reading which children experience in their homes and communities. They recognised the importance of extending definitions of reading and providing a more satisfying and challenging reading curriculum.

Some teachers developed as 'Reading Teachers' and became increasingly aware of their [own] reading preferences, habits, behaviours and strategies and explored connections between their own reading practices and those of the children. As a result, these professionals sought to build reciprocal reading communities, which focused on readers' rights and identities and fostered learner autonomy. As potent role models, they markedly influenced the children's commitment to reading.

Shared understandings were established between teachers, children and families about the changing nature of reading and everyday reading practices. These supported children reading for pleasure and generated new kinds of talk about reading, both with and amongst children. Where relationships with local libraries were fostered, there was evidence of significant impact on individual children's lives.

(ibid.)

In brief, teachers of reading should be familiar with and enthusiastic about the range of factual and imaginative literature available to the learners for whom they are responsible. Equally important is the continuing development of teachers' own experience of reading, at their level. The project's definition of 'Reading Teachers' is 'teachers who read and readers who teach'. When teachers are enthusiastic and wide-ranging readers themselves, they are better teachers of reading.

No end to it . . .

The message of this section of the chapter is that achievement in reading does not end with the acquisition of fluency in decoding words; neither does it come about simply from exposure to more text. Reading needs deliberate and continual development if our young readers are to match and surpass the demands made on them, now and in the future.

PISA (the Programme for International Student Assessment) makes regular international comparisons of educational performance. The section began with a quotation from the 2000 PISA report on reading. It ends with another:

> *Literacy is no longer considered an ability only acquired in childhood during the early years of schooling. Instead, it is viewed as an expanding set of knowledge, skills and strategies which individuals build on throughout life in various situations and through interaction with their peers and with the larger communities in which they participate.*
>
> (Kirsch *et al.*, 2002: 24)

One snapshot from the past: the Bullock Report

Chapters 1 and 2 record the circumstances in which the Bullock Committee was set up more than 40 years ago. We are frequently in a state of crisis about reading standards. The Bullock Report was only one of a series of reports commissioned over the past century in response to a perceived decline in standards of reading. On each occasion, government and the media have expected confirmation of the alleged decline, followed by simple recommendations that would solve the problem. On most occasions, the reporting group has come up with a more nuanced response to the question it had been asked.

A Language for Life, published in 1975, went far beyond its original, narrow brief, to examine the contemporary state of literacy teaching and to describe the kinds of teaching which would provide learners with the abilities in language and literacy that would sustain them for life.

> *We have also suggested that a wider and more demanding definition of literacy should be adopted. The existing criterion is determined by the reading standards of seven and nine year old children of many years ago on tests whose limitations are acknowledged. It should be replaced by a criterion capable of showing whether the reading and writing abilities of children are adequate to the demands made upon them in school and likely to face them in adult life.*
>
> (The Bullock Committee, 1975: paragraph 3.3)

The report recommended that the teaching of reading should be based on an analysis of the demands made on the mature reader. It argued for a coherent approach encompassing the full range of reading abilities. Crucially, it did not believe that learners should be introduced to the wider range of abilities only when they had mastered the basic skills of decoding. Rather, it advocated a reading curriculum in which the broad range of abilities is introduced from the start and is built on at increasing levels of sophistication as the learner develops.

The report offered an elegant definition, still relevant today, of the demands on a child's literacy:

> *What are these demands? This question is best answered in terms of three basic objectives, simple enough on paper but far from simple in the execution:*
>
> *(i) the pupil needs to be able to cope with the reading required in each area of the curriculum*
> *(ii) he should acquire a level of competence which will enable him to meet his needs as an adult in society when he leaves school*
> *(iii) he should regard reading as a source of pleasure and personal development which will continue to be a rewarding activity throughout life.*
>
> (*ibid.*: paragraph 8.2)

Implications for teaching

The report went on to explore the implications of these demands for the teaching of reading. One of the report's most celebrated sentences was a key driver of the language across the curriculum movement.

> *Since reading is a major strategy for learning in virtually every aspect of education we believe it is the responsibility of every teacher to develop it.*
> (*ibid*.: paragraph 8.9)

Bullock was received with considerable excitement by many in the educational community, and it spurred many schools to produce policies for language across the curriculum. Sadly, too often these policies existed only as written documents, and the process of translation into effective provision rarely happened on the scale required to realise the report's ambitions. Sustained attempts to build on the report's research and proposals have been rare over subsequent decades. Indeed, there has been a trend towards the kinds of definition of reading which the report explicitly rejected:

> *We believe that an improvement in the teaching of reading will not come from the acceptance of simplistic statements about phonics or any other single aspect of reading, but from a comprehensive study of all the factors at work and the influence that can be exerted upon them.*
> (*ibid*.: paragraph 6.3)

As discussed in detail in Chapter 2, the government's current policy with regard to early reading is based on a belief that systematic instruction in synthetic phonics is the only effective means by which young children learn to read, thus missing the point that learning to read is a broader, more complex task than could be achieved by any single 'method'. John Richmond's argument in Chapter 2, however, is not in any crude sense 'anti-phonics'. There *are* many grapho-phonic correspondences in the English writing system, and it is sensible for teachers to take advantage of this convenient fact. But very many English written words, and especially many of the commonest ones – those that young children will encounter most frequently – do not demonstrate straightforward grapho-phonic correspondences. They have to be learned by means in which phonics can play no part.

Furthermore, an excessive zealotry for phonics ignores one fundamental truth about reading, a truth that Bullock elegantly stated: that reading is essentially to do with the construction of meaning in the reader's mind, on the basis of the evidence provided by marks on a page or a screen.

> *It should be established from the beginning in the mind of the child that reading is primarily a thinking process, not simply an exercise in identifying shapes and sounds.*
>
> (*ibid*.: recommendation 73)

'Method', any method, is too narrow a term to do justice to the hypothesis-forming, rule-testing, rule-adapting, memory-employing, meaning-making complex activity which is reading.

Forty years on . . .

The achievement of a coherent understanding of the demands which reading makes on learners in different areas of the curriculum remains a key element of a successful primary school's approach to learning. The task for teachers and schools at Key Stage 2, put in other words than those used in *A Language for Life* but based on the principles spelled out in that report, is to use all the encouragement, resources and support schools can employ so that all learners gain the fullest pleasure, personal development, knowledge and understanding that reading can bring.

This in turn means:

- every school leader giving the highest priority to enabling all learners, regardless of their circumstances and starting points, to extend their experience, skills and use of reading;
- every teacher making sure that reading plays a central part in developing breadth and depth of knowledge and understanding in learning across all subjects.

The next three sections of this chapter cover the teaching of reading under three broad headings: reading for pleasure; reading for information; and reading imaginative literature. These categories correspond roughly to the way reading is often organised in schools, but they are of course by no means watertight. Pleasure is, or should be, a feature of reading both information and literary texts; information texts can be of the highest literary value; and imaginative literature can be mightily informative about all kinds of aspects of the real world.

Reading for pleasure

The active encouragement of reading for pleasure should be a core part of every child's curriculum entitlement because extensive reading and exposure to a wide range of texts make a huge contribution to students' educational achievement.

(All-Party Parliamentary Group for Education, *Report of the Inquiry into Overcoming the Barriers to Literacy,* 2011: 6)

How well do we do?

At the beginning of this century, the indications were that England was not doing well in promoting pleasure in reading. The 2003 national report for England of the Progress in International Reading Literacy Study (PIRLS) (Twist *et al.*, 2003), which compared 10-year-olds from 35 countries on a variety of literacy-related measures, showed that primary-school children in England were less confident about their reading ability and enjoyed reading less. Worse, 13 per cent of the children actually disliked reading, compared to an international average of 6 per cent. Similarly, when asked how confident they were about reading, only 30 per cent were highly confident about their ability, compared to an international average of 40 per cent (quoted in Clark and Rumbold, 2006: 10).

By the time of the 2011 PIRLS report for England, things were somewhat better:

England's performance in PIRLS 2011 was well above the international average and significantly higher than that seen in 2006. There was a wide range of achievement in England: the best readers were among the best in the world but there was a greater proportion of weaker readers than in many other high achieving countries. The difference between the reading achievements of boys and girls was greater than that seen in many other countries.

In common with a number of other high achieving countries, pupils'
attitudes to reading were less positive in England than the average inter-
nationally. The more able readers were more likely to enjoy reading and be
motivated to read than the weaker readers. Compared to 2006, fewer pupils
in 2011 reported never *or* almost never *reading for fun out of school. Over*
half of pupils in PIRLS 2011 reported reading for half an hour or more every
day out of school.

(Twist *et al.*, 2012)

In the same year, however, Ofsted, in its report *Moving English Forward*,
expressed concern about the neglect of reading for pleasure in schools and
pointed to what it saw as misconceptions in much current practice:

In recent years the view has developed, especially in secondary schools,
that there is not enough curriculum time to focus on wider reading or read-
ing for pleasure. Inspectors also noted the loss of once popular and effective
strategies such as reading stories to younger children, listening to children
read, and the sharing of complete novels with junior age pupils.

(Office for Standards in Education, 2012: 29)

The report of a recent survey of reading habits commissioned by Booktrust
(*Booktrust Reading Habits Survey 2013: A National Survey of Reading Habits*
and Attitudes to Books Amongst Adults in England) indicates that there is
a substantial gap in reading habits between the economically advantaged
and disadvantaged groups in the UK. The survey makes strong claims for
the personal and practical benefits of regular reading for pleasure. Its report
concludes:

Overall, the research highlights four justifications for initiatives to encourage
reading for pleasure from an early age, particularly among disadvantaged
groups.

- *People who read books are significantly more likely to be happy and*
  content with their life.
- *Most people who read books feel this improves their life. It also makes*
  them feel good.

- *People who were read to and encouraged to read as children are significantly more likely to read as adults, both to themselves and to their own children.*
- *Those who never read books live in areas of greater deprivation and with more children in poverty.*

(Gleed, 2013: 4)

What schools can do

In the light of these findings, what can primary schools do at the level of the whole institution to promote reading for pleasure? Despite the difficulties and obstacles, very many primary schools regularly and routinely find ways to make reading for pleasure a key part of school life. Here are two sets of guidelines for promoting reading across the school.

Nine things a school could do to promote reading

1 Do a **survey of reading habits** in the school in order to get precise information about what and how much is read and the sources that children get books from; and set up a system for monitoring changes in the nature and extent of independent reading as children go up the school.

2 Establish **a shared approach between primary and secondary schools** about provision for independent reading and work out how useful information about new secondary pupils' reading might be made available by primary schools.

3 Hold discussions with parents about voluntary reading and set up a **home-reading scheme**.

4 Form an **active library committee** (including pupils) to work with the teacher responsible for the library to ensure that it is: adequately stocked with books that children want to read; a place where books are displayed to full advantage and in ways children understand; an attractive and comfortable area; open for general use before school, during breaks and after school.

(continued)

(continued)

5 Devise **lists of useful and accessible books** to support and extend work in all areas of the curriculum; these books to be made available in classrooms as well as in the library, and the reading of them given the status of homework.

6 Organise **visits to local libraries and bookshops** in school time so that pupils all know their way into and around them. Establish secure ways for pupils to **buy books online**.

7 Run **regular book events**, during which special timetabling allows for: talks and readings by writers; exhibitions and sales; book-related activities and competitions.

8 Provide **a book-box** for each class so that children have immediate access to a supply of books which is: sufficient in quantity and wide enough in range and type for all children to make a reasonable choice; efficiently managed and maintained so that the books remain available and are regularly added to or changed.

9 Make **independent reading a regular fixture**, so that all children get a regular chance in school just to read – and with opportunities in this reading time for promotional activities and help for pupils who find reading on their own difficult.

(Adapted from Raleigh, 1982,
reprinted in Simons [ed.], 1996: 120–121)

The Power of Reading Project

The Power of Reading Project has been run by the Centre for Literacy in Primary Education (CLPE) since 2004. It is a whole-school development programme for primary schools through which teachers attend in-service training, have access to a wide range of quality children's literature and work with their colleagues to develop practice around the teaching of reading in their school. Over the 12 years of the project, the programme has involved teachers from more than 2,000 schools in over 50 local authorities in England. Every year, the project analyses data about children's achievement and progress and invites teachers to share examples of how they have changed school practice.

A recent CLPE publication summarises the project's findings:

Reading for pleasure – What works

1 Developing an ethos and an environment that excites, enthuses, inspires and values.
2 High-quality texts with depth and interest in story, character, illustration, vocabulary, structure and subject matter.
3 A read-aloud programme.
4 Teachers who are knowledgeable about children's literature.
5 Creating a community of readers with opportunities to share responses and opinions.
6 Planning for talking about books and stories, providing structures within which to do this.
7 Understanding the importance of illustration in reading both in terms of creating a text and responding to a text.
8 Using drama and role-play to help children to understand and access texts.
9 Working with authors and author/illustrators to understand the process of creating books.
10 Using literature beyond the literacy lesson – cross-curricular planning with quality literature as the starting point.

> (CLPE, *Reading for Pleasure: What We Know Works: Research from the Power of Reading Project*, 2014)[1]

Enjoy!

The last quotation in this section goes to the author Philip Pullman, who in a 2003 article in *The Guardian* attributed at least part of the blame for schools' lack of drive on reading for pleasure to the National Curriculum and official guidance on it:

> *I recently read through the sections on reading in Key Stages 1 to 3 of the National Literacy Strategy, and I was struck by something about the verbs. I wrote them all down. They included 'reinforce', 'predict', 'check', 'discuss' . . . and so on: 71 different verbs, by my count, for the activities that come under the heading of 'reading'. And the word 'enjoy' didn't appear once.*
>
> (Pullman, 2003, in Clark and Rumbold, 2006: 12)

Reading for information

The invention of reading

The origins of writing and therefore of reading appear to lie in the unromantic matter of tax records. Poetry, story and the narratives of history and religion could be carried perfectly well within an oral culture. As city states expanded in Mesopotamia, along the Nile and in India and China, the need for a record of what was grown and could therefore be taxed led to the development of written records. Thus reading for information has a long history. When we contemplate a tax form, we can at least console ourselves that we are part of the longest tradition of reading in the world. Every day, we are likely to refer to either paper or electronic text to get access to facts, information or processes.

The benefits

What are the benefits gained by effective readers for information? The following answer to the question is from New South Wales.

People who use information successfully display the following characteristics:

- *they are able to add to their core knowledge and frequently do so;*
- *they use a variety of information sources and the necessary technology;*
- *they are able to process the information which surrounds them;*
- *they are confident in their ability to use information effectively.*

(New South Wales Department of Education
and Training, *Information Skills in the School:
Engaging Learners in Constructing Knowledge,* 2007: 6)

Our ability to read for information efficiently has the capacity to make our daily lives easier and more enjoyable. All learners need to develop this ability; schools need to help them to do so.

Beyond the comprehension exercise

To be downbeat for a moment: in too many schools, for too long, reading for information has often been confined to what is in effect the old-style comprehension exercise. Pupils are presented with factual information, in the form of a piece of prose in a book or on a worksheet or on the whiteboard. They are then required to find and repeat small parts of that information by answering a series of closed questions.

It would be going too far to say that the old-style comprehension exercise is entirely without value. The retrieval of factual information is something that children and adults alike do all the time. However, if pupils' experience of reading for information is confined to the old-style comprehension exercise, it is likely that the learner will greet the task of taking on new information with diminishing enthusiasm.

Instead, pupils should be introduced to a range of different ways in which texts can be mined for their information, and become aware for themselves of what is common and what is different in the approaches the reader adopts. Consider the following example.

The EXEL project

The Exeter Extending Literacy (EXEL) project was funded by the Nuffield Foundation and based at the University of Exeter School of Education from 1992 to 1995. The project aimed to produce materials to help teachers to extend the literacy experience of junior-age (i.e. Key Stage 2) pupils. It developed a model for helping pupils to read information texts more effectively.

The model, dubbed EXIT (Extending Interactions with Texts), defines these processes. In the report of the project, *Extending Literacy: Children Reading and Writing Non-Fiction*, David Wray and Maureen Lewis are keen to emphasise that they do not see the processes as a linear description of what happens when we read for information, nor as stages through which pupils progress as they become more effective readers. They stress that authentic work with information texts is likely to involve all the processes, and not necessarily in the same order each time. In particular, they see 'a critical approach to literacy as being part of literacy teaching from the very beginning'. The processes they define are:

1 *Elicitation of previous knowledge. (What do I already know about this subject?)*
2 *Establishing purposes. (What do I need to find out?)*
3 *Locating information. (Where and how will I get this information?)*
4 *Adopting an appropriate strategy. (How should I use this source of information?)*

  5 *Interacting with text. (What can I do to help me understand this better?)*
  6 *Monitoring understanding. (What can I do if there are parts I do not understand?)*
  7 *Making a record. (What should I make a note of from this information?)*
  8 *Evaluating information. (Should I believe this information?)*
  9 *Assisting memory. (How can I help myself remember the important parts?)*
  10 *Communicating information. (How should I let other people know about this?)*

(Wray and Lewis, 1997: 7–8)

The project made strong connections between the reading and the writing of non-fiction texts, in particular promoting the use of 'writing frames' (skeleton outlines to scaffold and prompt writing) to give pupils a structure for communicating what they want to say.

RESEARCHING THE GREAT CREDITON FIRE

Wray and Lewis describe the work of a Year 4 class whose teacher ('Ms M') was involved in trialling the EXIT model. The class was studying the topic of change, in this case focusing on how the town they lived in, Crediton in Devon, had changed over time.

   The teacher wanted the class to learn to use a range of sources in studying how major events, such as the Civil War and a great fire of 1743, had affected the town. The class looked at a collection of resources, including books, artefacts and other materials, and the teacher elicited the knowledge the class had of the fire: not much, but enough to get started. She asked them to deduce what they could about the fire from the resources on display and then to form and pool questions to which they would seek answers, as well as ideas about where to seek them.

   In the account which follows, the processes outlined in the EXIT model are noted in curly brackets.

   Ms M produced ten historical sources including eyewitness accounts, newspaper reports, insurance company accounts, disaster fund appeals, and explained what each was but did not read them to the children. They were then told that they were each going to decide which question(s) they wanted to research and that their final piece of work would be displayed, along with the sources, on the wall in the corridor {establishing purposes, communicating information}. They were each given a QUADS [question/answer/details/

*source] sheet to record their work and in pairs or small groups were given a
set of photocopied sources to share.*

*Having decided on, and written down, their questions, the children turned
to the sources. They were encouraged to skim over the materials looking for
key words or phrases (e.g. 'fire', 'started', 'died') contained in their questions. Skimming was more sensible than close reading in this initial hunt for
answers {adopting an appropriate strategy}. Having key words to focus their
searching was especially important as the language was difficult for many
of the children. When the children found a section they thought might be
useful they were encouraged to read it aloud with each other and to work
together to try to understand what it was saying {interacting with text/
monitoring understanding}. The children were actively engaged in monitoring
their own understanding rather than turning instantly to the teacher to have
the text read to them, although of course this remained a final option.*

*Several of the children discovered that different sources gave different
information, for example about how many people died and how many build-
ings were destroyed, and this both demonstrated to them the importance
of recording the source but also the importance of questioning its credibil-
ity {evaluating information}. They were encouraged to try to think for themselves why a newspaper account from the next day might say twenty houses
were destroyed whilst an insurance company account written a week later
gave a different figure, and to decide which they thought was the more
accurate figure.*

*The children then shared their questions and answers in a session on the
carpet in order for them to get a complete picture of the event and to review
and revisit their research . . . Finally, as planned, the children produced a
final version of their work [on their QUADS sheets] to go on display {com-
municating information}.*

(Abridged from *ibid.*: 160–162)

Dealing with difficult texts

For many pupils, the problem is keeping pace with the increasing demands
that the reading of authentic material across the curriculum makes as they
move through school. Part of the solution to the problem is engaging the
pupils in deliberate discussion about what makes texts difficult and introducing ways of coping with them. *Spotlight on Literacy*, the teaching resource
from the English and Media Centre referred to earlier in the chapter, has a

helpful section on getting to grips with difficult texts and helping pupils to become more independent and resilient readers. The sequence includes:

- *running a 'reading clinic', which involves pupils and teachers bringing examples of texts they find difficult and discussing the features that account for the difficulty;*
- *use of 'performed reading', using different strategies to highlight key points and messages;*
- *stepping back from the detail to establish the bigger picture of what the text is about;*
- *using simple grids to identify 'what I know already', 'what I want to know' and 'what I've learnt';*
- *using skimming and scanning to investigate and locate particular items of information;*
- *evaluating the usefulness of different pre-prepared summaries of information in a text;*
- *re-presenting a difficult text for a different audience in order to focus on making key points accessible;*
- *sub-editing a text by giving it headlines, sub-heads and pull-quotes;*
- *paying close attention to the grammar of selected sentences in order to pick through the meaning and the style of the piece;*
- *giving the pupils key words, fragments and prompts before they see the text as a whole;*
- *asking the pupils to summarise as they go along, to pose questions about what they have read so far and to speculate and predict what is coming next;*
- *providing a focus for independent reading by asking pupils to identify a key passage or to sum up the argument in a few words;*
- *encouraging pupils to formulate, pool and then try to answer interesting questions about the material they have read.*

(Bleiman *et al.*, 2013: 283–288)

Many of these approaches, especially those involving visual organisers such as simple grids, skimming and scanning, explicit focus on grammatical form, and the use of key words and summaries, would be particularly effective with EAL learners. Weaker EAL learners benefit from more able readers' re-presenting of difficult texts. There is more discussion of the needs and achievements of EAL learners in Chapter 9.

Reading imaginative literature

whatever else the pupil takes away from his experience of literature in school he should have learned to see it as a source of pleasure, as something that will continue to be a part of his life. The power to bring this about lies with the teacher, but it cannot be pretended that the task is easy.

(The Bullock Committee, 1975: paragraph 9.28)

We come now to a central responsibility of the primary teacher concerned with language: the teaching of literature.

Key questions

The teaching of literature has always been a controversial matter. Some of the controversy has taken place at an academic level, but it has also attracted strong political interest; hence the tendency of politicians to impose their preferences as to which texts should be taught in schools. Going back in time, the development of the study of English literature as an academic subject coincided with a fierce debate in the late nineteenth and early twentieth century about English identity.

One problem with the debate is that all too often it gets bogged down in arguments about which texts should be taught. This is an important question, but it is not the only one. Teachers need to think about the 'why' as well as the 'what': about the purposes of their teaching in terms of their pupils' developing capabilities.

We could categorise the reading and the teaching of literature in three ways. It is to do with:

* engaging the reader with the text;
* understanding the text's rhetoric;
* relating the reader's perspective to that of the text.

Engaging the reader with the text

The first of the three categories is closely related to reading for pleasure, as discussed earlier in the chapter. Our first and most enduring response to a literary text is to engage with it. If we fail to engage with the text, unless it is one we are forced to read, for example as part of an examination syllabus, we are unlikely to persevere with it.

It is valuable to choose some texts that reflect and explore the experiences and cultures present in the classroom. Children respond to seeing their own world explored in fiction, drama and poetry. However, it is also vital to nourish ambition in young readers. Literature is produced by writers from many different cultures and countries. This cultural diversity and richness should be represented in the reading pupils do in school, whether for wider pleasure or close textual study. By the age of 11, pupils should have a sense that there is a remarkable source of enjoyment and stimulation out there in literature, and that this source is being enriched all the time by writers from a diversity of cultural backgrounds.

Children need the opportunity not only to read widely but in some depth. They should from time to time have the chance to read a number of texts by one author, in one genre or exploring one theme. They need to read or hear whole texts (see the next sub-section), an experience which need not always be followed by detailed discussion or writing.

Pupils right across the range of attainment should have the experience of reading or hearing high-quality, demanding literary texts. The fact that a reader may not be fluent does not mean that he or she cannot enjoy, with help, a complex work of literature. The aim is to ensure that all pupils have experienced writers of this quality and make informed choices about what they like; most important of all, that they are ambitious as readers and do not place artificial limitations on what might or might not interest them.

Whole-class reading

'Whole-class reading', where the teacher reads a complete literary text to the whole class, has been under pressure in recent years. Given the demands on teaching time and the need for schools to demonstrate measurable progress in learning, it can appear a luxury. Its value should not be underestimated. It allows the developing reader to hear how good expressive reading aloud can enrich the experience of a text. Done skilfully, reading aloud accentuates the listener's excitement, suspense and pleasure. For many children at primary school, being read to in this way is one of their most memorable experiences. For some, it is an experience not replicated elsewhere.

A complete text is not necessarily a full-length novel. It could also be a picture book, a short story or a narrative poem. Sometimes the teacher may invite pupils to read sections. Sometimes he or she may stop to ask questions and invite comment. But in this kind of reading, the most important thing is impetus. The listeners need to feel that they are being engulfed, absorbed by the experience.

Understanding the text's rhetoric

It is a teacher's responsibility to help young readers come to understand how a text works. If they care what happens to a character – that is, if they are engaged – how has the author made them care? If they are saddened by a poem, how has the form, structure, language and content produced this feeling? This is the province of rhetoric, the ancient study of how language can achieve an emotional and intellectual impact on listeners and readers. What might it include?

Vocabulary

The study might include close attention to the choice of words, the vocabulary. Why *this* word, and what weight or implications might it have? It is sometimes hard to say. Teachers need to provide structure and support. One way of doing this is to allow pupils to choose alternative words and compare their responses to them. This activity might take the form of a cloze exercise where synonyms are available to fill the spaces. Another approach is to look at two or more translations of the same poem or passage, or two or more retellings of the same fable, to compare the ways in which different authors have chosen their words and to discuss the effects of the different choices.

Grammatical structure

It is in the context of looking at texts to see how meaning is made, how particular readers' responses are elicited, that it makes best sense to introduce the study of grammatical structure. The study of the structures of simple, compound and complex sentences, for example, is best done by looking at how these structures contribute to the meaning and impact of a worthwhile and engaging text. Pupils might substitute simple sentences for compound or complex ones, or vice versa, and consider the differences. Or they might discuss the impact on the narrative of a shift in tense. Pupils can also use their own and each other's writing to consider the impact of different grammatical choices. (See Chapter 6 for a detailed discussion of effective grammar teaching.)

Narrative structure

Above the level of words and sentences, readers should be introduced to the way in which the overall structure of a narrative supports the tension of a story, or its pathos or humour. This can be done from the simplest to the most complex of narratives. From an early age, pupils can grasp the management of time in a story. They can understand the impact of a circular narrative. They can recognise the way in which episodic structure might enhance or detract from a story's suspense. They can be shown how the use of voice impacts on a narrative, by being introduced to the distinction between an author and a narrator. They can be offered activities that focus on the difference between a first-person and a third-person narrative.

Learners are able to appreciate narratives before they are able fully to analyse them. This implicit appreciation needs to be harnessed to the development of explicit understanding.

Terminology

In studying the rhetoric of texts, pupils' implicit appreciation of the effect of a text is being guided towards explicit understanding. Some appropriate critical terminology by which to describe how a text has made meaning, has achieved its impact on them as readers, will help them along the way. The terms 'topic', 'introduction', 'development', 'conclusion', 'argument', 'assertion', 'evidence', 'example', 'plot', 'character', 'climax', 'author', 'narrator', 'first-person', 'third-person' are all potentially appropriate examples, depending on the kind of writing being discussed and the age of the pupils.

Relating the reader's perspective to that of the text

The third aspect of the teaching of literary texts involves setting the reader's values and assumptions in relation to those of the text. It offers the potential to call into question the values and assumptions of even the greatest literary works. Equally, it offers an opportunity for the reader to question her or his own values. Writing in the late sixteenth century, Michel de Montaigne observed that 'A speech belongs half to the speaker, half to him who hears it'

('On Experience', in *Essays*, Penguin, 1993: 372). Meaning is constructed in dialogue. The speaker or writer may be able to control what he or she intends to mean but cannot control the meaning actually made by the hearer or reader.

Debating with the text

Part of what we gain from reading literary texts is the ability to see the world – for a time at least and even if only partially – through someone else's eyes, someone else's consciousness. It is also an aspect of pupils' developing competence as readers that teachers can nurture and develop, helping pupils to make conscious the previously unconscious, helping them debate with the text.

As with all aspects of the teaching of literature, this is not teaching to be reserved only for the fluent and sophisticated reader. From the very start, young children bring their own experience of the world to the stories they hear, the texts they have read to them and those they read for themselves. They respond to the narrative and to the characters with their own assumptions and values, just as more sophisticated readers do. When young readers comment on and discuss the behaviour of characters, the relationships between them, the settings in which they appear, the conversations they have, there is the opportunity to reflect on these assumptions and values.

Teachers of course have a responsibility to protect children from texts that are not appropriate to their age or are likely to cause real hurt or offence. However, pupils' reading should not be confined to texts that are unproblematic, that offer only those values that can be easily accepted. The relationship between the text and the reader is a two-way street. While the reader may challenge the text, the text should be allowed to challenge the reader. Teachers should ensure that, over time, pupils are introduced to some texts that do that.

Designing a literature curriculum

The development of a literature curriculum across the age range 7 to 11 should include all three of the elements discussed in this section. It should:

- engage learners and extend the range and ambition of their reading;
- equip them with the skills and language to understand and analyse how texts achieve their effects on readers;
- give them the knowledge and confidence to interrogate the values and assumptions of the text in an informed, open-minded and confident manner.

Such a curriculum will involve the selection of texts to suit the particular purpose of the learning. Such an approach takes us beyond decisions about which books a 7-year-old or an 11-year-old should read (necessary as those decisions will be) to more dynamic questions such as:

- Which texts will engage this group of readers and extend their reading horizons?
- Which texts will best illustrate structural and linguistic features which this group of readers can usefully study?
- Which texts will provide this group of readers with the best opportunities for discussing the writer's and their own perspective?

The school library

The school library is the heart of the school which itself has learning at its core; and good libraries can empower the learner. The resources in a library can allow our imaginations to run free, introduce us to new experiences and promote access to knowledge and enjoyment.

(Department for Education and Skills, *School Libraries: Making a Difference*, 2004, quoted in Office for Standards in Education, *Good School Libraries: Making a Difference to Learning*, 2006: 4)

What's become of it?

School libraries make a vital contribution to the promotion and development of reading. The factors that make for good libraries were described in simple terms in an HMI survey published in 1989:

Better libraries:
- *are easy to get to and pleasant to be in;*
- *provide what readers want to read;*
- *are well matched to what learners have to learn;*
- *are well equipped to help the learning process;*
- *have skilled, enthusiastic staff who know how libraries work and have the time to see that learners' needs are met;*
- *develop and use pupils' skills as librarians;*
- *are funded to take sensible heed of costs and replacement needs;*

- *attractively present well-chosen stock which relates to learners' ages, abilities and interests;*
- *make good use of the expertise and stock of Schools Library Services;*
- *look regularly at what they have and how it is being used;*
- *are rooted in the active belief of all staff, clearly stated, that the library is essential to the healthy growth of learning and that the library and its use are the responsibility of all teachers and of all others concerned with promoting learning.*

(Department of Education and Science,
*Better Libraries: Good Practice in Schools – A survey
by H.M. Inspectorate,* 1989: 6, original emphasis)

The 2006 Office for Standards in Education survey which carried the quotation at the beginning of the section found that:

Funding for libraries varied markedly, even across the schools with good libraries. The survey found a direct link between well-funded libraries and effectiveness. However, gaps in resourcing were less significant overall than under-use or poor management.

(Office for Standards in Education, 2006: 2)

A 2010 report from a commission on school libraries set up by the National Literacy Trust and the Museums, Libraries and Archives Council was scathing in its comments on the current national picture:

School libraries are an underutilised resource, often perceived by headteachers to be a low priority. What should be a vital ingredient of our schools' system is marginalised and seems not to be connected with the acknowledged educational priorities of literacy and information skills supporting knowledge acquisition, which are their core business.

(National Literacy Trust and Museums, Libraries and Archives
Council, *School Libraries: A Plan for Improvement,* 2010: 5)

The research showed that, while some headteachers and governing bodies saw the school library as an essential element of their school development plan, many others had given little thought to the part it could be playing in the life of the school. In the consultation groups, headteachers who did not currently regard the library as a priority did not do so out of hostility but simply because they had not thought of it as a strategically useful resource.

(*ibid.*: 8)

The unevenness of both the extent and the quality of provision is a matter of major concern. Inequality of access to books and other resources as between schools is a fundamental failing.

Staffing

Crucial to the quality of school libraries is the question of staffing. The International Federation of Library Associations and Institutions guidelines for school libraries state:

> *Research has shown that the most critical condition for an effective school library program is access to a qualified school library professional.*
>
> (International Federation of
> Library Associations and Institutions, 2015: 18)

The School Library Commission (National Literacy Trust and Museums, Libraries and Archives Council, 2010) and various advocacy organisations for libraries have repeatedly made the point that without dedicated staffing, too many school libraries are underused and waste resources and potential. Most secondary schools do find the funds for library staff; unfortunately, this is rarely the case in primary schools. Some primary schools and local authorities have found creative solutions to the problem. Some share library staff between schools. In some authorities, the school library service provides peripatetic staff to work in schools. Some schools use volunteers, including parents. Here is a description of the excellent library service to primary schools provided in the London Borough of Tower Hamlets:

> *Many primary schools in Tower Hamlets have a professional librarian managing their library and developing a reading culture in school. Children who read for pleasure are better able to access the curriculum and achieve higher standards. Working for anything from 3.5 hours to 35 hours each week, a professional librarian will:*
>
> *1 give long-term consistency and quality in your library;*
> *2 ensure value for money from improved use of your school's resource collection;*
> *3 buy good-quality books using their professional judgement to make the most of your budget;*
> *4 establish a reading year of events, clubs and activities to promote reading for pleasure;*

5 *teach library and information skills in liaison with teaching staff;*

6 *manage the library computer system;*

7 *ensure you get great value for money from your subscription to the schools library service;*

and much more!

(Tower Hamlets Schools Library Services, 2015)

The School Library Association offers extensive advice to primary and secondary schools (School Library Association, 2015). It has established the School Librarian of the Year Award to recognise and highlight best practice.

However the staffing is achieved, the teacher responsible for the library is enormously influential in promoting books and other resources to staff and pupils, both individually and as classes, as well as being part of any programme teaching about how to read for information.

The present situation in England

The new National Curriculum for English has the following overall aims for reading at all Key Stages. Pupils should:

- *read easily, fluently and with good understanding;*
- *develop the habit of reading widely and often, for both pleasure and information;*
- *acquire a wide vocabulary, an understanding of grammar and knowledge of linguistic conventions for reading, writing and spoken language;*
- *appreciate our rich and varied literary heritage.*

(Department for Education, 2014a: 14)

These intentions are unarguable.

Key Stage 2

The statement on reading in the introduction to the orders for Years 3 and 4 is sensible:

[Pupils] should be developing their understanding and enjoyment of stories, poetry, plays and non-fiction, and learning to read silently. They should also

be developing their knowledge and skills in reading non-fiction about a wide range of subjects. They should be learning to justify their views about what they have read: with support at the start of year 3 and increasingly indepen- dently by the end of year 4.

(*ibid*.: 34)

The paragraph on reading in the introduction to the orders for Years 5 and 6 is equally so:

[Pupils] should be able to prepare readings, with appropriate intonation to show their understanding, and should be able to summarise and present a familiar story in their own words. They should be reading widely and fre- quently, outside as well as in school, for pleasure and information. They should be able to read silently, with good understanding, inferring the mean- ings of unfamiliar words, and then discuss what they have read.

(*ibid*.: 42)

As at Key Stage 1 (see Chapter 2), the detailed statutory orders on reading are divided into 'Word Reading' and 'Comprehension'.

Nothing in the comprehension orders prevents teachers from teaching well. The approach to reading for information, with its awareness of the diversity of strategies by which young readers gain information from texts, can be wel- comed. Also to be welcomed is the emphasis on reading a diversity of literary and non-fiction texts, and the mention of reference texts such as dictionar- ies. The comprehension orders at Key Stage 2 are a good example of statute which enables.

The word reading orders, however, are curious – and so brief that they can be quoted in full. Here are those for Years 3 and 4:

Pupils should be taught to:

- *apply their growing knowledge of root words, prefixes and suffixes (etymology and morphology) as listed in English Appendix 1 [the statutory appendix concerned with spelling], both to read aloud and to understand the meaning of new words they meet;*
- *read further exception words, noting the unusual correspondences between spelling and sound, and where these occur in the word.*

(*ibid*.: 36)

The equivalent orders for Years 5 and 6 are confined to the first only of these two bullet points.

There is good value in the study of etymology and morphology, offered at an appropriate level of difficulty for the age range in question. However, confined as they are to the word reading orders, there is a danger that etymology and morphology will be taught in isolation from the study of whole texts. It is the study of whole texts (not necessarily long texts) which provides the most meaningful contexts in which those aspects of language can be discussed.

The significant thrust of the guidance on the reading of words is however to be found in the introductions to the orders both for Years 3 and 4 and for Years 5 and 6. For Years 3 and 4:

As in key stage 1, however, pupils who are still struggling to decode need to be taught to do this urgently through a rigorous and systematic phonics programme so that they catch up rapidly with their peers. If they cannot decode independently and fluently, they will find it increasingly difficult to understand what they read and to write down what they want to say. As far as possible, however, these pupils should follow the year 3 and 4 programme of study in terms of listening to new books, hearing and learning new vocabulary and grammatical structures, and discussing these.

(*ibid.*: 34–35)

For Years 5 and 6:

It is essential that pupils whose decoding skills are poor are taught through a rigorous and systematic phonics programme so that they catch up rapidly with their peers in terms of their decoding and spelling. However, as far as possible, these pupils should follow the upper key stage 2 programme of study in terms of listening to books and other writing that they have not come across before, hearing and learning new vocabulary and grammatical structures, and having a chance to talk about all of these.

(*ibid.*: 42)

In other words, if the medicine did not work by the age of 7, offer more of the same until the age of 9; if has not worked by then, repeat the prescription until 11. However, these two sets of guidance do include the correct advice that pupils who are still having difficulty learning to read words should, as far as possible, nonetheless be included in the activities which their more advanced peers are being offered.

Chapter 2 discusses in detail how children learn to read. The chapter is highly critical of the preoccupation with synthetic phonics as the only means by which children perform this feat. It freely acknowledges that the recognition of grapho-phonic correspondences is indeed one of the routes into reading; the argument is by no means 'anti-phonics'. However, it also points to the limitations of phonics when relied on exclusively, and lists a number of other routes into reading which young children should be shown. Most important of all, the chapter emphasises the central importance of the gaining of meaning in reading from the earliest beginnings, whatever a child's current level of fluency as a reader. These principles apply with even greater force to those pupils who come into Key Stage 2 as unconfident readers. They need to be shown the whole gamut of routes into reading, not offered a single nostrum whose repeated application will produce diminishing returns.

Age-related requirements

There is much to welcome in the new National Curriculum requirements for reading from 7 to 11. However, they run into the difficulty – as do all similar efforts to describe language development in age-related terms – that they do not properly reflect the essentially recursive nature of language learning. There is no compelling logic as to why some skills and activities are located in Years 3 and 4 and others in Years 5 and 6. For example, at Years 5 and 6 pupils should increase 'their familiarity with a wide range of books, including myths, legends and traditional stories, modern fiction, fiction from our literary heritage, and books from other cultures and traditions' (Department for Education, 2014a: 44). In fact, such a list could equally apply to Years 3 and 4, as long as the texts chosen were suitable for the age group.

To take another example, the orders state that Years 5 and 6 pupils should learn 'a wider range of poetry by heart' (*ibid.*: 45). The use of the word 'wider' suggests that there must have been a requirement at Years 3 and 4 that pupils learn a more limited range. But no; there is no mention of learning by heart at Years 3 and 4. Done well, the learning of poems by heart enhances a love of poetry. What is the rationale for an appropriately worded requirement not appearing in the demands made at Years 3 and 4? Younger pupils can learn simpler or shorter poems; older pupils longer and more demanding poems.

Generic key skills and knowledge should be visited and revisited at ever increasing levels of complexity. Artificial age distinctions may constrain the curriculum on offer and lead to a dislocated experience for pupils. Though there is good matter in the reading orders at Key Stage 2, there is little coherence in a developmental sense; rather, sets of activities and skills are piled into lists. The best hope is that teachers will set the orders in a richer and wider context, informed by their fuller understanding of what they are aiming for in the teaching of reading.

'Learning to read' and 'reading to learn'

The most acute shortcoming in the orders concerns the relationship between 'learning to read' and 'reading to learn'. In this respect, the orders could lead to a dislocated reading experience for children at Key Stage 2, in which the skills of learning to read fluently are isolated from the wider intellectual and imaginative processes involved in reading for meaning; or in which the wider processes are neglected until such time as the child has learned to decode fluently. Such a state of affairs would be contrary to what is known about language and learning in general and about reading in particular.

An alternative

In Chapter 11, readers will find an alternative curriculum for reading 7 to 11, which retains the features of the statutory orders which can be welcomed, while addressing the shortcomings which have been discussed in this chapter.

To conclude . . .

As the Bullock Report puts it:

> we have been anxious to establish the principle that young children should acquire from the beginning the skills that are employed in mature reading. These skills will obviously be used for more elaborate and demanding purposes as the child grows older, but the pattern is one that can be established early . . . The development of reading skills is a progressive one, and there are no staging points to which one can attach any particular ages.
>
> (The Bullock Committee, 1975: paragraph 8.1)

The teaching and the uses of reading for learning need to be set in the broader context of what is now known about the development of language. Reading is from its earliest stages a complex and holistic intellectual and imaginative activity. This central truth needs to be reflected in the way it is taught. 'Learning to read' is not an activity to be divorced from 'reading to learn'. Rather, 'learning to read' and 'reading to learn' are processes which should enhance each other.

Schools and teachers need to consider the full range of purposes for which and approaches by which pupils are asked to read. A curriculum which represents these purposes and approaches will develop in pupils the capacity to enjoy literature and to read for information in an efficient and productive manner. It will nurture in them the priceless habit of reading for pleasure. If a primary school is to offer such a curriculum in practice, it needs to adopt a whole-school strategy, fully supported, resourced and monitored by the school's senior leaders.

Effective teachers of literature ensure that pupils are engaged in their reading; they equip pupils with the analytical skills to understand how texts achieve their emotional and intellectual impact; and they help pupils to interrogate both the assumptions of the texts and the assumptions that they, the readers, bring to those texts.

A well-resourced, properly staffed, constantly used school library is essential to a school's effectiveness as a reading-promoting place.

The principles summarised here, if enacted, represent an agenda by which primary schools could enable their pupils to achieve satisfying success as readers: an achievement which will massively enhance the quality of their later lives.

Note

1 Reproduced by permission of the Centre for Literacy in Primary Education, www. clpe.org.uk.

4 Writing 3 to 7

John Richmond

Summary of main points

Successful entry into literacy depends on developing competence in spoken language. In the first years of their lives, children are learning to talk; and they are concurrently learning to recognise and use graphic systems: drawing, writing and number. They experiment with these systems while learning to talk.

The beginning writer, to be successful, must employ all the resources of her or his retentive memory and generalising brain.

A great deal of informal, unconscious learning about writing comes from reading and being read to. Oral and written stories, poems, songs and rhymes have a key role to play in this learning.

While recognising the powerful forces at work in children's unconscious literacy learning, the teacher has a vital part to play through appropriately pitched conscious instruction.

The teaching of writing requires an understanding of all the characteristics and needs of a writer at work, and an understanding of the multiple demands that adults make on children when we ask them to write.

Teachers should encourage the confident voices of early writers.

Teachers should provide the supports and the direct teaching necessary to bring children, without undue haste and without creating undue anxiety, to an understanding of the conventions of the writing system appropriate for their age, and to a relaxed control of the physical act of handwriting.

The premature introduction of instruction in some of the abstract categories in which adults discuss writing (for example grammatical categories and spelling rules) can be harmful to the confidence of the young writer, and counter-productive even to the purpose – to lead the child to correctness – for which those categories have been introduced.

Young children should have experience of writing which is active, participatory, social and collaborative. There should also be occasions for writing when quiet, reflective individual effort is required.

Young children should be introduced to an appropriate range of the kinds of writing which exist in the world and be encouraged to try out some of that range for themselves. The range should both confirm and represent the linguistic, social and cultural diversity of the classroom, and allow for exploration of real contexts and imaginary worlds beyond the classroom.

The range of children's writing, and the means by which the writing is displayed and distributed, should employ digital and electronic equipment and media as well as traditional physical equipment and media.

All these principles apply with equal force to learners of English as an additional language (EAL) (about one in six children in the age group with which this book is concerned). However, children who have begun to read and write in another language and are learning to write in English are additionally engaged in the complex process of making comparisons between writing systems. There is likely to be a conscious transfer of knowledge and skill from one written form to another. As well as the other benefits they bring, appropriate books in the first language and in bilingual editions can help the comparison of the writing systems of English and the other language(s).

The world of writing

In considering early literacy, we might describe beginning writing as 'the other side of reading'. In fact, 'the other side' is a wrong metaphor, suggesting as it does two sides of a coin, either of which may be viewed but neither of which looks at the other. Early reading and early writing are mutually interpenetrating and interactive. They feed off and into each other.

Let us start with a rehearsal of some familiar underlying information.

Speech and writing

Speech emerged hundreds of thousands of years before writing was invented. The first civilisation to invent writing, in about 3500 BC, was Sumer, in the southern part of what is now Iraq. (Egypt, China and the Maya civilisation in what is now Mexico later invented their own writing systems.) Even though 5,500 years is a long time, it is but a blink by comparison with the length of time which has passed since people first developed the power of speech.

Literacy may be based on and may be an extension of speech, but it is not just a visible form of speech. Across all languages which have writing systems, there are significant differences between the characteristic forms of speech and the characteristic forms of writing; and the phrase 'characteristic forms' covers a great variety and a wide range in each case. Relaxed, informal speech between friends is different from speech exchanged at a job interview. A chatty letter – or, these days, a text or a tweet – is written differently from an answer in an examination paper. There are, indeed, some forms of speech which come close to or are identical with writing, such as a speech. But they are exceptions. Speech and writing are close relations, but not identical twins. Speech has a grammar through which it realises meaning in ways as complex and as rich as does writing. As babies learn to listen and speak, they are laying the foundations for their literacy learning. The most significant event in the process of becoming literate is the realisation that the marks of written language have a relationship with the sounds of spoken language.

Early writing and early reading

In recent decades, there has been much discussion about the exact nature of the interaction between reading and writing in the early development of literacy. Which comes first?

The received view was that reading comes first. It is the 'receptive' mode for the written language, with writing the 'productive' mode, just as listening is the 'receptive' mode for the spoken language, with speaking the 'productive' mode; and babies certainly do a lot of listening before they produce their first words. It is also true that writing is nurtured by reading. Reading is the daily evidence that writing exists and has been done by other people.

However, more recent work (some of which is summarised later) has shown that the relationship between early reading and early writing is not one-way. Children do not have to wait until they have achieved a certain level of competence as readers before they can usefully start to write. Children can begin to write, draw and experiment with number well before the age of three. These are symbolic activities: they stand for things, people, animals, actions or states in the real or imagined world.

Spoken words and gesture are also symbolic activities: the spoken word 'milk' stands for a certain white liquid; a baby's hand movement towards a mug of milk stands for a desire to drink the milk. If drawing is play with marks, writing is the drawing of spoken words, which – to repeat – are symbolic activities themselves. Writing, or emergent writing – for we are a long way from worrying yet about mastery of conventions of spelling or other features of the adult writing system – takes its place in this network of symbolic acts which very young children learn and learn about. Writing helps very young children to 'fix' experiences which have been mediated through spoken language, whether these experiences come direct from life or from hearing (and watching) stories, songs, rhymes and poems.

Children who write, in however embryonic a fashion, are immediately reading their writing, or having it read to them by an adult who should offer a positive response to it, in which case the 'clinch' between writing and reading is made. So a child coming into literacy may do so by learning about writing through reading or by learning about reading through writing; and most commonly by a combination of the two routes. It is doubtful that any individual's exact experience of becoming literate is identical to any other's. This doesn't matter. The important thing is that the 'clinch' between reading and writing should be made.

The need to mean

Whatever an individual's exact experience, there is one universal element in any proper understanding of literacy, whether looked at through the primary perspective of reading or of writing, and this is *the need to mean*.

The need and desire to mean are fundamental throughout a person's experience not just of *learning* to read and write, but of reading and writing throughout her or his lifetime, of putting those competences to work for the host of purposes for which they are used in the world.

Whatever learning contexts teachers provide for the development of young children's literacy, whatever explicit advice or instruction they give to young children, the most important question they can ask themselves is: 'Is this context, advice or instruction promoting the child's facility as a maker of meaning?' If teachers can say that it is, then they need to worry much less about precise teaching methods, or about whether such-and-such is a good teaching resource or not. All sorts of methods and resources can be used well or badly.

As it enters into literacy, the child's learning brain receives information; it remembers; it dynamically extrapolates from the information, inferring patterns and making generalisations; it experiments with and revises its generalisations in the light of experience and mistakes (it might be helpful to put a hyphen into this last word: 'mis-takes'); it builds up an ever more complex network of experiences of literacy on which it can draw and to which it can compare future experiences of literacy.

This is what happens when the child's learning brain is operating as it can and should. In order for what happens in reality to be close to what can and should happen, one crucial positive factor needs to be at work: the literacy acts a child engages in need to be authentic and have a clear purpose. To make the analogy with speech, children learn to speak by being surrounded by natural speech and by being invited to interact with speakers from whom, in normal and happy circumstances, they receive responses, including large amounts of praise. If children's earliest exposure to spoken language were with artificially constructed alternative versions of speech, many 5-year-olds would be left with serious difficulties as speakers.

The process of learning to write

Becoming literate is a different process from learning to speak. Learning to speak is an almost entirely unconscious process, although interactions between the child and the adult will involve moments of conscious reflection on what has been said. Powerful unconscious processes are engaged as young children learn to read; but in reading, conscious reflection on words, groups of words and whole texts is also essential for most learners.

Writing is a yet more conscious process, especially with beginners. Young writers are not only aware in a broad sense that they are writing; they are also conscious of having to perform many of the individual acts, including motor acts, which yield a piece of writing. As competence increases, acts which at the outset were conscious begin to be performed with less conscious effort. Examples of this shift would be the habit (in English) of writing strings of words from left to right and top to bottom, or the use of the fine motor movements involved in developing a personal handwriting style, or the ability to spell once unfamiliar words without thinking about it.

The detailed workings of these processes – how and when deliberate, conscious acts become unconscious competences; how conscious teaching is incorporated into and advances unconscious competences – are mysteries. In the case of the EAL learner who already has some level of literacy in a language other than English, this process of transfer from conscious acts to unconscious competences involves the comparison of writing systems at a more conscious level, as it does with the learner's reading.

Mysterious these detailed workings may be; nonetheless, one broader truth emerges clearly. All the big generic powers of the learning brain – especially the ability to generalise and hypothesise from particular experiences – are simultaneously at work as the child writes, and these powers are laying down a network of interacting competences which will, as the writer becomes more skilled and experienced, operate at the unconscious level.

Helpful guidance on early writing

This section contains summaries of and quotations from work on early writing going back many decades and originating in several countries (the UK, the USA, New Zealand, Russia, Argentina). The work offers valuable general guidance – some theoretical, some practical – to the teacher of young writers today.

The Plowden Report

Balance content and correctness

The relationship between correctness and content in writing is at least as complex, as multi-faceted, as that between the achievement of comprehension in reading and the reader's strategies to achieve that comprehension; and this relationship in writing is established at a more conscious level than is the case with reading.

I have already quoted from the Plowden Report, *Children and their Primary Schools*, in Chapters 1 and 2. To read its findings and recommendations on writing is to be reminded of the essential virtue of a holistic view of a complex activity like writing. There is a ringing endorsement of the need for experience to lie at the heart of children's writing:

> *What is most remarkable now in many infant schools is the variety of writing: writing arising out of dramatic play, writing associated with and explaining the models that are made, writing which reflects the sharpening of the senses, 'the peppery smell of the lupins', 'the primroses clustered so closely that the stalks can't be seen', the writing that derives from the special occasion, the tortoise brought in for the day – 'I could hug him and snug him and our teacher wanted to tell us the story of the hare and the tortoise but we had all heard it before'. Much of the writing derives from the experiences of individual children, much from the excitement of a shared visit, 'the day*

that most fascinated me', a visit to a zoo which led after a longish spell of time to a description of a snake 'slithering slowly through the long grasses. Up, up, up the tree he coiled and rested his head on his tall slim body'. Less frequently the spirit and language of a story are caught, 'one day however the prince was lucky for he found to his joy on the topmost branch of an oak the Golden Bird and he said in a joyful voice "Great Golden Bird, come down and let me pluck a feather from your breast so I may marry the princess". The Golden Bird shivered . . .'.

(The Plowden Committee, 1967: paragraph 601)

This, if you like, is classic Plowden, of the sort that some reactionary commentators were later keen to sneer at. The report is equally clear about the importance of correctness, while being aware of the limitations of that term; it understands, crucially, that the teacher's approach to correctness has to be enacted with a developmental awareness:

Care should always be taken not to discourage children, particularly the younger and the less able, by too much criticism. What should children be told about their work? They ought to know if they have succeeded in sharing their meaning and, however tactfully, what impact the meaning made. Teachers should, that is to say, be at least as much concerned with the content as with the manner of what is said . . . Often the probing question is the best comment. Some 'correction', if so inadequate a word must be used, should be directed towards inaccuracies, not so much the careless slips that everyone makes throughout life, as the repeated errors in sentence construction, in punctuation and in spelling which get in the way of communication. Similarly such techniques as paragraphing can be taught when it can be made clear to children that the technique will serve their purpose in writing.

(*ibid*.: paragraph 609)

A profound understanding of the role of the effective teacher in calling forth and then responding to children's writing is to be found in these paragraphs. Much more detailed work has been done since they were written. But for a statement of principle on the matter, no one has subsequently improved on 'Teachers should . . . be at least as much concerned with the content as with the manner of what is said'.

The Bullock Report

Writings emerge from talk

The Bullock Report, already quoted in the three preceding chapters, introduces its discussion of early writing via a reminder of writing's origins in children's talk.

> *The continual reinterpretation of all that a child knows in the light of what he comes to learn is a characteristic of the talk that occurs in make-believe situations of his own creation. This takes many forms, from domestic scenes in the home corner to improvisations on storybook and television themes of heroes, adventurers, giants and witches. It is fed by nursery rhymes and singing games, by the stories that teachers and children tell and the poems they read. Talk of this kind is a consolidating activity, a way of reordering experience to make it acceptable. Into this context of purposeful, sociable and consolidating talk, the infant teacher introduces the written language.*
>
> (The Bullock Committee, 1975: paragraph 5.22)

Bullock, like Plowden, is clear about the importance of giving young writers the opportunity to write on a diversity of topics and in a diversity of styles:

> *There is, even in the earliest stages, no lack of things to write about. Young children will write about their homes and families, their pets and other animals, and the highlights of their day-to-day experience. They will write about a football match, a street accident, a snowfall or a thunderstorm, a visit to hospital, a television programme they have watched, or the things they bring into school, and they will write stories on fantasy themes involving witches or bandits, ghosts or gunmen. They describe objects or processes that have interested them, and in this way much of their writing arises from the practical activities in school. At the same time, they develop a language adapted to the expression of feeling, a language of implicit rather than explicit statement; in short, a form of 'poetic' writing . . . Thus, writing serves them to give expression to their own versions of what is, and to create fascinating alternatives in terms of what might be. Across this range of purposes, however, their writing in these early stages is likely to remain expressive; it is likely, that is to say, to retain a close affinity with their speech. To begin to write is to put to a new use those linguistic resources that have so far been developed entirely by speaking and listening.*
>
> (*ibid.*: paragraph 5.23)

Writing displayed in the classroom is also an important source of information:

> *Captions or labels of use and interest to the children are often to be found in the classroom. At first, the labels are accompanied by pictures that carry the same message, but as reading proficiency increases there will no longer always be the same need for pictures. In some classrooms the walls become a kind of glossary of useful words in useful groupings, and the material changes as the interests of the class change and develop. Captions written by the children on maps or diagrams or models add to the verbal display. Where the whole effect is colourful and attractive, the right climate is produced for the development of pleasure in writing and reading and pride in the appearance of the handwriting. The seeds are here for later developments. The nature of the books will change; what began as a full-page picture with caption will become by degrees a written page with illustrations, and then, where appropriate, a page of text unadorned.*
>
> (*ibid*.: paragraph 5.22)

Marie Clay

Children take on the task of writing on all fronts simultaneously

Marie Clay's *What Did I Write?* was first published in 1975, the same year as the Bullock Report, and has been many times reprinted. In the book, Clay shows, with the help of numerous examples of young children's drawing and emergent writing, most of them presented in facsimile form, how young children are trying out hypotheses about what writing can do for them:

> *The theme of this book is the child's gradual development of a perceptual awareness of those arbitrary customs used in written English.*
>
> (Clay, 1975: 2)

Like all the wisest writers on any aspect of children's language development, Clay warns against the easy but wrong assumption that children's patterns of learning in a particular area are simple versions of an adult's way of describing that area:

> *I doubt whether there is a fixed sequence of learning through which all children must pass and this raises further doubts in my mind about the value of any sequenced programme for reading or writing which proceeds from*

an adult's logical analysis of the task and not from an observation of what children are doing, and the points at which they, the children, are becoming confused.

(ibid.: 7)

Children approach the task of writing on all fronts simultaneously:

Observation of children suggests that they do not learn about language on any one level of organization before they manipulate units at higher levels. A simplification achieved by dealing firstly with letters, then with words, and finally with word groups may be easy for teachers to understand but children learn on all levels at once.

(ibid.: 19)

Clay makes it clear that her aim is not to offer advice on the teaching of handwriting, the learning of the alphabet, or practices such as the child's dictating to the teacher and then tracing over or writing under the teacher's writing. She is trying to see development through the eyes and brains of the young writer, and she recommends that teachers should try to do the same:

It is hard for the experienced reader to realise that a space is a signal.

(ibid.: 53)

Errors are interesting. They often signal that a child is reaching out to some new facet of written expression, and that he needs help towards some new learning.

(ibid.: 58)

Many of the 'errors' in children's creative writing at this early stage must be regarded as indicators of this flexibility which is essential for the complex learning to be mastered.

(ibid.: 63)

More important than anything else is the need for teachers, whatever kinds of formal instruction they offer, to recognise the sense behind children's as yet non-conventional writing:

Adults seem to be reluctant to bother with a jumbled set of letters in early writing or a story that has been written from right to left. They prefer not to read what the child is saying until he presents it in an easily read form. Those who make the effort will find a rich commentary on each child's earliest learning about print encapsulated in his accumulated attempts to write.

(*ibid.*: 15–16)

Don Holdaway

Development is approximation towards correctness and control

Towards the end of *The Foundations of Literacy* (1979), Don Holdaway offers a succinct description of a key developmental process, which he calls 'approximation'.

> **Approximation** *Such complex developmental tasks as reading and writing, which take many years to master, are characterized by gradual approxima-tion towards 'correct' performance. The crude division of responses into right and wrong, which is so deeply set in the practices of schooling, flouts this crucial principle, which may be seen as the efficient learning of any developmental task. Provision for appropriate approximating necessarily implies longitudinal monitoring and recording of actual behaviour rather than the results of isolated exercises or 'right/wrong' tasks.*
>
> (Holdaway, 1979: 190)

The summary which follows refers to observational work discussed earlier in the book:

> *During the leisurely period of three to four years of active literacy-learning before school entry most of these children [the children who have been studied] become fascinated with print as a mystery that is well worth solving. They begin to play with writing in the same way as they play with reading, producing writing-like scribble, the central feature of which, for them, is that it carries a message. They learn to write their names, and explore creating letters and letter-like symbols with a variety of writing devices. They show intense interest in the print around them on signs, labels, advertisements, and TV, and often imitate these forms in inventive ways . . .*
>
> *Many of the same principles that we have been studying in reading-like behaviour of pre-schoolers are also clearly evidenced by very young children who have been exploring writing in a developmental environment in which approximation was tolerated.*
>
> (*ibid.*: 47)

The 'reading-like behaviour' to which Holdaway refers is young children's wonderful habit of 'telling out loud' the story of a book whose overall structure and whose main events they know, even though the words they speak are not the exact words printed on the page.

Emilia Ferreiro and Ana Teberosky

Young writers learn by hypothesis

In *Literacy before Schooling* (1982), two Argentinian researchers, Emilia Ferreiro and Ana Teberosky, offer fascinating insights into the early literacy of young Spanish-speaking children in Buenos Aires. (Their findings on reading go hand in hand with their findings on writing, but it was the latter that caused the most stir when the book was published, probably because there was less literature on early writing at the time than there was on early reading.)

The authors show, as a result of careful, disciplined observation of children's emergent writing, that children construct a series of hypotheses about what writing is as they move towards conventional understanding.

Very early, as children start to distinguish between drawing and writing, they hypothesise that *words need to correspond in size to the things they represent*. The bigger the thing, the bigger or longer the word needs to be. (As readers, the children that Ferreiro and Teberosky observed believed that in order for a text to be readable it must have a minimum number of characters, ranging from two to four, with three being the minimum for most of them.)

Then children move to the hypothesis that *different things must be represented by different combinations of marks*. If the children observed only had access to a limited number of marks, these had to be pressed into service in different combinations to write the word the child wanted to write.

Next, they attempt to assign a sound value to each of the letters that compose a piece of writing; they hypothesise that *each letter does the job of standing for a syllable*.

Next, a conflict arises: *if one letter stands for a syllable, does that not contradict the children's hypothesis as readers, that a minimum number of characters, and certainly more than one, is needed to make meaningful text?*

Next, children emerge from that conflict to an understanding that *letters of the alphabet represent sounds*:

> *Alphabetic writing is the final step of this evolution. In reaching this level children have broken the code; they understand that each written character*

corresponds to a sound value smaller than a syllable, and they systematically analyze the phonemes of the words they are writing.

(Ferreiro and Teberosky, 1982: 209)

Ferreiro and Teberosky are quite clear that this stage of development, delightful as it is to see, is exactly the reason why teachers should *not* then impose a regime of phonics teaching, because nearly all their phonetic invented spellings *are* examples of frequently occurring grapho-phonic correspondences. And they are 'wrong'. There is another stage to be gone through, beyond the first five, during which the child adapts her or his understanding to the realities of conventional orthography, which is very far from the plain sailing of regular grapho-phonic correspondences.

Ferreiro and Teberosky worked within Jean Piaget's theory of cognitive development, which says that children construct an understanding of the world around them, and then experience discrepancies between what they already know and what they discover in their environment, discrepancies which they have to assimilate (see, for example, Piaget and Inhelder, 1969). Ferreiro's and Teberosky's essential advice to teachers is not that there should be no instruction, but that instruction should take account of the hypothesis-making, hypothesis-revising nature of the learning brain.

Lev Vygotsky

Young writers discover the symbolic function of writing

In the very last paragraph of *Literacy before Schooling*, its authors write:

> As we were finishing this research, we discovered that without knowing it we were doing what Vygotsky [1978b] clearly pointed out decades ago: 'The first task of scientific investigation is to reveal this prehistory of children's written language, to show what leads children to writing, through what important points this prehistorical development passes, and in what relationship it stands to school learning'.
>
> (Ferreiro and Teberosky, 1982: 286)

Although not published in English until 1978, in a collection of his papers entitled *Mind in Society*, the paper to which Ferreiro and Teberosky refer is 'The Prehistory of Written Language', written by the great Russian psychologist Lev Vygotsky in the early 1930s. In 14 short pages, this paper lays out a theory, based on the close observations which Vygotsky and his colleagues had conducted, of how young children get to the point of writing and of understanding what writing does. Possibly for the first time ever, the paper grasps the idea which Ferreiro and Teberosky fleshed out in so much more detail more than 40 years later, and which I have already summarised: that out of the symbolic acts which children learn from babyhood onwards – speech, play and drawing, which are all acts which represent or symbolise other things – comes the understanding that writing is another way of symbolising other things, in this case the language which up to a certain point the child has only encountered as sounds.

Vygotsky's three practical conclusions are:

> *it would be natural to transfer the teaching of writing to the preschool years. Indeed, if younger children are capable of discovering the symbolic function of writing . . . then the teaching of writing should be made the responsibility of preschool education . . .*
>
> *writing should be meaningful for children . . . an intrinsic need should be aroused in them, and . . . writing should be incorporated into a task that is necessary and relevant for life;*
>
> *writing should be taught* naturally *. . . the motor aspect of this activity can indeed be engaged in in the course of children's play . . . writing should be 'cultivated' rather than 'imposed'.*
>
> (Vygotsky, 1978b: 116–118)

Anne Haas Dyson

Writing is social

Anne Haas Dyson has written extensively about early writing. In *Multiple Worlds of Child Writers: Friends Learning to Write* (Dyson, 1989) and *Social Worlds of Children Learning to Write* (Dyson, 1993), she lovingly and carefully describes the emerging powers of young writers (at kindergarten through to Grade 3) in two schools in San Francisco. Dyson studied the children's development over a three-year and a two-year period respectively. The words 'Friends' and 'Social' in the titles of the two books signal a useful corrective to what has perhaps been up to now an over-emphasis on writers as individuals in this chapter; Dyson presents young writers as collaborators and as encouragers and critics of each other's work.

In both schools, the children had a strong teacher who understood the essentials of how children learn to write. Some of these have already been stated.

First, learning to write is part of children's dawning realisation that writing is a symbolic act, arising from and connected to their existing use of other symbolic acts: talk, dramatic play and drawing.

Second, the desire and need to write is driven by the desire and need to express meaning and to communicate that meaning to others.

Third, an effective classroom is a community of readers and writers, a network of readers and writers, critics, commentators, encouragers, admirers.

Fourth, the journey towards confident control of the conventions of the writing system (clear handwriting, correct spelling, appropriately placed punctuation, grammatical consistency within and between sentences) is helped by the practices and tools which the teacher and other adults in the room provide. These include: dictation of short texts to accompany drawings; teacher modelling of writing; discussion of conventions using sentences which the teacher puts on the board; over-writing and then under-copying of adult writing to develop clear handwriting; learning the alphabet and making alphabet books; the labelling of journal books, mailboxes and personal 'cubbies' with children's names; displays of spellings of common words around the room; and the use of personal dictionaries.

Effective Teachers of Literacy

Effective teachers enable pupils to create meaning using text

Effective Teachers of Literacy (Medwell *et al.*, 1998) is the report of a project conducted by researchers at the University of Exeter and the University College of St Mark and St John. The project was commissioned by the UK government's Teacher Training Agency. Its purpose was 'to help the Teacher Training Agency and teachers in England to understand more clearly how effective teachers help children to become literate'. A total of 228 primary-school teachers were identified as effective teachers of literacy 'on the basis of a range of data including pupil learning gains'. These teachers responded to 'a questionnaire survey of [their] qualifications, experience, reported beliefs, practices and preferences in teaching literacy'. Of these, 26 were observed teaching literacy lessons and were interviewed 'about the content, structure and organisation of the lessons observed and about the knowledge underpinning them'. There was also 'a "quiz" designed to test teachers' subject knowledge about literacy'.

Both quantitative data and qualitative data were collected to build up as full a picture as possible of the knowledge, beliefs and teaching practices of a group of teachers identified as effective at teaching literacy. Similar data was [sic] also collected from a sample of 'ordinary' teachers (referred to as the validation group) and from a group of student teachers (novice teachers). Thus the findings from the effective teacher sample could be compared and validated against those from the two other teacher groups.

(Medwell *et al.*, 1998: paragraph 1.3)

The first of the project's main findings is crucial. Effective teachers of literacy tended to:

believe that it is important to make it explicit that the purpose of teaching literacy is enabling their pupils to create meaning using text. While almost all teachers would also endorse this aim, the effective teachers of literacy we studied were very specific about how literacy activities at the whole text, word and sentence levels contributed to such meaning creation.

(*ibid.*: paragraph 1.5)

Throughout the report, it is clear that the difference between effective and less effective teachers of literacy (the researchers' validation group) is that the former teach about the technicalities and conventions of the English writing system – whether in the context of lessons about reading or about writing – as essential aids to the achievement of a larger purpose, which is to create meaningful and satisfying texts as writers and to gain satisfying meaning from texts as readers.

The effective teachers of literacy mentioned aspects of knowledge about writing (that it carries meaning, has a range of purposes and has an audience) most often. The validation teachers mentioned letter formation most often . . . this suggests a different view of the starting points in teaching early writing and the effective teachers seemed concerned for children to understand the purpose and role of writing from the outset so that they could, for example, see the need for technical skills such as forming legible letters as a means towards communicating meaning in writing.

(*ibid.*: paragraph 2.7)

The effective teachers of literacy tended to place a high value upon communication and composition in their views about the teaching of reading and writing: that is, they believed that the creation of meaning in literacy was fundamental. They were more coherent in their belief systems about the teaching of literacy and tended to favour teaching activities which explicitly emphasised the deriving and the creating of meaning. In much of their teaching they were at pains to stress to pupils the purposes and functions of reading and writing tasks.

(*ibid*.: paragraph 3.10)

effective literacy teachers were observed using modelling extensively . . . One reception teacher told us a little about why she modelled writing for her class:

'I noticed when you demonstrated writing you talked about the capital letters, the pronoun I and exclamation marks. Why?'

'It's something I do from the day they arrive at school. I demonstrate writing. I talk about what is happening on the flipchart and they begin to pick up adult conventions without a "formal" lesson. It's our everyday approach.'

'Do you do it often?'

'Oh yes, whenever I am demonstrating, not just in writing. I am always talking about the conventions of writing and what I am doing and I feel they are learning an awful lot more if they realise that it is just part of writing and reading. When they are reading to me we discuss where the full stops come and commas and speech marks. I am trying to train them to an awareness of everything so that if they question they will learn. But if no-one points things out to them they might not even ask.'

(*ibid*.: paragraph 4.4)

In summarising their conclusions, the authors of the report write:

The effective teachers of literacy placed a great deal of emphasis on presenting literacy to their children in ways which foregrounded the creation and recreation of meaning. Because meaning was such a high priority, they tried wherever possible to embed their teaching of the crucial technical features of literacy (how to do it) in a context where the children could see why they were learning about such features.

(*ibid*.: paragraph 8.7)

Understanding Spelling

Spelling is a multi-faceted process involving many different kinds of knowledge

Understanding Spelling (O'Sullivan and Thomas, 2000) is the outcome of a three-year longitudinal study of children's spelling conducted by the Centre for Language (now Literacy) in Primary Education.[1] O'Sullivan and Thomas worked with teachers and pupils at three London primary schools. The book is a powerful and practical account of success, difficulty and development in children's spelling, covering the whole primary age range. The quotations here relate to the learning of spelling by children up to the age of seven.

The authors point to teachers' need for detailed advice on spelling, a need they identified when they began to work with the schools.

> *At the beginning of the spelling project, it became apparent that many teachers felt unsure about how to teach spelling in a constructive way. Some were concerned about inhibiting children's writing by focusing too closely on their spelling. They tended to see teaching spelling mainly as a question of correcting errors, rather than a way of developing an interest in, and attention to, words and their structures.*
>
> (O'Sullivan and Thomas, 2000: 9)

In their review of earlier work on spelling, the authors describe how the excitement generated by such excellent writers as Ferreiro and Teberosky (1982) and Bissex (1980) had distracted some teachers.

> *A fascination with children's early and original spellings dominated discussion. There was a need for a broader view of learning to spell and a clearer understanding of the range of strategies that children need in order to become competent spellers. There unquestionably is a basic developmental dimension to children's progress in spelling, but children always need information, support and teaching to help them move on in their learning. The hard question is always how this teaching can be provided most effectively, so that it connects with children's understandings.*
>
> (O'Sullivan and Thomas, 2000: 13–14)

One general answer to this hard question is that 'becoming a speller [is] most likely to be a multi-faceted process involving many different kinds of knowledge, and that children [are] likely to be different in their learning of spelling' (*ibid*.: 17).

Two of these kinds of knowledge are very broad: knowledge acquired from reading and knowledge acquired from writing. Although diverse and pleasurable experiences of reading are not, in the case of most children, a *sufficient* basis on which to become successful spellers, they are in all cases a *necessary* basis. One cannot become a good speller without wide, diverse and pleasurable experiences of reading. The *sufficient/necessary* distinction applies equally to writing. Although to have varied and satisfying experiences of writing does not *guarantee* success in spelling:

> *The children in the project who made most progress in spelling were those who had a wide range of opportunities to write, who wrote at length and who were helped by their teachers to become enthusiastic writers. Our analysis of the case-study children's texts showed that, as their texts got longer, the percentage of their misspellings declined and their attempts at unknown words improved.*
>
> (*ibid*.: 19)

Then there are more specific kinds of knowledge which children variously draw on in their development as spellers. Notable amongst them are:

- *phonological knowledge, 'a growing awareness of the sounds of words, and of the various ways that words can be split up, for example into syllables, onsets and rimes, phonemes';*
- *letter name and alphabetic knowledge, in which children's early introduction to the names of the letters of the alphabet and to the spellings of their own name is over-generalised and '[plays] an important part in children's spelling in the earliest stages, but their use is a strategy which is normally abandoned relatively quickly';*
- *a repertoire of known words, learnt and retained as wholes;*
- *knowledge of visual patterns, in which children come to recognise the commonest letter combinations in English, and realise that there are words which sound alike and are spelled alike, words which sound alike but look different, and words which look alike but sound different; this knowledge is linked to an understanding of analogy in spelling patterns, in which through hypothesising about groups of words which 'belong together', such as* beat, meat, cheat, seat, *but then realising that a hypothesis can be over-extended (*late *and* mate *don't help with* great *or* wait*), children learn about 'rules' and 'exceptions' (or, in more accurate adult terms, more reliable and less reliable patterns);*

- *syntactic knowledge, as in the realisation that the -ed and -ing endings of verbs do the same grammatical job for many verbs;*
- *semantic knowledge, as in the recognition of frequently used prefixes and suffixes which change, extend or reverse meaning.*

(ibid.: 18–31)

All these kinds of knowledge, and mixtures of them, are at work in the conscious or unconscious mind of the developing speller. The teacher's job is to recognise the need for particular kinds of knowledge, and then to address that need, consciously, in the context of enjoyable encounters with writing. The writing may be the children's, or the teacher's with the children's (as in shared writing with the teacher scribing onto a flip chart or whiteboard and the children helping), or someone else's (as in the close study of a story by a published writer).

An analogy between learning to write and learning to read

Inquiry into Meaning: An Investigation of Learning to Read (Chittenden and Salinger with Bussis, 2001) is, as its title states, concerned with early reading. It reports on a study of how some 80 children in schools in the USA learned to read and how their teachers helped them to do so. However, the book is also relevant to early writing, because it offers a profound understanding of the relationship between the gradual acquisition of a skill and the performance of any complex action (for example, writing) to which the skill contributes.

> *Any skill exercised by a beginner will necessarily be more awkward and less proficient than the same skill performed by an experienced individual. But the only way for a novice to gain the proficiency that comes with experience is to practice the skill, using whatever relevant resources he or she commands. Nothing else suffices in the long run, because acts of orchestration and coordination are functions of the brain that apparently can be learned only through repeated attempts to perform them. Learners may want to concentrate on different aspects of the action at times (the flow or the accuracy), and they must limit their ambitions at first, but practicing the action is what counts.*

(Chittenden and Salinger with Bussis, 2001: 40)

What do these authorities have in common?

This long section needs a short epilogue. The consensus uniting the authorities whose work has been summarised is that the encouragement of strong voices and the effective teaching of writing as a system are complementary not opposite principles. Success comes when young writers are given opportunities to compose and communicate ideas, experiences and narratives, real and imagined, which matter to them and whose written expression gives them pleasure and a sense of achievement. With these essentials established, matters like grammatical consistency, spelling, punctuation and handwriting cease to be merely 'the basics' or 'technicalities'. They become the writer's equipment, and the gaining of mastery of that equipment itself becomes a source of pleasure and brings a sense of achievement.

The last quotation from the section on *Effective Teachers of Literacy* encapsulates the consensus.

> *Because meaning was such a high priority, [effective teachers] tried wherever possible to embed their teaching of the crucial technical features of literacy (how to do it) in a context where the children could see why they were learning about such features.*
>
> (Medwell *et al.*, 1998: paragraph 8.7)

A simple model of the writer

Here, in diagrammatic form (Figure 4.1), is a simple, three-pronged model of the writer. It owes much to the wisdom of theoreticians and practitioners quoted in the last section.

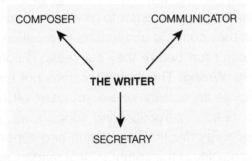

Figure 4.1 A simple model of the 'personality' of the writer.

Composer: Writing is almost never the simple transcribing onto paper of language already formed in the head. In the act of writing, writers discover what they mean; they formulate understanding in a way not available to them before they began to write.

Communicator: Most of the time, writers write in the expectation of having an effect on someone else. (Sometimes, admittedly, writers write solely for themselves. Often, writing is both for themselves and for other people.) All writers need regularly to know – whether their readership is a single person or an unknown number of readers, whether their purpose is ephemeral or long-term – that their writing has been noticed and has made a difference.

Secretary: Writers work within the writing system of the language they are using. The system has evolved over hundreds of years (and continues to change) for a host of reasons: for example, the influence of other languages; the practices of scribes; the rise of print; the efforts of some groups to reform spelling.

'Composer', 'communicator' and 'secretary' are equally important facets of the 'personality' of the writer. Less effective teachers tend to neglect the composer and the communicator in the writer, and are preoccupied with producing good secretaries. If young writers have limited or no opportunity to experience composition and communication, there is no inherent point in becoming even the most accurate of secretaries. More effective teachers, of which thank goodness the English-speaking world has many thousands, understand the need to nurture all three facets of the writer's 'personality'. The interplay between them applies to writers at all ages and stages.

The teacher's task: help them to start off running

Ineffective teaching approaches and materials engage children with abstracted features of the written language in order to give them practice for an imagined future moment when they come to understand or produce the real thing.

The truism 'they can't run before they can walk' is sometimes applied to early literacy learning. Wrong. The metaphor does not hold. The learning of language and literacy is an activity where you start off running. Of course, the beginning writer needs instruction and support, as does the beginning reader. Effective teachers offer that instruction and support so that children can participate more quickly in the community of readers and writers that they are entering.

The greatest obstacle to writers' entry to that community is fear of the pen and the page or the screen. If children have been so over-burdened with anxiety about correctness that their voices have been stifled, they will by the age of seven already have developed defensive strategies which mean that they write as little as possible, and within as narrow and constrained a set of limits as possible, in order to minimise the risk of failure and the censure that comes with that. The desire to minimise the risk of failure actually increases the likelihood of failure, because a writer cannot progress unless he or she is prepared to take the risks that come with the production of continuous texts.

Progress in writing comes not from avoiding mistakes, but from producing writing which is then sympathetically discussed. During the course of the discussion, mistakes and their correct equivalents can be pointed out.

On the other hand, it is not sufficient for children simply to be told to write, for the writing to be received and superficially commented upon, and then for nothing to happen until the next command to write. Sympathetic discussion of children's writing will include attention to the structure and organisation of a piece as a whole, to the structure and organisation of sentences within the piece, and – as appropriate given a particular child's level of competence and confidence – attention to spelling, punctuation, grammar and handwriting. There is a direct relationship between strength of voice in a writer and willingness to accept and absorb positive criticism. The more confident writer can take that criticism, because he or she has understood the importance of taking a reader into account. Some of that 'taking into account' involves concern for convention.

If this degree of attention to children's writing means that, overall, less quantity is produced, so be it. The benefits in terms of quality will soon be apparent.

What should young children write?

The Plowden Report made some suggestions:

> *writing arising out of dramatic play, writing associated with and explaining the models that are made, writing which reflects the sharpening of the senses . . . writing that derives from the special occasion . . . writing [derived] from the experiences of individual children . . . from the excitement of a shared visit . . . [from] the spirit and language of a story . . .*
> (The Plowden Committee, 1967: paragraph 601)

As already noted on page 110, the Bullock Report made some more suggestions:

> *Young children will write about their homes and families, their pets and other animals, and the highlights of their day-to-day experience. They will write about a football match, a street accident, a snowfall or a thunderstorm, a visit to hospital, a television programme they have watched, or the things they bring into school, and they will write stories on fantasy themes involving witches or bandits, ghosts or gunmen. They describe objects or processes that have interested them, and in this way much of their writing arises from the practical activities in school.*
>
> (The Bullock Committee, 1975: paragraph 5.23)

Don't forget digital

To these we could add many other possibilities. Generic range is important from the start. Within that range, we should remember that computers, the interactive whiteboard, portable digital appliances and the internet now mean that all the genres of writing appropriate for young children may be realised in electronic as well as in printed and handwritten form. So diaries could take the form of blogs; stories or poems or recipes, which could be contained in illustrated home-made books, could also be composed, illustrated and displayed electronically, by individuals or as a class's joint effort; in partnership with another school anywhere in the world where English is understood, writing plus still pictures or short films can be exchanged as email attachments or on memory sticks or as compressed files.

Here are some more kinds of writing which young children could attempt:

- letters (to other children, to characters in a story, to authors, to real-life figures such as the school's lollipop man or lady);
- descriptions of pictures which the children have been shown or which they have painted themselves;
- responses to music;
- accounts of favourite television programmes;
- poems (whether inspired by direct experiences or by events in a story or written as alternative versions of poems by children's poets which the teacher has read aloud);
- playscripts recording the words of improvisations (which have often been inspired by shared texts);

- diaries;
- writing in role as historical or mythical figures;
- notices about kindness and respect of the 'at school we . . .' sort;
- observations about things growing in the school garden;
- recipes before or after a class cooking session;
- reports of science experiments;
- notices and signs showing adults and children around the school.

The present situation in England

This section examines the government's statutory framework for the Early Years Foundation Stage and the National Curriculum for English's statutory requirements for writing at Key Stage 1, to see how they compare with the view of the teaching of early writing presented in the chapter so far.

Statutory framework for the Early Years Foundation Stage

The current version of the government's statutory framework for the Early Years Foundation Stage has this to say about writing:

> *children use their phonic knowledge to write words in ways which match their spoken sounds. They also write some irregular common words. They write simple sentences which can be read by themselves and others. Some words are spelt correctly and others are phonetically plausible.*
>
> (Department for Education, 2014c: 11)

That is all. The writing guidance has been influenced by the previously given guidance on reading:

> *children read and understand simple sentences. They use phonic knowledge to decode regular words and read them aloud accurately. They also read some common irregular words. They demonstrate understanding when talking with others about what they have read.*
>
> (*ibid.*: 11)

So far as the government is concerned, everything to do with the earliest beginnings of writing proceeds from phonics. None of the understandings offered or quoted in this chapter has any place in the government's view of the beginning writer.

Key Stage 1

In its new National Curriculum orders for English (Department for Education, 2014a), the government makes perfectly clear its priorities with regard to writing at Key Stage 1: transcription (by which it means spelling and handwriting) comes first. It may be suggested that the order in which requirements are laid out is less important than what is in the requirements themselves. Perhaps, but the symbolism of the order is powerful. It is saying to teachers 'Deal with this first'.

Spelling

At the very beginning of the requirements for spelling, readers are directed to 'English Appendix 1'.

Appendix 1 is on spelling and is statutory. It contains an unrealistic and theoretically wrong insistence on the teaching of formidably long lists of spelling patterns. For Year 1 alone, 46 separate spelling patterns must by law be consciously taught. The number drops to 26 for Year 2, to 17 for Years 3 and 4, and to 10 for Years 5 and 6 (though children at Years 3 and 4 and at Years 5 and 6 must also learn the spellings of a prescribed list of 100 words in each case).

The error in this requirement begins with the simple fact that the number of patterns which must consciously be taught decreases as children get older. This is exactly the wrong way round: wrong for everyone, and especially wrong for EAL learners who arrive at school at any stage later than Year 1, who presumably would be required to 'catch up' by learning an even greater number of spelling rules as fast as possible. Young children need maximum exposure to and maximum practice in real written language. They need to be shown a limited selection of spelling patterns relevant to their actual or likely needs as writers, as the authors of *Understanding Spelling* (O'Sullivan and Thomas, 2000), already quoted, clearly say. It is as children get older, and as their familiarity with actual written language increases, that they will be able to apprehend and make sense of a wider variety of spelling patterns.

This demand for the learning of huge numbers of spelling patterns by 5-, 6- and 7-year-olds is a case, if ever there was one, of an adult, analytical view of language inappropriately imposed on the psychologically integrated way in which young minds perceive reality, including the reality of written language.

It will prove unworkable in the classroom. Unfortunately, it will not merely be unworkable, not merely a waste of a certain amount of teachers' and learners' time. The repeated attention to large numbers of analytically isolated spelling patterns will actually confuse and discourage some young writers, causing them to decide that the obscure codes and rules they are being asked to learn are an essential entry qualification which must be acquired in advance before they can be shown into the world of writing. That way failure lies.

If we glance back at all the authorities quoted in the section 'Helpful guidance on early writing', we can see that their consensus – encourage strong voices and teach about writing as a system in the context of that encouragement – is precisely the opposite of what the government proposes when it comes to spelling.

The government's obsession with spelling patterns in writing is the twin of its obsession with grapho-phonic correspondences in reading. This twin obsession keeps tripping over the problem of the complex and often unpredictable relationship between the sound and the written mark in English. Chapter 2 willingly acknowledges that there *are* grapho-phonic correspondences in English, lots of them, and that teachers should make use of this convenient fact in those cases where the correspondences apply. But the chapter also warns against making excessive claims for these correspondences. A teacher who teaches that spelling patterns are always or nearly always regular in English words, and that this regularity is always or nearly always a function of symbol-to-sound correspondences, is misleading the children.

In his *Early Spelling*, Gunther Kress writes: 'I want children to learn to spell. I think that the most damaging procedure is to pursue an incoherent route with authoritarian vigour' (Kress, 2000: 79). The authoritarian quality of the vigour has increased since Kress wrote those words.

A better approach to the teaching of spelling, drawing especially on *Understanding Spelling*, is outlined in the alternative curriculum in Chapter 11.

Handwriting

By comparison with the spectacular misjudgements in the new orders for Key Stage 1 to do with spelling, the handwriting requirements are modest and perfectly sensible. *Understanding Spelling* offers a helpful expansion on these requirements:

Handwriting teaching, particularly in groups, helps children to establish the correct shape and formation of letters and to practise common letter patterns.

- *Short frequent teaching and practice sessions are most effective.*
- *Each letter should be introduced with demonstrations of how it is formed (the teacher needs to demonstrate with her or his back to the children). Children can trace the letter in the air before practising it on paper.*
- *Letter recognition can be supported by multisensory approaches such as modelling plasticine letters, tracing in sand, making letters from play dough, using templates.*
- *Letters can be taught in groups according to their formation, e.g. i l t u y / r n m h b p k / c a d g q o e / s f / v w x z j, or according to frequency of use by teaching common letters first, such as i, t, p, n, s.*
- *Always teach letters using the exit stroke, to allow for ease of joining.*
- *Later on, use letter strings and patterns which link to a weekly focus in hand-writing practice sessions.*
- *Alphabet strips (lower and upper case) using correct letter formation should be on children's tables during writing.*
- *Later [still], well known songs, rhymes, poems and proverbs can be used for [handwriting] practice.*

(O'Sullivan and Thomas, 2000: 77)

Punctuation

The requirements for punctuation, which appear in the new orders themselves and in the statutory Appendix 2, are also in themselves perfectly sensible.

(The punctuation requirements are unhelpfully grouped with grammar and vocabulary in Appendix 2: three unlike things yoked together. Spelling and punctuation belong more easily with each other, both being aspects of orthography. They are sets of conventions strictly related to the written language, although punctuation is often an indicator of grammatical choices that a writer has made.)

The orders for punctuation do not impose unrealistic expectations on young learners, and they could be taught largely within the context of children's actual writing and reading.

Shared writing and reading sessions are perfect opportunities for teaching about punctuation. In jointly reading a text, the children can have their attention drawn to the decisions writers have made about full stops, capital letters, commas, apostrophes and speech marks, and can discuss the jobs that these marks do. In jointly composing a text with the teacher, the children can respond to the teacher's leading questions such as 'Isn't there something missing here? Do we need a punctuation mark? What kind of punctuation mark? Wait a minute; this is the beginning of a sentence. What do we need?'

Grammar

Chapter 6, on grammar and knowledge about language, starts from the proposition that grammar is not simply a province of the country of writing. Some of that chapter is highly relevant to the teaching of writing up to age seven.

The government's wrong-headedness about grammar teaching at Key Stage 1 parallels its wrong-headedness about the teaching of spelling. An extraordinary overload of grammatical concepts and terminology must consciously be taught and learned. At Year 1, for example, children must learn, objectively and consciously, about plural noun suffixes, about 'suffixes that can be added to verbs where no change is needed in the spelling of root words', and that the prefix 'un-' changes the meaning of verbs and adjectives. At Year 2, for example, they must learn, again objectively and consciously, about subordination, coordination and noun phrases, and 'how the grammatical patterns in a sentence indicate its function as a statement, question, exclamation or command'.

This will not work. Most teachers will do their best to meet statutory requirements, as they always have done, but a price will be paid. Too much time will be given up to separate grammar teaching at an unrealistically advanced level, at the expense of time given to the teaching of writing, which should include attention to all the aspects of convention and control which developing writers need: to the manner as well as the matter of what they write.

Readers will find a sufficiently demanding but realistic set of alternative proposals for the teaching of grammar at Key Stage 1 in Chapter 11. They exemplify the most important teaching principle in this area: that grammatical conventions and terminology should be introduced in the context of the study of authentic and pleasure-giving texts, including texts which the children have produced themselves. The reader can easily see how the same kinds of practices recommended above to do with the teaching of punctuation could also be employed in the teaching of the modest collection of grammatical concepts and terms appropriate for Years 1 and 2. Done that way, the learning of grammar can become an enjoyable part of children's responses to and study of texts.

Vocabulary

In the general introduction to the programmes of study and attainment targets for English, there is a sensible paragraph on the learning of vocabulary:

Opportunities for teachers to enhance pupils' vocabulary arise naturally from their reading and writing. As vocabulary increases, teachers should show pupils how to understand the relationships between words, how to

understand nuances in meaning, and how to develop their understanding of,
and ability to use, figurative language. They should also teach pupils how to
work out and clarify the meanings of unknown words and words with more
than one meaning. References to developing pupils' vocabulary are also
included within the appendices.

(Department for Education, 2014a: 16)

It is curious, then, that no mention of vocabulary is made in the sections entitled 'Writing – vocabulary, grammar and punctuation' at either Year 1 or Year 2.
In both cases, the reader is directed to English Appendix 2, where the use of
the term 'vocabulary' in practice simply means 'terminology'. It is obvious that,
to the extent that aspects of writing are consciously taught, teachers will use
terminology. In reality, vocabulary, as proposed in Appendix 2, is not a separate matter from grammar, punctuation or spelling. It is simply the language in
which those things are discussed. Given that, apart from the paragraph just
quoted, there is no reference to vocabulary in the sense of the lexis of the
language in which children write, it is not helpful to treat vocabulary as a separate category. The absence of any detailed reference to children's developing
mastery of vocabulary as lexis is another weakness of the new orders.

Composition

The composition requirements for writing at Key Stage 1 are oddly brief. They
require some writing practices to be welcomed: for example, planning, evaluating, re-reading, proofreading, sharing writing with others. But little is said
about *what* children should write. At Year 1, they are required to write sentences: nothing more. At Year 2, it is true, they are required to write 'narratives
about personal experiences and those of others (real and fictional)', to write
about 'real events', to write poetry and to write 'for different purposes' – a
vague category which could include all writing. This is an inadequate account
of the diversity of purposes for which and the diversity of forms in which children should by the age of seven be writing. To say that the very important
question '*What* should children write?' is insufficiently attended to would be a
kindness. Here is yet one more weakness of the new orders. I offered a fuller
answer to the question earlier; and the fuller answer also appears in the alternative curriculum in Chapter 11.

The limits of 'professional autonomy'

In the contrast between elements of writing that are attended to in excessive detail and those that receive too brief and general a treatment, there is a similar disparity to that in the statutory requirements for early reading.

When concerned with the broader competences (comprehension in the case of reading and composition in the case of writing), the government is content to allow teachers a certain latitude of action; no doubt ministers and their advisers would speak of 'professional autonomy' at this point. But when it comes to details of method (phonics, spelling patterns, grammatical analysis), areas in which teachers have a right to expect to be granted professional autonomy, that autonomy is entirely absent. Teachers are being marched through sets of minutely sub-divided orders like a training platoon on its first outing; no straying from the route map is allowed. This is exactly the wrong way round.

Government has a right to describe the broad aims of a curriculum and the major features of its content. It has a right to say what degrees and kinds of competence it expects most learners to attain at particular stages in the course of schooling. It has a right to pursue these ends with a sense of urgency: there is evidence from HMI reports and elsewhere that there are already wide disparities in achievement in writing at the end of Key Stage 1. For example, the Office for Standards in Education's *Moving English Forward* (2012), already quoted in Chapter 3, says in paragraph 2, Part A:

> a sizeable minority of pupils [at the end of Key Stage 1] have not acquired the necessary basic skills in literacy when they move into Key Stage 2. Girls perform better than boys and the gap is greater in writing.
>
> (Ofsted, 2012: 8)

However, the government has no business micro-managing method. In doing so in this case, it has revealed the poverty of its understanding of an aspect of teaching and learning in the school curriculum. The set of requirements for writing 3 to 7 presented in Chapter 11 is a practical alternative to that poverty. The requirements envisage a proper balance between the encouragement of strong voices in young writers and teaching which helps them towards confident control of the conventions of the writing system.

To conclude . . .

Several times in the course of this book a distinction is made between two terms frequently used in discussions of pedagogy: *theory* and *method*. Theory is to strategy what method is to tactic. The one sees the broad picture; the other represents a narrower decision to act in a particular way on a particular occasion. Teachers should have a working theory which, when called upon, they can explain and justify; the intention of this chapter has been to help readers – teachers of writing to children at the most decisive stage of their education – towards greater clarity in taking possession of such a theory.

Young children should in the course of their development as writers be shown how to write conventionally as well as confidently. Fortunately, thousands of teachers of young children understand well the principle that confidence, the use of the strong voice, and experience of authentic, pleasure-giving continuous texts is the only effective basis on which children's control of the conventions of the writing system can be advanced. I pay tribute to those teachers. Unfortunately, most teachers working in primary schools in England are currently obliged by law to engage in the unrealistically advanced and abstract teaching of some elements of writing, notably spelling and grammar.

Some of the requirements for writing at Key Stage 1 simply will not work. There is a danger, in the meantime, that some young children will be so befuddled and discouraged by the succession of abstractions and rules which the law requires teachers to teach that they will see writing (and reading) *as* this succession of abstractions and rules. These children will decide therefore that writing and reading are burdensome and mysterious processes, not primary sources of pleasure and fulfilment, and will in future only undertake them under duress. We have seen for too many years the damage that such decisions can cause.

The alternative curriculum for writing 3 to 7 offered in Chapter 11 offers better-balanced guidance as to the subtle relationship between meaning and system, between voice and control, between the development of active competence in the learner and the use of explicit teaching by the teacher, than that in the frequently unsatisfactory new National Curriculum orders.

Note

1 Reproduced by permission of the Centre for Literacy in Primary Education, www. clpe.org.uk.

5 Writing 7 to 11

John Richmond

Summary of main points

The purpose of the teaching of writing is to develop in children a confident control of the medium and a sense of the pleasure that writing can bring.

The teaching of writing requires an understanding of all the characteristics and needs of a writer at work, and of the multiple demands that teachers make on learners when they ask them to write.

Competence in writing – at whatever level – precedes analysis of writing, not the other way round. This is true of language generally. Analysis of or specific attention to conventions of the writing system should take place in the context of the examination of whole, meaningful texts, whether these are texts produced by the pupil as a writer or those encountered by the pupil as a reader.

Learners' developing competence and confidence in handling forms of and purposes for writing will come about as a result of copious reading of high-quality texts – factual, instructional, persuasive and imaginative – which teachers should provide.

Preparation for writing should often involve oral work in various forms: paired, group and whole-class talk; role-play, improvisation and drama. Oral work in any of these forms can also be an outcome of writing.

Writers should have opportunities to write for a range of different purposes and in a range of different formats, sometimes individually and sometimes in collaboration with other writers.

Writers should be familiar with the process of redrafting in order to bring about a better and more satisfying final product.

Writers should write for readerships which, while including the teacher as the most important reader, are not confined to the teacher.

Teachers should show learners that they write too.

The modelling of writing, including the study of how other writers have made successful and pleasure-giving texts, should be a feature of the teaching of writing.

Recent, fast-moving advances in digital technology have transformed and will continue to transform the possibilities for the production and exchange of writing, and for the combination of writing with other modes, for example images and sound.

Teachers' interventions in pupils' writing should be concerned, first, with what the pupil has written in terms of the content and the overall structure of a piece.

Teachers' interventions in pupils' writing should be concerned, next, with the degree of correctness shown in the writer's handling of the writing system: with spelling, punctuation, layout and the grammatical order and forms of words in sentences.

There is always pattern in error. Teachers' attention to error in pupils' writing should have the principal aim of developing in writers the self-critical awareness which will enable them increasingly to attend to error themselves. That is, writers should be shown how to make their implicit knowledge of the writing system active in the critical examination of their writing.

Pupils at Key Stage 2 should be helped to develop a clear, relaxed handwriting style, if they have not already done so by the age of seven. From Key Stage 2 onwards, pupils should learn keyboard skills so that they can type on a computer at least as fast as they can handwrite.

All these principles apply with equal force to EAL learners (about one in six pupils in the age group with which this book is concerned). However, pupils who have begun to read and write in another language and are learning to write in English are additionally engaged in the complex process of making comparisons between writing systems. There is likely to be a conscious transfer of knowledge and skill from one written form to another, and sometimes features originating in the first language will appear in EAL learners' English writing. Appropriate books in the first language and in bilingual editions can help the comparison of the writing systems of English and the other language(s), in addition to the other benefits they bring.

Writing – at large and in school

This chapter goes beyond the early stages of writing, to consider the progress of children who are travelling in the direction which should lead them to full competence as writers. What are the waymarks along the journey? What is the best advice and help teachers can offer them as they go?

Writing at large . . .

There is no evidence that writing is on the wane in our society. Books, maga-zines, newspapers, journals and booklets continue to pour forth in immense quantity. If it was true 300 years ago that someone with a good library and the leisure and money to use it and add regularly to it could know more or less everything that there was to know, it is now true that to keep up with devel-opments even in one sub-branch of the total output of writing, whether it be sociolinguistics or cookery books or detective fiction, is beyond most of us.

The arrival and explosive growth of digital technology in recent decades relies very heavily on the written word in its websites, blogs, wikis and social-media exchanges, often in conjunction with images (still or moving), spoken language and music, and in the millions of emails and texts written and received every day. Every computer and mobile telephone and most portable digital appli-ances have some kind of device (physical or electronically displayed typewriter console, alphanumeric keyboard . . .) to enable the user to write.

. . . and in school

The production of writing remains, and seems likely to remain, a hugely impor-tant and immensely time-consuming part of a child's schooling. There are negative as well as positive reasons for this. Negatively, there is no doubt that a close relationship exists between writing and control in classrooms. Many teachers – perhaps all – have sometimes used writing as a means of con-trolling or calming a group of noisy or difficult pupils. If that occasional and understandable expedient becomes a regular practice, and writing comes to be associated in learners' minds as a dreary duty or a mild form of punishment, then something is badly wrong.

On the other hand, teachers also know that writing, although not without its pains and frustrations, can be a deeply pleasurable and fulfilling activity; and teachers who enjoy writing and write seriously for various purposes want their pupils to experience the pleasure and fulfilment that writing offers. In success-ful classrooms, learners regularly experience such pleasure and fulfilment.

Correctness versus creativity?

In the 1970s, there was a debate amongst teachers about how best to help their children to write better. At its worst, the debate was sterile, with two sharply divided groups each claiming a monopoly of truth for its position. One group insisted that there had been a loss of nerve at some unidentified point in the 1960s, leading to a dereliction of duty on the part of the other group, and that a return to the basic groundwork of grammar drills, spelling and punctuation exercises and (in primary schools) handwriting practice was urgently needed. Writing should once more be stringently marked and graded, and every error pointed out to the writer; if teachers failed to do these things, how would the pupils learn?

The other group was sure that the methods of the first group had been tried and found wanting, and that the important priority was to provide an environment in which children were stimulated and encouraged to write, drawing especially on their own experience. The one group was doggedly pessimistic, the other determinedly optimistic: pupils' writing would develop and improve, said the optimistic group, given the right learning environment.

There is a degree of parody in this account, but it contains enough truth to be worth the recalling. Later, a more mature and more useful position began to develop, based on the realisation that the written language has characteristics which require an understanding which is broader and more eclectic than the orthodoxy of either group.

Writing: profoundly creative . . .

Like the spoken language, the written language is a profoundly creative affair. People every day compose and write down sentences, paragraphs, whole texts which have never been written down before. Written language is creative too in the sense that it enables us to fix in the world, to make concrete ideas, feelings and opinions which we were uncertain of, or didn't even know we had, until we wrote them down. In *Aspects of the Novel*, E. M. Forster (2005 [1927]) summed up the capacity of writing to do these things in his rhetorical question: 'How can I tell what I think till I see what I say?'

In these circumstances, any attempt to reduce the teaching of writing to the learning in advance of a set of rules or formulae which can then be permutated to produce the real thing is bound to fail. If anything, the opposite would be truer: young writers have an overall intention to write something, whether of their own free will or because the teacher has told them to, and, in the course of fulfilling that overall intention, they encounter the thousand details and demands of actually making marks sensibly on paper or on a screen.

Once young children have mastered the physical act of writing, their further development as writers requires that they have opportunities to write in meaningful contexts which make sense to them and which bring them a sense of achievement, with the help of constant exposure to other people's writing in the form of reading.

. . . and profoundly structured

But it is equally true that the written language is a profoundly structured affair.

If a reader is suddenly confronted with an abandonment of structure and convention – if rools the and structre's the of langauge writen decide we brake to – he or she is going to have difficulty understanding what the writer means. And beyond the level of the sentence, the reader does not expect a leading article in *The Times* to be written in the style of a teenage music magazine, or a report on a football match suddenly to turn into a general lament about the ills of contemporary society.

Language may be creative, but it's not anarchic, and it depends on an enormous amount of consensus between writer and reader about conventions of form and meaning. Teachers who understand both the profoundly structured nature of writing *and* its rolling, unpredictable creativity are in a good position to help their pupils with it.

Craft and art

Writing is a craft as well as an art. The difference between a craft and an art is that the good craftsperson always knows what he or she is doing, whereas the good artist frequently does not.

In reality, most constructive activities have both craft and art about them: makers are working confidently, pleasurably within themselves, using known and trusted skills; they are also daring, pushing open doors to as yet unexplored rooms, frightening the first time, less frightening the next. In writing, craft and art are tangled together in the process, and writers make both sorts of decision – those that are calculations and those that are gambles – all the time.

Just as it is important not to see calculation and gamble, craft and art, as unfriendly opposites, so it is important not to see them as hierarchically related either, with craft the poor relation and art the exalted muse. At the most accomplished level, the poet takes no less pleasure in the formal qualities of a poem than in its meaning, or mood, or intensity of feeling. At the level with which teachers are frequently concerned, pupils who see that they have learned to punctuate, or to handle a complex sentence, or simply to write a page which looks nice, may gain as much from that sense of achievement as from the pleasure of having authentically expressed a strong personal feeling or articulated a complex idea on paper.

In other words, when children develop as writers, their development happens most effectively on a broad front, in several areas at once, and development in one area is often supportive of development in another. On the other hand, young writers sometimes identify priorities for themselves for the time being, which become temporarily more important than anything else. The priority in question may be anything from neat handwriting to managing a balanced argument in a piece of discursive prose.

Teachers also, and often, set priorities for their pupils. The priorities that teachers set should reflect, over time, the broad front of competences and skills a writer needs. Effective teachers are not narrowly preoccupied with only one set of competences and skills: those of correctness.

The demands made on pupil writers

What do teachers need to know and do in order to teach writing effectively?

None of the answers to this question offered in this and the following four sections will be discrete or watertight. The content of one will sometimes leak back or forward into the content of another. This may not make for theoretical elegance, but a consolation will be that the answers, overlapping and cross-referring as they will sometimes do, are like the activity of writing itself, which is neither learned nor most effectively practised as a result of being chopped up into categories in advance, but can be helped by the discussion of those categories, and the terminology associated with the categories, along the way.

Many of the following ideas originated in work I did, in collaboration with colleagues, when I worked on the National Writing Project, which ran from 1985 to 1990 and was funded by the School Curriculum Development Committee. The aim of the project was to improve the quality of the teaching of writing in all areas of the curriculum in primary and secondary schools in England and Wales.

In the years since 1990, the digital technological revolution which was beginning during the 1980s has gathered extraordinary pace. Children make familiar use of a multiplicity of digital electronic devices and media in ways which would have bewildered most teachers 30 years ago, and continue to challenge many today. Everything in this and the next four sections is intended to apply equally to writing employing digital technologies as to writing employing traditional, physical equipment and means of publication.

The first of the answers to the question 'What do teachers need to know and do in order to teach writing effectively?' is that teachers should *recognise the complexity of what they ask pupils to do when they ask them to write*.

Imagine that it is an ordinary day at school, and that the class has been set a writing task. At the end of the lesson, the teacher receives 30 pieces of writing. He or she reads them. In reading, the teacher might consider any of the aspects of writing represented in the diagram on page 142, and consider some of issues raised there (Figure 5.1).

The categories contained within those boxes are not chronological in order of acquisition, or hierarchical in order of importance. Eight-year-olds may be learning to write fairy stories. They have accumulated a sufficient stock of fairy stories and fables, have understood some of the conventions of the genre sufficiently well, to attempt to write one. It may be that the 8-year-olds' sentences are simple rather than complex, that the piece contains several spelling errors, and that there are some errors the 8-year-olds do not make because they have not even got to the stage of attempting the constructions within which such errors might be made. But the young writers are still writing fairy stories, and as such are attempting to handle that difficult quality called genre.

So it is not a case of building blocks of words going to make sentences, going to make paragraphs, going to make whole texts, and the process happening sequentially over time. Neither is this the case when 11-year-olds write up the report of a science experiment. The categories that we might isolate in order to see more clearly – and to help writers to see more clearly – what is happening in a piece of writing are not the categories that the writers perceive in doing a piece of writing.

With that qualification in mind, let us look at the boxes in the diagram. When a teacher asks a child to do a piece of writing, the request is to: manipulate a pen, pencil or computer keyboard; order words in groups so that they make grammatical sense; observe the conventions of the English spelling and punctuation systems; maintain cohesion within a piece of writing, so that it holds together as a vehicle of meaning rather than being merely a sequence

A Piece of Writing

THE TASK
Is the piece carried through and finished?
Did it require more than one draft?
How consistent is it from beginning to end in terms of the requirements
of all the other boxes?

**AWARENESS OF
THE READER**
Who is the writer writing for? Does the
writing implicitly or explicitly show an
awareness of its potential readership?

**HANDWRITING OR
KEYBOARD SKILLS**
If the piece was handwritten, is the
handwriting easily legible?
If the piece was word-processed, how
advanced are the writer's skills?

**WHO IS 'SPEAKING'
THROUGH THE WRITING?**
Is the piece personal or impersonal?
Does it operate in the third person, in the
first person with the writer speaking as
herself or himself, or is the narrator not the
writer but 'speaking' in role? How skilfully
and consistently does the writer handle one
of these options, or a different option?

**LAYOUT, PRESENTATION
AND MEDIA**
How firm is the writer's grasp of the
conventions and possibilities of layout
and presentation in this piece?

VOCABULARY
What evidence of variety, aptness,
accuracy or power in the writer's
choice of vocabulary?

OVERALL IMPACT
What is the piece – factual, imaginative
or a hybrid – saying to the reader?
How effectively is it doing its
job of communicating information,
ideas, a point of
view, emotional power?

CONTROL WITHIN A SENTENCE
Errors, miscues and confusions:
how many and what sort?†
What variety of sentence introductions?
What variety of sentence lengths?
What variety of sentence structures?
How well are these handled?

**THE FORM OF
THE WHOLE TEXT**
How firm is the grasp of the overall
structure of the piece being attempted
(whether it be a story, playscript, poem,
factual description, discursive essay,
text for a speech, diary or blog, letter,
report of science experiment,
set of instructions . . .)?
Is the writer able to manipulate mood in
imaginative writing, showing a feeling for
the poetic, the startling, the rhetorical?
Does the writer present argument, opinion
or polemic logically and persuasively?
Is the writer accurate and clear in reports
and instructional writing?

CONTROL BETWEEN SENTENCES
What are the relationships between
sentences? Are they: *temporal/sequential*
('Once upon a time . . . The next day . . .
Many years later . . .'); *causal*
('She would not speak to him. This made
him very unhappy.'); *concessive*
('Some people say there are too many
immigrants coming to this country.
But I think . . .'); *rhetorical* ('His heart
began to beat faster. The palms of his
hands were damp. His fingers twitched.');
or of some other kind?
How well does the writer handle them?

Figure 5.1 Aspects of writing considered by the teacher.

†See the list of errors, miscues and confusions on page 156.

of discrete and unconnected sentences; be aware of conventions of genre while also remembering that those conventions are open to challenge and change; keep in mind the person or people for whom the piece is being written; and maintain the necessary stamina to see the job through. That is quite a list of demands, which must be met simultaneously.

Readers are invited to improve on the effort opposite; it is there as a prototype. (The note at the bottom of the diagram, referring to a list on page 156, is an early signal of something to be discussed in more detail later: the fact that there is always pattern in error.)

The 'personality' of the writer

Chapter 4 offered the following simple model of the 'personality' of the young writer. It is also included here (Figure 5.2) because it works for young writers throughout their schooling and extends to the most sophisticated writing adults do. Readers may care to turn back to Chapter 4 to see the descriptions offered there of the three features of the writer's 'personality' in the model.

Reconciling the three facets of the writer's 'personality'

As I say in Chapter 4, 'composer', 'communicator' and 'secretary' are equally important facets of the 'personality' of the writer. Effective teachers, of which thank goodness the English-speaking world has many thousands, understand the need to nurture all three facets of the writer's 'personality'. Each must be respected and given the chance to flourish. Each interpenetrates with the others. There will be times when one or other of the three is uppermost in the

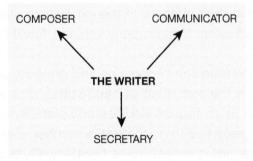

Figure 5.2 A simple model of the 'personality' of the writer.

mind of the writer. Draft observational notes on a science experiment, jotted down prior to writing a report, belong principally to the writer's characteristic as composer. A letter written to a children's author about a book that the class has just read belongs principally to the writer's characteristic as communicator. A lesson in which the teacher uses a piece of prose to show how commas are used in complex sentences belongs principally to the writer's characteristic as secretary. But it can easily be seen how the 'lesser' characteristics in each of these three examples still have their part to play.

Redrafting

The description in Chapter 4 of the 'composer' facet of the writer's 'personality', and the quotation from E. M. Forster above, use different forms of words to say that the act of writing helps writers to articulate understanding in a way not available to them before they began to write. This articulation is often helped when writers have more than one chance to complete a piece of writing to their and the teacher's satisfaction. Over the last 30 years, there has been a major and welcome move away from the custom that pupils only ever had one go at a piece of writing, which was then judged by the teacher and forgotten about by the time the teacher issued an instruction to do another piece of writing.

This is a big step forward. Adults who write seriously for any purpose in their lives (a group which includes but is not confined to professional writers) work on a piece of writing until they're more or less satisfied with it. Pupils who are enabled to work on a piece of writing until they are more or less satisfied with it derive a similar satisfaction, generating a similar motivation to go on and write again, write better. They may in the process produce less quantity in total. The benefit in terms of quality far outweighs the disadvantage of a reduction in quantity. One of the reasons why many adults in the world do as little writing as possible is that their memory of the experience at school is of one-off attempts, abandoned rather than properly finished, few if any of which yielded satisfaction.

However, any good idea can become an arid orthodoxy if implemented too rigidly. To encourage the redrafting of handwritten or word-processed writing is not the same as to require endless complete longhand or on-screen rewrites. Not every piece has to go through a number of drafts. The right kind of flexibility in this regard is similar to the flexibility adults who write seriously offer themselves: some pieces need more reworking; some arrive at a satisfactory state more quickly.

To restate the positive: the process of distance-taking from their work, of becoming good critical readers of their writing – in which the drafting process plays a crucial part – is an essential trait of the 'personality' of mature and maturing writers.

A community of readers and writers

The section 'The demands made on pupil writers' concentrated on a piece of writing. The section 'The "personality" of the writer' concentrated on the writer. This section concentrates on the classroom. Here, again presented diagrammatically (Figure 5.3), is a model of what a writing classroom can and should be.

A range of audiences and means of publication

The teacher remains an immensely important audience for pupils' writing: probably the most important for most pupils. But the teacher should not be the pupils' only audience. Beyond the teacher, the readily available, day-to-day audience for pupils' writing is the other people in the classroom.

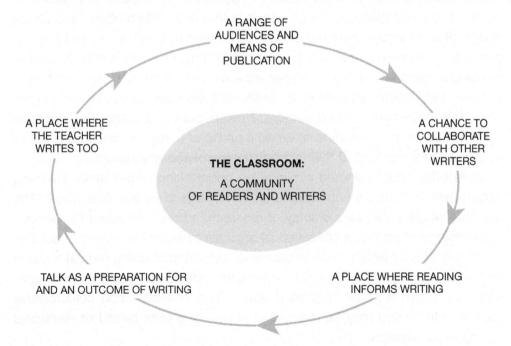

Figure 5.3 What a writing classroom can and should be.

Those who have gone beyond the classroom have found great benefits in, for example: pupils writing for younger children; pupils writing for a specific readership in the local community; letter, email and audio-visual exchanges with other schools (including schools in other countries).

Means of publication include: reading out loud, wall displays, a class folder with transparent loose-leaf holders containing recent writing from everyone in the class, word-processed and duplicated booklets of illustrated writing. To these long-established means we must add more recent electronic ones: e-books, websites and blogs, wikis, podcasts and other audio-visual presentations – on whiteboards, tablets and other appliances – in which writing is combined with sounds and images.

The means of publication – oral, handwritten, printed or electronic – will sometimes be ambitious; the audience will sometimes be beyond the classroom. But most of the time, the means of publication and the audience for writing should be straightforward for the teacher to organise with the community of readers and writers immediately available.

A chance to collaborate with other writers

Collaboration with other writers does not usually mean a group of pupils writing the same one piece by committee. It is true that writers often need peace and quiet and the chance to get on with something by themselves. But equally, pupils who write only and ever as a solitary effort, never as a contribution to a collective endeavour, fail to experience the way in which much writing in the real world comes into being. Scientific and educational books and papers very often have two or more authors. Newspapers and magazines combine the efforts of many contributors. When a group of teachers produces a policy statement of some kind at their school, it is a collaborative effort.

Quite often, pupils should similarly be undertaking group tasks involving writing, with individuals contributing different parts to an eventual whole. The eventual whole could be a display of research, a brochure about the school, an anthology of poetry, a collection of argument pieces on a topic of controversy: any activity which involves planning, allocation of tasks, mutual support and criticism, leading to a product where individuals can see their own contributions within a larger finished product. This collective and collaborative approach to writing may be realised in paper- and print-based or electronic means of publication.

A place where reading informs writing

The next section discusses the range of kinds of writing pupils should encounter and try out for themselves. It touches on the importance of models in giving pupils examples of how different kinds of writing have been achieved. Here, we cite one piece of research which looked in detail at how pupils' reading of one kind of writing, literary texts, influenced their own writing of literary texts.

The Reader in the Writer (Barrs and Cork, 2001) is the report of a year-long research project, organised by the CLPE,[1] which studied the writing of Year 5 and 6 children in five primary schools. The project aimed to discover whether exposure to high-quality literary texts affected those children's own writing of literary texts. If it did affect the children's writing, did it improve it? If it did improve it, in what ways was the improvement demonstrated?

The research found that exposure to high-quality literary texts did significantly improve the children's literary writing. In particular, to quote or paraphrase some of the project's conclusions:

- *Children's reading of literary texts encouraged them to write differently, moving out of what might be termed their 'home style' into new areas of language.*
- *Children's experience of writing in first person, but not as themselves, helped them to assume different voices and enter areas of language that they did not normally use.*
- *Teachers in the project classrooms believed strongly in the value of continuing to read aloud to older children and regarded this as an important way in which they could bring texts alive for them and engage them with literature.*
- *Discussion around a text helped children to articulate aesthetic responses to the writing.*
- *Drama work led to strongly imagined writing in role.*
- *The most effective teachers helped children to plan their writing by offering 'open structures' which were supportive but not overly formulaic.*
- *Effective teachers put a great deal of emphasis on encouraging children to work on their writing together, for instance through the use of response partners or writing partners.*
- *Texts with strong clear narrative structures, such as traditional or folk tales, were helpful to all children, and especially to children for whom English was an additional language.*

- *Emotionally powerful texts, several of which were introduced to children in the course of the year, helped writers to adopt other points of view, and to explore the inner states of characters, more readily.*

(Barrs and Cork, 2001: 210–216)

This work is confined to the use of literary texts with children in two upper-primary years. However, the lessons from the work are clear and generalisable. As a result of reading or listening to high-quality texts, and aided by opportunities for engaging with texts through talk and drama, pupils' confidence and competence in writing texts of this kind themselves, and their sense of the options available to them in doing so, are greatly enhanced.

Talk as a preparation for and an outcome of writing

Other sections in this chapter imply and sometimes state that oral work in all its forms – paired, group and whole-class talk; role-play, improvisation and drama – are very often essential preparations for effective writing. It's also true that the spoken language in these and other forms – for example, spoken presentations of various kinds to the class and to wider audiences – can be outcomes of writing, satisfying to the writer/reader/speaker and to the readers/listeners/spectators too.

A place where the teacher writes too

Teachers of writing should write too. Some of their writing should be shared with their pupils; from time to time, teachers should actually write in the classroom so that pupils can see that they do it; on occasion, teachers should write 'in public', using an easel with large paper or an interactive whiteboard, inviting the collaboration of the class.

The benefits are various. The intention is not, of course, to say to pupils 'If only you could write like me, how lucky you would be'. There is the general truth that teachers teach by example as much as by instruction. If pupils see teachers writing, they are more likely to conclude that writing is worth the time and effort. They may even be interested in teachers' experiences and opinions, as teachers should be interested in theirs. If pupils see teachers engaging with the process, struggling with the difficulties, glad of the rewards, that example will support them when they find writing hard. When teachers show pupils that writers have the right to change their minds, they are teaching an important lesson. Teachers have a more advanced control of writing and the writing system than pupils do, from which the latter can learn. Finally, teachers' recent experience of writing themselves is bound to inform the quality of their teaching of it.

A broad and varied repertoire for writing

The fourth answer to the question 'What do teachers need to know and do in order to teach writing effectively?' concentrates on the repertoire of kinds of writing which pupils should have the opportunity to experience. There is no correct number of kinds of writing which pupils should encounter. There are many different ways of naming and grouping kinds of writing.

Purposes, forms and media

We could list kinds of writing in terms of the *purposes* they serve, in terms of the *forms* they take, and in terms of the *media* by which they are communicated to a readership.

Purposes for writing could include: to recount (a series of events); to re-present (information gleaned from a variety of sources); to explain (the workings of a piece of technology); to instruct (the reader in making a cake); to advocate (a cause); to discuss (a controversial issue, with things to be said for and against a proposition); to narrate (a fictional or factual story, or one which mixes fact and fiction); to distil (a thought or idea in concise terms); to respond (to an aesthetic experience of some kind); to remember (facts or experiences which would be forgotten if they were not written down).

There are ten purposes in this list. The number is deliberately round and arbitrary; the reader will wish to add to or subtract from the list. The names given to the purposes here are negotiable: does the reader prefer 'debate' to 'discuss', 'report' to 're-present', 'argue' to 'advocate'? Improvements and amendments are welcome.

Let the list of forms also number ten. Forms of writing could include: chronological account, factual description, discursive essay, poem, prose story, playscript, diary, letter, speech (as in 'a speech'), set of instructions. The same flexibility applies here as to purposes; the reader should feel free to add or subtract and to rename.

The purposes for writing could be fulfilled in many of the forms. The forms of writing could achieve many of the purposes.

The media by which purposes for and forms of writing can communicate with a readership (media which will profoundly affect both purposes and forms) include: handwritten script on paper, word-processing on screen, physical book-making, wall display, poster campaign, blog, mobile phone text, email, staged presentation of script, filmed presentation of script.

Here are another ten possibilities in a third dimension of the universe of writing. There are now 1,000 theoretical combinations of purpose, form and medium (though some combinations are implausible or impractical). Pupils should encounter and attempt a sample of the possible combinations.

We could present the interaction of purposes, forms and media in a Venn diagram (Figure 5.4 on page 151).

The teacher's constituency

The teacher's job in designing schemes or sequences of work is not, first, to make a list of purposes, forms and media and then to find excuses for employing them. The job is to decide, first, on the activities and topics which will constitute that work, and then to think imaginatively about how writing, in the fullness of its variety of purposes, forms and media, may play a part in it.

That said, teachers do have a constituency. They should be able to describe the range of kinds of writing which pupils should encounter across a year, across a Key Stage. Otherwise, the tendency is for that range to be narrow and familiar.

Learners of any human competence learn partly or wholly as a result of seeing how other humans have mastered that competence. There is no reason why this should not be as true of, say, learning to write a piece of persuasive argument or a ballad in quatrains or the text of a speech or an explanation of a scientific process as it is true of playing football or painting a watercolour or cooking an omelette or riding a bicycle. In all these examples, the apprentice will make mistakes or perform with imperfections in the course of the development of the particular competence. Learning by imitation and adaptation of the achievement of more competent masters or mistresses of the art, craft or activity is an essential part of the process.

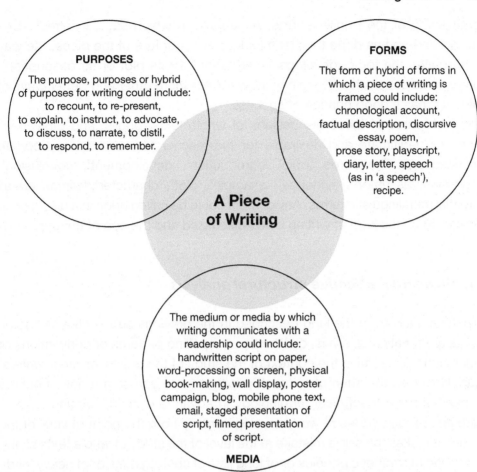

PURPOSES

The purpose, purposes or hybrid of purposes for writing could include: to recount, to re-present, to explain, to instruct, to advocate, to discuss, to narrate, to distil, to respond, to remember.

FORMS

The form or hybrid of forms in which a piece of writing is framed could include: chronological account, factual description, discursive essay, poem, prose story, playscript, diary, letter, speech (as in 'a speech'), recipe.

A Piece of Writing

The medium or media by which writing communicates with a readership could include: handwritten script on paper, word-processing on screen, physical book-making, wall display, poster campaign, blog, mobile phone text, email, staged presentation of script, filmed presentation of script.

MEDIA

Figure 5.4 The interaction of purposes, forms and media.

Pupils come to handle a broad range of kinds of writing by being shown a variety of authentic, pleasure-giving examples of the repertoire which the teacher wishes them to encounter. Some of these examples will have been written by published writers; some by other pupils and by the teacher. The models shouldn't be presented as examples of perfection; neither should there be the suggestion that, for example, one particular written discussion of whether or not animals should be kept in zoos is the only way to conduct such a discussion. Examples can show that there is more than one way to tell or retell a fable. There is more than one way to put a case in a piece of polemic or to discuss a controversial issue in a discursive essay. Poems come in numerous shapes and sizes and speak to the reader in different tones of voice.

Once pupils have been shown examples of a form of writing, they can try their hand at it themselves. It is then useful for the teacher to lead a discussion about some of the pupils' efforts. An approach which says, in effect, 'See how so-and-so has done this; let's look at the structure of the piece, the way it introduces the topic, develops its argument (or its plot or its description), comes to its conclusion. Does it work well? Are there other and better ways of doing it?' has a good chance of success.

In the course of these discussions of whole texts, pupils' and other people's, it is legitimate and desirable for the teacher to introduce appropriate metalanguage. The words 'topic', 'introduction', 'development', 'conclusion', 'argument', 'assertion', 'evidence', 'example', 'plot', 'character', 'climax' are all potential metalinguistic terms. Any of them could be called upon in a discussion, depending on the kind of writing being discussed and the age of the pupils.

Effective and ineffective structural analysis

Structural analysis of the kind described in the previous sub-section is useful, just as grammatical analysis, or attention to spelling patterns or conventions of punctuation, is useful in the context of the study of the pupils' or other writers' texts. However, the attempt to teach pupils to write across a range of genres by offering them theoretical terminology in advance of actual writing will fail. Such an approach doesn't work developmentally from the point of view of the learner. It makes the same mistake at the level of the study of whole texts as the imposition of synthetic phonics or of long lists of spelling rules or of heavy loads of decontextualised grammatical terminology makes in those fields of learning.

It is tempting for those with an adult and analytical understanding of a field of learning to suppose that the understanding they have is also the way in which a learner comes to apprehend that field. It is not. Apprentice writers need to find their way towards full control of the characteristics of a particular kind of writing by trial and error. Transitional efforts at factual genres such as advocacy, discussion, instruction or report may include, for example, awkward mixtures of the personal and impersonal, switchings between present and past tense, and comings and goings of the active and passive voice. Only by allowing these awkward mixtures to present themselves and to be commented on will pupils move towards consistent control of the characteristics of a particular factual genre.

There should be no worry, initially at least, about pupils' 'lack of originality', about their imitation of style or structure in the writing of others, including that of established writers. Originality originates in imitation. Masters and mistresses, present in the classroom or introduced from outside, teach apprentices, who come to develop their own style, their own way of handling structure, their own 'signature'.

Generic boundaries

Kinds of writing, whether expressed in terms of purposes, forms or media, are not watertight categories, each with a set of separate characteristics. Kinds merge into and intersect with each other. The dividing lines are smudgy, not sharp. It is unhelpful to become over-specific about the necessary character-istics of a certain type of writing.

An effective understanding of instruction

The great majority of developing writers' learning comes from experience: of talking, listening, reading – and writing. Chapter 4, however, acknowledged that learning to write also requires much conscious activity in young children. As children move beyond the early years, and as their experience of speech and of the written language (through reading and writing) broadens and diver-sifies, the learning that they take from this experience is continuous, very powerful and mainly unconscious. No child can learn to write without such experience. It works from the little – where to put commas in sentences – to the large – what are the structural characteristics of a successful piece of factual explanation, or narrative or argument.

But for most pupils, learning to write is not only a matter of experience. Teachers also have an essential job of instruction to do. The fifth answer to the question 'What do teachers need to know and do in order to teach writing effectively?' is concerned with the nature of that instruction: with the quality of teachers' interventions in pupils' writing (see Figure 5.5 on page 154).

Teach by illustration not abstract definition

This principle was asserted in the previous section in the context of the dis-cussion of the structural analysis of whole texts. Pupils do not learn how to control an element of writing by being given definitions and rules in isolation from the act of writing. Definitions and rules are abstractions, attempts to

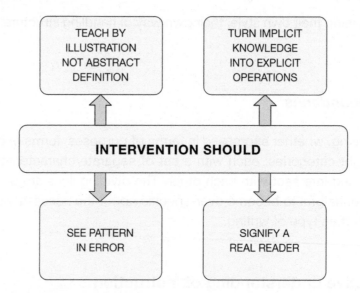

Figure 5.5 Teachers' interventions in pupils' writing.

analyse reality. There is nothing wrong with analysis; but it is only effective when there is some already existing level of competence. Pupils learn by seeing examples of how other writers have used speech marks or paragraphs, or discussed a controversial issue, or described a scientific process or composed a poem. Other writers should include other pupils and the teacher, as well as published writers.

   To the unconscious learning about writing which comes from seeing the work of other writers in wide reading, there must be added a closer kind of reading in which the teacher takes a text, shows it to the class and leads a discussion about its characteristics. What is it in the content and overall structure of the writing and in its finer details such as choice of vocabulary, complexity (or simplicity) of its sentences, appropriate (or unconventional) use of punctuation which makes it work well? Once pupils have understood how a thing has been made, they will be in a better position to make a similar thing themselves. As acknowledged earlier, a 'similar thing' to the style and structure of a model is not to be criticised on grounds of lack of originality; close imitation is often a staging-point on the way to an individual 'signature'.

Turn implicit knowledge into explicit operations

Pupils know more about writing than they know that they know. Their implicit understanding of an element of writing – the understanding they have from all their other experiences of language – is in advance of their ability regularly and reliably to control that element under the pressure of production. The teacher should appeal to that implicit understanding in asking the learner to perform a conscious operation on the text; to be a critic or a detective. 'We've got a bit of a problem with the marking of sentences – with full stops and capital letters. There are about six places on this page where you haven't marked the sentences right. Can you find them?' Most pupils can find most of them.

See pattern in error

There is no such person as a writer, however unsuccessful, whose writing is just a mass of ignorance and confusion. There are always a few things – maybe no more than two or three – which are causing the major difficulties. The teacher's skill is in looking past the superficial symptoms, seeing the pattern in the error, and attending with the writer to the two or three things which matter most at this particular moment in the writer's development.

'Progress in Pat's Writing' (Richmond, 2012b) is a study I made of the development of a 15-year-old girl's writing over a period of 12 months. The study revealed a hierarchy of frequency of error in Pat's writing, with a small number of categories accounting for the overwhelming majority of individual cases. It was immediately clear that if I could attend with Pat to this small number of categories, which in her case were to do with the incorrect marking of sentences, the misspellings of certain words, the incorrect use of speech marks, the occasional omissions of words, and the uncertain use of commas, Pat would make rapid progress, which she did. Still more important was my realisation that Pat's implicit knowledge of the conventions of the writing system was far in advance of her ability regularly and reliably to observe those conventions as she wrote. She certainly knew more about writing than she knew that she knew.

So once I formed the habit of, as it were, turning Pat into an error detective on her own work, using the kinds of prompts suggested in the previous subsection, Pat soon became an efficient sub-editor of her writing. Of course, there were also occasions when I simply taught; these went hand in hand with the occasions when Pat, having been shown how to be self-critical, taught herself.

Later, when I was working on the National Writing Project, I studied the writing of pupils in primary schools in three local authorities to see if my discoveries with Pat also applied to younger writers. I found that they did. I drew up the following list of categories of common error, miscue and confusion.

The list of these features is ordered by frequency in the work of the writers with whom I worked.

1   incorrect marking of sentences;
2   misspellings;
3   uncertain control of tense;
4   grammatical derailment – the sentence doesn't hold together grammatically;
5   incorrect marking of speech in a narrative;
6   omission or duplication of words or phrases;
7   omission or redundant use of commas;
8   omission or redundant use of apostrophes;
9   omission of capitals or their redundant use in mid-sentence;
10 omission of question marks;
11 splitting a word: 'neighbour hood'; or shunting together a phrase: 'afterall';
12 confusion over similar- or identical-sounding very common words: 'there'/ 'their', 'when'/'went', 'were'/'where';
13 uncertainty about singular/plural, particularly when a word has an irregular plural form: 'woman'/'women'.

The insight that pupils can apply their implicit understanding of the conventions of writing in explicit self-critical interventions in their work is of central importance in moving practice away from the model of the teacher as the only assessor and examiner of writing.

Signify a real reader

When pupils are engaged in writing for a purpose they understand and for an audience they care about, they are usually determined to get the conventions right too. The single most important principle of intervention is that teachers should behave as real readers; their first response should be to what the writing is saying.

Instruction as applied to spelling, punctuation and layout, handwriting and typing, and grammar

It should be clear by now that this and the previous chapter advocate a holistic approach to the teaching of writing: one that holds together attention to content, structure and system. However, it will be useful to say something specific here about some aspects of writing commonly lumped together as features of the writing system, while pointing out straight away how unhelpful is that lumping together.

Spelling, punctuation and layout are indeed specific to the writing system. Handwriting and typing are motor skills required for the visible realisation of writing. Grammar underlies all language, spoken and written. In all these cases – even with beginning writers, for whom a higher degree of conscious learning is required than is the case for beginning talkers or readers – the heavy load of learning is carried by experience of language; the lighter but still significant load is carried by instruction in language.

Spelling

The advice on spelling offered here significantly overlaps with and sometimes repeats advice offered in Chapter 4.

Pupils come to have a secure grasp of spelling by recognising and remembering the way words are spelled in the context of meaningful sentences and texts. 'Meaningful sentences and texts' should not be taken to mean only the writer's own sentences and texts. The phrase means all the meaningful sentences and texts which pupils encounter as readers and produce as writers (before, in the latter case, encountering them as readers of their own writing). So, most important of all, effective teachers ensure that their pupils read copiously all manner of worthwhile and pleasure-giving texts.

Here are some more detailed recommendations about the teaching of spelling.

As acknowledged in Chapters 2 and 4, there *are* grapho-phonic correspondences in English, and teachers can make use of this convenient fact in those cases where the correspondences apply. But they also need to be careful not to make excessive claims for these correspondences. If they claim that spelling patterns are always or even nearly always regular in English words, they are misleading the pupils.

It can be helpful to display on the classroom walls lists of words, included in meaningful sentences, which – to use language appropriate to a pupil at Key Stage 2:

- look like each other and sound like each other;
- look like each other but do not sound like each other;
- sound like each other but do not look like each other.

It is important for teachers to be aware of accent variation across the country. The examples in each of the three lists will vary depending on where the school is. We noticed in Chapter 2 that 'blood' and 'book' sound different in the south of England, the same in some parts of the north of England and different again in others. Some EAL learners make no difference in pronunciation between certain words – for example 'ship' and 'sheep' – when most first-language English speakers do.

Words with unusual spellings which commonly give difficulty can be displayed on the classroom walls in the context of meaningful sentences.

Pupils should be shown the use of dictionaries, printed and electronic, appropriate for their age group.

It's helpful for pupils to have their own spelling books, physical or electronic, in which they accumulate spellings which they have needed in the course of their writing.

Pupils should be shown what to do when they're not sure of a spelling (for example, they could go to a word bank or dictionary, classroom-made or published; they could ask a friend; they could write out the word in different ways before looking it up or asking an adult). Once new correct spellings are in the spelling book, pupils can practise them using the Look–Say–Cover–Write–Check routine:

> **Look** at the word carefully and mark any parts of it which are causing you problems. **Say** the word to yourself. **Cover** the word and close your eyes; remember the word by trying to see it in your head; say it slowly in a way that helps you remember how to spell it. **Write** the word down, keeping the word you looked at covered. **Check** the spelling to see if you have got it right. If you haven't, try again or try working with your spelling partner.
>
> (O'Sullivan and Thomas, 2000: 81)

When pupils write on computers, they can use the spellchecker and note down in their spelling books the words which the spellchecker corrected. (But they should be warned that spellcheckers are not infallible; they cannot detect homonyms or homophones.)

Before a class is to undertake a writing task, the teacher can ask for, contribute and display a collection of words that will be useful in the task.

When the teacher writes publicly for and with the pupils, using paper-based or electronic equipment, he or she can draw them into discussion of how to spell particular words that they and the teacher suggest.

To repeat an earlier recommendation, pupils should be encouraged to become their own and each other's 'spelling detectives'. If they are told that there are a certain number of spelling errors in a piece of writing, and asked to try to identify and correct them, they will be able to do so in many cases. If their independent efforts or the help of their friends fail to produce a correct spelling, the teacher will provide it.

Punctuation and layout

As with the teaching of spelling, conscious teaching of punctuation is best done in the context of the study of meaningful sentences and texts. Once again, these sentences and texts include but are not confined to the learner's own writing.

Often, in the course of the whole-class study of a piece of writing, the teacher can point out a writer's correct and effective use of punctuation, and draw attention to its value in making clear the writer's meaning. Punctuation is best understood as an aid to meaning. It can be an indicator of grammatical choices.

Sometimes, a pupil's writing can be shared (with the writer's agreement) with the whole class. The writing will contain some errors of punctuation (and perhaps of spelling too). After a discussion of the qualities of the content of the writing, the teacher can invite the class to help the writer to identify and correct the errors.

Examples of the use of features of punctuation (for example, capital letters to begin a sentence or as the first letter of a proper noun; apostrophes to indicate possession or abbreviation; commas to separate items in lists or to isolate phrases or clauses; semi-colons to separate phrases or clauses in long sentences) can be displayed around the classroom, always as features of meaningful phrases, clauses or sentences.

Print and the internet have so rich a diversity of presentation and layout that it is easy to show pupils models of how texts can be organised, presented and enhanced as appropriate by the use of boxes, different fonts and colours, diagrams and illustrations.

Handwriting, typing and word-processing

By the age of seven, children should already have had plenty of handwriting practice and be on the way to developing a relaxed, clear and individual handwriting style. However, there is evidence (for example, in the Office for Standards in Education's *Moving English Forward*, 2012) that many children at Year 3 and beyond, and especially boys, still need frequent opportunities to practise their handwriting. Chapter 4 quotes the detailed advice on handwriting which appears in *Understanding Spelling* (O'Sullivan and Thomas, 2000) and which also applies to the teaching of handwriting in the lower years of Key Stage 2.

It is often helpful for children who need practice in handwriting to copy texts, so that they are concentrating purely on the physical formation of letters and words, without the pressure of composition. There will in some cases be a need for the teacher to reinforce this basic competence and to help the child to hold a pen or pencil more firmly and naturally.

The most effective way to encourage good handwriting is to show children the importance of attractive final copy for some of their writing (see the remarks in the section 'The "personality" of the writer' about redrafting). The desire to 'look good in public', whether the public is an audience in the child's class or beyond, unites the physical act of writing with the wider sense that writing is *for* someone, for a readership whom the writer wishes and needs to impress.

It is a curiosity of officialdom's nervousness and uncertainty about the digital revolution which has profoundly affected all of us – teachers and learners alike – that there is no acknowledgement of the existence of the digital world in the new National Curriculum orders for writing at Key Stages 2 (see the critique of this failing in the new orders later in the chapter).

Just as children should be helped at Key Stages 1 and 2 to develop a clear, relaxed handwriting style, so should pupils from Year 3 onwards be helped to develop equivalent keyboard skills.

A desirable stage in the development of handwriting is 'automaticity' – a level of fluency which means that the physical act of forming letters and linking them in words is operating at a largely unconscious level, so that the writer's brain can be occupied with other important matters such as composition. Equivalently, if pupils writing on computers are stuck at the 'hunt and peck' stage of typing letters, they will not be engaging with larger tasks such as wrangling with a text's overall structure or thinking about the needs of their audience. During Key Stage 2, pupils should have some instruction in typing and word-processing, whose aim should be that they can compose at the keyboard at least as fast as they can handwrite.

Grammar

Chapter 6 contains a detailed discussion of the place of grammar teaching within the English, language and literacy curriculum, and of the relationship between grammar teaching and pupils' achievement in writing. This subsection considers grammar only in the context of teachers' interventions in pupils' writing to correct grammatical errors.

In the list on page 156 above, the third and fourth categories of error, miscue and confusion which I found in working with pupils relate to grammar: 'uncertain control of tense' and 'grammatical derailment – the sentence doesn't hold together grammatically'.

The most effective teaching of grammar, as it relates to errors in pupils' writing, is – with the help of appropriate terminology such as 'present tense', 'continuous present (the "-ing" form)', 'past tense', 'first-person verb ending', 'third-person verb ending' – to point out the error, and to appeal to the pupils' underlying grammatical understanding as speakers of English. The usual reason why a writer has made a grammatical error is that, in composing a part of a text, the need to compose has made too heavy a demand on the process of transcription, causing the writer to produce a word-form or an arrangement of words which he or she would never have produced in speech. By appealing to the writer's profound understanding of the grammar of her or his first language, the teacher turns the writer into a critical reader of the text.

Pupils who are learning English as an additional language, and pupils who have access to a non-standard variety of English in their speech repertoire, will sometimes produce grammatical forms in their writing which owe their existence to the grammar of a first language or of a non-standard variety of English. There is more on this in Chapters 9 and 10.

Writers experiencing difficulty

This section has dwelt at some length on aspects of difficulty in writing. Readers looking for separate and different advice on teaching writing to reluctant or failing writers will not find it here. A pupil who is having difficulty with writing is likely to need a more explicit, more individual, more closely guided version of one or more of the interventions just recommended. However, three general principles apply to reluctant or failing writers:

1 The greater the difficulty, the more urgently the writer needs to be shown the *possibility* of what he or she can achieve.
2 The frailer the confidence, the higher should be the quotient of *encouragement* in the teacher's mix of encouragement and criticism.
3 The further a writer still has to go before attaining anything like the competence which we would expect from most writers of her or his age, the more he or she is likely to need *models* rather than *analysis*.

A working theory of the teaching of writing

The last five sections have offered answers to the question 'What do teachers need to know and do in order to teach writing effectively?' Between them, the answers amount to the statement of a working theory for the teaching of writing. In short, effective teachers:

- hold in their minds the complexity of the task which confronts pupils when they are asked to write;
- are concerned for content as a first priority, allowing a concern for correctness and control to emerge as a consequence of that concern;
- provide a broad and diverse range of contexts for writing in which pupils write in a range of forms, for a variety of purposes, making use of a diversity of media, intended for a variety of audiences (including, of course, the teacher) within and beyond the classroom;
- make full use of the possibilities offered to writers by digital technologies;
- teach about aspects of the writing system principally by showing examples of how writers have handled those aspects successfully; and
- manage the writing classroom as an environment which replicates as closely as possible the conditions in which writers operate well.

The present situation in England

This section examines the extent to which the new National Curriculum orders for writing at Key Stage 2 are likely to encourage the kind of teaching which helps pupils towards confidence and control as writers by age 11.

Overall

Paragraph 6.3 of the new National Curriculum orders for English at Key Stages 1 to 4 (Department for Education, 2014a) has this to say in general about writing:

> *Pupils should develop the stamina and skills to write at length, with accurate spelling and punctuation. They should be taught the correct use of grammar. They should build on what they have been taught to expand the range of their writing and the variety of the grammar they use. The writing they do should include narratives, explanations, descriptions, comparisons, summaries and*

evaluations: such writing supports them in rehearsing, understanding and consolidating what they have heard or read.

(*ibid*.: 11)

We can isolate the key lexical words from the first three of these sentences: 'stamina', 'skills', 'spelling', 'punctuation', 'grammar', 'writing', 'grammar'. The current government's essential vision of the effective teaching of writing resides clearly in these words. In the fourth sentence, and well down the pecking order, we see that pupils must also write across a certain rather narrow and arbitrary range of forms.

This statement of priorities, and the balance of teaching approaches it envisages and commands, are a world away from the understanding of writers and the writing process advanced in this chapter.

Meanwhile, the orders are in denial about one of the fundamental characteristics of the social reality in which pupils at Key Stage 2 live and move, in and out of school: that of the use of digital technologies and media to compose, receive and respond to writing. There is nothing about writing enterprises which involve collaboration. Nothing about the combining of writing with other modes such as sound and image. In this respect, the new orders for writing greet the present and the future by firmly turning their back on both.

At Key Stage 2

(Some of this critique is similar or identical to that offered in Chapter 4.)

At Key Stage 2, the orders for writing make the same distinction between transcription (which in the document means 'spelling and handwriting') and composition (which means 'articulating ideas and structuring them in speech and writing') as was made for Key Stage 1.

Again, as for Key Stage 1, there are two statutory appendices: Appendix 1 on spelling and Appendix 2 on vocabulary, grammar and punctuation.

Spelling

At both lower (Years 3 and 4) and upper (Years 5 and 6) Key Stage 2, the government's priorities are clear. Transcription comes first and, within transcription, spelling. Chapter 4 refers to 'an unrealistic and theoretically wrong insistence on the teaching of formidably long lists of spelling patterns' at Key Stage 1. It is true that the number of spelling patterns which have to be consciously taught drops from 46 in Year 1, to 26 in Year 2, to 17 in Years 3 and 4, and to 10 for Years 5 and 6. At the same time, children at Years 3 and 4 and at Years 5 and 6 must learn the spellings of a prescribed list of 100 words in each case.

The learning of 17 and then 10 isolated spelling patterns and the spelling of 100 isolated words over each of the two two-year periods of Key Stage 2 do not in themselves represent loads as heavy as those to be imposed at Key Stage 1. But these requirements demonstrate a continuing determination to superimpose an adult, analytical view of language on the psychologically integrated way in which young minds perceive language, and then generalise from their perceptions.

To take the very first example from the requirements for Years 3 and 4, the abstract learning of the rule that *multi-syllable words* double their *final single consonant* when adding a *suffix which begins with a vowel* when their *single final vowel* is *stressed* ('forget', 'forgetting', 'forgotten'), but not when their final syllable is *unstressed* ('garden', 'gardener', 'gardening') is a harder intellectual task than to come to spell those words correctly as a result of becoming familiar with them in the context of their normal use.

Moreover, children must learn that this rule only applies when there is a *single* final stressed vowel. It does not apply to 'retreat', 'retreated', 'retreating'. It only applies when the *very last letter* is a consonant; not when the last syllable is stressed but the word ends with an 'e': 'create', 'created', 'creating'. It only applies when there is only *one* consonant at the end of a word: not 'conflict', 'conflicted', 'conflicting'. It only applies when the suffix begins with a vowel: 'fulfil', 'fulfilling' but 'fulfilment' (except in America – 'fulfillment'). This process of sub-division and exclusion – 'Only then, not then, only stressed, not unstressed, only single, not double, only stressed without a final 'e', not with a final 'e', only when the suffix begins with a vowel' – is interesting at the level of adult orthographics. Such patterns do exist. In this case, adult orthographics are imposed on children for reactionary educational reasons because of a defective understanding of learning on the part of policy-makers.

One of the requirements for Years 5 and 6 almost induces a smile. It admits that the method to be dunned into children has severe limitations:

> Use **–ant** and **–ance/–ancy** if there is a related word with a /æ/ or /eɪ/ sound in the right position; **–ation** endings are often a clue.
> Use **–ent** and **–ence/–ency** after soft **c** (/s/ sound), soft **g** (/dʒ/ sound) and **qu**, or if there is a related word with a clear /ɛ/ sound in the right position.
> There are many words, however, where the above guidance does not help. These words just have to be learnt.

(*ibid*.: 67)

Despite the difficulties, most teachers will do their best to teach the patterns and the word lists, perhaps a few per week over a period of time, and children will do their best to learn them. Unfortunately, that is not how children come to have a secure grasp of spelling. The section 'An effective understanding of instruction' discusses some of the ways in which pupils *are* helped to a secure grasp of spelling; the essentials of the list are repeated in the alternative curriculum in Chapter 11.

Handwriting

As at Key Stage 1, the requirements for handwriting at Key Stage 2 are perfectly reasonable, although the requirement at Years 5 and 6 that children should '[choose] which shape of a letter to use when given choices' is mysterious. There is no mention of the desirability of children learning keyboard skills from Key Stage 2 onwards, as mentioned in the section 'An effective understanding of instruction', so that they can type and word-process at least as fast as they can handwrite.

Composition

By contrast with the excessively detailed prescriptions which apply to spelling (see above) and to grammar (see below), the composition requirements for writing at Key Stage 2 are curiously inadequate. This inadequacy may well come as a relief to teachers; at least the orders do not actually prevent good teaching. They require some of the writing practices which have been advocated in this chapter (for example planning, drafting, evaluating, editing, proofreading, sharing writing with others). This is welcome. But there is an almost complete silence about *what* children should write. There are three mentions of 'narratives' (one at Years 3 and 4 and two at Years 5 and 6) and one of 'non-narrative material' at Years 3 and 4; apart from these, there is no account at all of the generic range of writing which children should attempt – a matter addressed at length in the section 'A broad and varied repertoire for writing'. There is no mention at all of writing using digital technologies, or of writing which combines with other modes such as sounds and images to achieve its effect. To say that the very important question '*What* should children write?' is insufficiently attended to would be a kindness. It has been largely ignored.

Grammar

The next chapter argues that the overload of grammatical concepts and terminology to be imposed on teachers and children at Key Stage 2 is unrealistic and pedagogically wrong. The new requirements betray the same back-to-front understanding of the relationship between competence in language and analysis of language as that demonstrated by the requirements with regard to spelling.

There should be a modest and realistic set of expectations for the amount of explicit grammatical knowledge which children should have attained by the time they leave primary school. In fact, the grammar requirements for Key Stage 2 in the National Curriculum orders that were statutory until July 2014 (and until July 2015 for Year 6) did the job well enough:

> *To read texts with greater accuracy and understanding, students should be taught to identify and comment on features of English at word, sentence and text level, using appropriate terminology [for example, how adjectives and adverbs contribute to overall effect, the use of varying sentence length and structure, connections between chapters or sections].*
>
> (Qualifications and Curriculum Authority, 2000: 20)

> *Pupils should be taught:*
>
> (a) *word classes and the grammatical functions of words, including nouns, verbs, adjectives, adverbs, pronouns, prepositions, conjunctions, articles;*
> (b) *the features of different types of sentence, including statements, questions and commands, and how to use them [for example, imperatives in commands];*
> (c) *the grammar of complex sentences, including clauses, phrases and connectives;*
> (d) *the purposes and organisational features of paragraphs, and how ideas can be linked.*
>
> (ibid: 23–24)

Punctuation

As at Key Stage 1, the requirements for punctuation, which appear in Appendix 2 of the new orders, are reasonable and realistic. The section 'An effective understanding of instruction' noted that it is unhelpful to group punctuation, grammar and vocabulary – three unlike things – in Appendix 2. Spelling and punctuation belong more easily together, both being aspects of orthography. It is true that punctuation is often an indication of grammatical choice; but both punctuation and spelling are conventions strictly related to the written language.

Vocabulary

As at Key Stage 1, the term 'vocabulary', which it might be imagined has to do, for example, with a writer's choice of vocabulary in writing a story, an essay or a description, in fact means 'terminology' in the government's lexicon, with the possible exception of the requirement that children at Years 5 and 6 must be made consciously aware of subjunctive forms ('recognising vocabulary and structures that are appropriate for formal speech and writing, including subjunctive forms'). Terminology applies to all aspects of language. It is not helpful to isolate 'vocabulary' as an item in the sense that the government uses the term.

To conclude . . .

Writing is a mode of communication best understood in terms of wholes rather than parts. A single text is evidence of the effort of the writer to say something, to marshal thought, to communicate that marshalled thought to a reader, to draw on examples – consciously imitated or unconsciously internalised – which may offer help in the marshalling, to conform to the conventions of the writing system insofar as he or she has come to understand them, to sustain the physical effort of putting linked groups of words on paper or on the screen. That is what all writers, including pupil writers, do. Teachers can most effectively teach writing by recognising that wholeness.

The learning which pupil writers undertake is best understood as a journey in which equipment will be provided progressively along the way rather than all supplied in advance.

The universe of writing is a family of forms best understood in terms of nuances of difference rather than hard edges. The kinds of writing in the world, some of which pupils should encounter and try out for themselves in the course of their schooling, exist as part of a connected and interactive network, not as isolated, unique entities. Some of these kinds have been created or transformed by the digital revolution.

The stance of the new National Curriculum orders for writing at Key Stage 2 with regard to the assertions of the three paragraphs above is wrong or inadequate in important respects. This chapter has discussed these shortcomings in detail. They will one day need to be addressed by government and the profession.

In Chapter 11, readers will find an alternative curriculum for writing 7 to 11 which better represents what we know about how children are best helped to competence and confidence as writers than do many features of the new orders for writing at Key Stage 2. The alternative nonetheless willingly acknowledges those features of the new orders which can be welcomed.

Note

1 Reproduced by permission of the Centre for Literacy in Primary Education, www. clpe.org.uk.

6 Grammar and knowledge about language

John Richmond

Summary of main points

Competence in language precedes analysis of language, not the other way round. Competence in language is implicit knowledge of language, brought about by a host of influences which affect the learner, consciously and unconsciously, and by a range of kinds of instruction and intervention by the teacher.

The teaching of grammar is a valuable and interesting activity, so long as it is pitched at an appropriate level of difficulty for the learners in a class, so long as it occurs in the context of the study of worthwhile texts, and so long as it engages learners actively in investigating language in use. Grammar teaching out of the context of pupils' broader language learning is useless.

The principal benefit of grammar teaching is on learners as readers and as people who discuss texts, including their own.

The teaching of grammar sits best within the overall study of language as a phenomenon. To understand grammatical concepts and terminology is to understand one aspect of language as a system shared by its users. The knowledge about language which pupils should acquire is broader than that, however. This broader knowledge could be categorised in five ways, each of which interact with the others:

- variety in and between languages;
- history of languages;
- language and power in society;
- acquisition and development of language; and
- language as a system shared by its users.

The government's new legal requirements on grammar teaching will at some point need to be changed to make their demands on primary-school pupils more modest and realistic. Chapter 11 offers such an alternative curriculum – rigorous but realistic – for the teaching of grammar and knowledge about language at Key Stages 1 and 2.

'The grammar question'

In this chapter, I come to an argument about teaching which – along with the argument about how to teach early reading – has caused the most debate and controversy, provoked the most intense outpourings of outrage, of all the areas of English teaching and language education addressed in this book. It is the grammar question.

There is an argument for dealing with grammar as an element of writing. The argument runs that discussions about grammar nearly always arise in the course of discussions about writing, and that the new National Curriculum requirements for grammar form part of the programmes of study for writing at Key Stages 1 and 2.

Grammar – not simply to do with writing

My reason for addressing grammar in a separate chapter is simple. It is that grammar, as I also say in the two chapters on writing, is not simply a province of the country of writing. It is often lumped together with spelling and punctuation (for example in the grammar, punctuation and spelling test taken by pupils at Year 2 and Year 6 in primary schools in England), but grammar is a bigger and broader thing than either spelling or punctuation.

This is not to underestimate the importance of spelling and punctuation, which are key elements of the English writing system. Punctuation, it is true, can also be an indicator of grammatical choices, again as acknowledged in the two chapters on writing. For example, in the sentence, 'Although the sun was shining brightly, I went to the cinema', the comma after 'brightly' indicates the end of the subordinate clause beginning 'Although . . .'. In the sentence, 'There wasn't a cloud in the sky; conditions were perfect', the semi-colon in the middle of the sentence indicates that there are two syntactically balancing and semantically interrelated main clauses on either side of it.

Grammar enables meaning

Grammar is nothing less than a fundamental language system within which words – spoken and written – are enabled to make sense, are imbued with meaning, as an outcome of the order in which they are arranged (syntax) or as an outcome of the way they change their form (morphology).

Grammar makes links

Furthermore, beyond the level of the written sentence or spoken utterance, writers and speakers make grammatical choices, and readers and listeners infer those grammatical choices, to give sense to or make sense of the structure of whole written texts or pieces of spoken discourse. For example, the reader of a chronologically narrated short story understands that the sentences and paragraphs which form the story proceed via linear time. The same reader, reading a piece of argumentative journalism in a newspaper, understands that the sentences and paragraphs which form the piece proceed via the writer's appeal to her or his sense of reason or logic. The grammatical linkages between sentences and paragraphs in the argumentative journalism will be different from those in the short story.

Grammar belongs to speech as much as to writing

Speech is not an imperfect version of writing. Typically, there is more informality and less explicitness in most forms of speech than in most forms of writing, but these are tendencies on a continuum. There are examples of more formal and more explicit speech (a political speech or an oral judgement in a court) and less formal and less explicit writing (an email exchange between friends).

Grammar teaching helps readers

Strange as it may seem, the principal direct benefit to a learner in conceptually grasping grammatical terms lies not in her or his future writing, but in her or his future encounters with texts: in her or his reading and discussion of that reading. This is another way of putting the argument for not discussing grammar merely as an aspect of writing: the principal direct benefit of teaching it is to be seen more in future acts of reading than in future acts of writing.

'But,' I hear my own reader saying, 'acts of reading are very often acts by which a reader reads her or his own writing; surely by this route explicit grammatical understandings can benefit the learner as a writer.' I shall come back to this good point in a moment.

The positive role of grammar teaching

Let me say something clear and positive about the role of grammar in the language education of children. Grammatical analysis, taught at the right level of complexity for a particular stage of pupils' development, is interesting and useful.

Why is it useful? Because to be able to speak about language, to have a technical language with which to discuss and describe language, a meta-language, is as useful as it is to have a technical language with which to speak about any other area of human endeavour. To have technical vocabulary at one's command brings a sense of mastery and clarity to the person so equipped.

Why is grammatical analysis interesting? Too obvious an answer, really: language is perhaps the most delicate and remarkable of human achievements, and to study some of its elements – including the way that words join together in groups and change their form so that they make sense – is therefore self-evidently worthwhile.

Halliday's three kinds of language learning

Marie Clay, in a chapter entitled 'Getting a Theory of Writing' in *Explorations in the Development of Writing* (Kroll and Wells [eds], 1983), elegantly summarises some earlier work by Michael Halliday:

> Halliday (1975) has provided an argument for the interrelatedness of language processes . . . He described three aspects of language learning: (1) language learning or constructing the system we know as the child's mother tongue, (2) learning through language as the child constructs his/her picture of the world and using language as a social process to acquire and share meaning, and (3) learning about the nature of language itself. He saw all three processes as largely subconscious but brought to the level of consciousness in education so that they can be consolidated and expanded. Learning to read and write are major tasks in such expansion. According to Halliday the three language processes should be allowed to take place side by side because they reinforce each other, and they should take place as social processes shared between the child and significant others. These three processes of constructing symbol systems,

using these to explore the world and experience, and exploring the sym-
bols themselves may be, at another level of abstraction, what we under-
stand by education itself, he says.

(Clay, 1983: 274–275)

Halliday proposes that his third aspect of language learning can reinforce the other two. So do I. I have already said that having a command of metalanguage helps the learner as he or she encounters texts, as long as it is appropriate to her or his stage of development. I should go a little further and happily acknowledge that the texts that the learner will read will include some that he or she has written. And here the interaction between the learner as writer and the learner as reader is complex and mysterious.

Good writers are generally careful and critical readers of their own writing. If I have acknowledged that it is useful for readers to have access to technical terms, including grammatical terms, surely a learner reading her or his own writing and using or thinking about grammatical terms, or having them pointed out by the teacher, will thereby benefit as a writer. Yes; this is a benefit arising from the writer's growing sense of mastery of the craft, of the precision in criticism which the appropriate use of grammatical and other technical terms supplies.

The myth of grammar teaching

There is the positive welcome for the idea that appropriately pitched teaching about grammar aids learners as people who read and discuss texts, including texts which they have produced themselves. Let us now flip this much-rubbed coin and put the other side of the argument. Here it is, bluntly expressed in pseudo-mathematical terms (Figure 6.1):

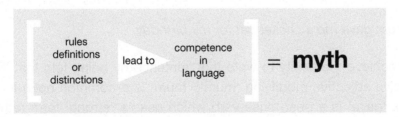

Figure 6.1 The myth of grammar teaching.

(This expression, and one more diagrammatic model which appears later in the chapter, are taken from my 'What Do We Mean by Knowledge about Language?' in *Knowledge about Language and the Curriculum: The LINC Reader* [1990], edited by Ronald Carter.)

This is the nub of it. Decades have gone by, as we shall see shortly, and the problem has not been solved. There is no peace. Politicians, journalists, academic writers, regretful at the loss of an imagined past of certainty and correctness, and enraged writers of letters to newspapers all insist, in effect, that the word at the right-hand end of the expression should be 'truth', not 'myth'.

Some of these people sincerely believe, with Samuel Johnson, that 'tongues, like governments, have a natural tendency to degeneration' and, with him, resolve: 'we have long preserved our constitution, let us make some struggle for our language' (Preface to *Dictionary of the English Language*, Johnson, 1975). They may also believe, in effect, that the teacher's role is 'to refine our language to grammatical purity', which is what Johnson claimed he had been doing for two years in his twice-weekly periodical *The Rambler* (*The Rambler 208*, Johnson, 1752), and which was also one of his missions in compiling his dictionary. I respect these sincere believers, while disagreeing with them. Governments are *un*like tongues in their natural tendency to degenerate. There are those in power in our own day who make statements such as Johnson's because they can see the popular advantage of advancing them; whether or not they are truthful or reasonable is of secondary interest to them.

Competence precedes analysis

Here are two examples of writing which I've collected from classrooms in recent years. They are powerful evidence that competence in written language *precedes* analysis of written language, not the other way round.

The Year 2 child who wrote:

My mum gave me a cricket bat for my birthday.

did not achieve the ability to write that sentence by being told that 'My' is a possessive adjective modifying 'mum', 'mum' is a common noun in subject position, 'gave' is a past-tense verb which uses a 'strong' form rather than the 'weak' *-ed* ending used by other verbs, 'me' is an indirect object pronoun (though its form is identical to a direct object pronoun as in 'My mum hit me with a cricket bat.'), 'a' is the indefinite article, 'cricket', though usually a noun when referring to the game, is here an adjective modifying the common noun 'bat', the three-word phrase 'a cricket bat' is a direct object phrase governed by 'gave', 'for' is a preposition expressing purpose and governing 'my birth-day', 'my' is once again a possessive adjective modifying the common noun 'birthday', and the three-word phrase 'for my birthday' is adverbial, modifying 'gave' in terms perhaps temporal, perhaps expressing purpose.

The writer of the sentence about the cricket bat was seven. Here is an 11-year-old writer:

The school that I would like would be one where the teachers asked you what you wanted to learn that day.

Did our utopian Year 6 child learn to write that sentence as a result of receiving lessons in advance on the use of the conditional mood and modal verbs, as in 'would like would be'? Surely she could not have written 'one where the teachers asked you what you wanted to learn that day' without prior knowledge that that group of 13 words is a subject complement to 'The school that I would like', and that the group of 13 words includes a smaller group of 7 words – 'what you wanted to learn that day' – which is a noun clause in object position? Surely (to switch for a moment from grammar to rhetoric) I could not have written the previous sentence without being taught in advance that irony is the occupation of the space between an apparent and an underlying reality? Surely she could. Surely I could.

If grammatical analysis were prior to grammatical competence, our lives would not be long enough to achieve even the most elementary degree of competence in written or spoken language, because the grammatical conventions, rules, structures of language – even of apparently very simple written sentences or spoken utterances – turn out to be extraordinarily subtle, complex and sometimes ambiguous when analysed.

'She walked down the street.': pronoun, verb, preposition, article, noun.
'She put down the pen.': pronoun, verb, adverb, article, noun.

At first glance, here are two very simple and very similar sentences. The first, third and fourth words of each are identical. Quite young children could easily have written either sentence. We can equally easily see that the correct use of 'down' in the two sentences does not require an advance understanding that in the first case 'down' is a preposition and in the second an adverb within the phrasal verb 'put down'. Phrasal verbs are a category which may be tested by moving the adverb to another place in the sentence to see whether the sentence is still grammatical. 'She put the pen down' is equally grammatical to 'She put down the pen'. 'She walked the street down' is not equally grammatical to 'She walked down the street'. Users of language don't usually have the time for great swathes of this kind of prior analysis.

Snapshots from the past

Plowden on grammar

The Plowden Report, *Pupils and their Primary Schools* (The Plowden Committee, 1967), puts grammar teaching firmly in its place. It is an aid to but not the main priority in the teaching of writing in primary schools:

> *Already the linguist has done a good deal to clarify the vexed question of the role of grammar in teaching English by his distinction between 'prescriptive' and 'descriptive' grammar. Speech is how people speak, not how some authority thinks they ought to speak. The test of good speech is whether any particular use of language is effective in the context in which it is used, not whether it conforms to certain 'rules'.*
>
> (The Plowden Committee, 1967: paragraph 611)

we offer the following propositions for the consideration of teachers:

(a) *Children are interested in words, their shape, sound, meaning and origin and this interest should be exploited in all kinds of incidental ways. Formal study of grammar will have little place in the primary school, since active and imaginative experience and use of the language should precede attempts to analyse grammatically how language behaves.*

(b) *The time for grammatical analysis will come but it should follow a firmly laid foundation of experience of the spoken and written language. When 'rules' or generalisations are discussed these should be 'induced' from the child's own knowledge of the usage of the language. The theory of grammar that is studied should describe the child's language and not be a theory based on Latin, many of whose categories, inflexions, case systems, tenses and so on do not exist in English.*

(c) While there is no question of the teaching of linguistics in the primary school, some work in linguistics at colleges of education or in refresher courses will help teachers to a sound view of how language works.

(ibid., paragraph 612)

Bullock on grammar

The Bullock Report, *A Language for Life* (The Bullock Committee, 1975) has much to say about the teaching of grammar. For example:

Since the beginning of this century a good deal of research has been devoted to [the question of whether exercises in themselves and by themselves will improve the child's ability to write], and though many believe its results to be inconclusive some of the individual experiments have carried much conviction. One such study [by Harris, 1963] is particularly worth singling out for attention. One class in each of five schools was taught formal grammar over a period of two years, a corresponding class in each school having no grammar lessons during that time. The latter took instead what might be described as a 'composition course', consisting of practice in writing, revising, and editing, and an inductive approach to usage. At the end of the period both groups were given a writing test and a grammar test. In the writing test the 'non-grammar' classes gained significantly higher scores than the 'grammar' classes, and overall there was no effective correspondence between high scores in the grammar test and improvement in writing.

We do not conclude from this that a child should not be taught how to improve his use of language; quite the contrary. It has not been established by research that systematic attention to skill and technique has no beneficial effect on the handling of language. What has been shown is that the teaching of traditional analytic grammar does not appear to improve performance in writing. This is not to suggest that there is no place for any kind of exercises at any time and in any form. It may well be that a teacher will find this a valuable means of helping an individual child reinforce something he has learned. What is questionable is the practice of setting exercises for the whole class, irrespective of need, and assuming that this will improve every pupil's ability to handle English.

(ibid., paragraphs 11.18 and 11.19)

'[T]he teaching of traditional analytic grammar does not appear to improve performance in writing.' That broad truth remains valid today despite furious attempts by governments since it was written to deny it.

Katharine Perera on grammar

Katharine Perera's *Children's Writing and Reading: Analysing Classroom Language* (1984), already quoted in Chapter 1, is written by a linguist, for teachers. It contains a most detailed description of the grammar of English. It contains an equally detailed discussion of the development of grammatical competence in children before and during their school years. Perera believes that teachers should know these things. She is rightly concerned to correct the misunderstanding that, when children arrive at school, already having achieved a remarkable mastery of many of the grammatical structures of their language, the job is more or less done. As I say in Chapter 1, she shows, with evidence, that the job is very far from done, and that many more complex grammatical structures remain to be mastered.

But the striking thing is that this linguist, who also understands a great deal about learning, has this to say about the explicit teaching of grammar:

> To suggest that a framework of grammatical knowledge can be of benefit to teachers is not to suggest that it should be formally taught to children. Since the beginning of the century, a body of research has accumulated that indicates that grammatical instruction, unrelated to pupils' other language work, does not lead to an improvement in the quality of their own writing or in the level of their comprehension. Furthermore, the majority of children under about fourteen seem to become confused by grammatical labels and descriptions . . .
>
> Although some teachers of older secondary pupils may want to introduce a systematic study of grammar, generally speaking, the 'planned intervention in the child's language development' [a quotation from the Bullock Report] that is advocated in this book can be implemented by means of demonstration and example, without the use of technical terminology or batteries of exercises.
>
> (Perera, 1984: 12–13)

More reviews of 'the grammar question'

Two significant large-scale reviews of the available research on the question 'Does explicit grammar teaching make for better writers?' (Hillocks, 1986 and

Andrews *et al.*, 2006) found no evidence that grammar teaching, *offered outside the context of the study of authentic texts*, makes for better writing.

Hillocks and Smith are rather blunt about the non-effect of grammar teaching on writing:

> *Why does grammar retain such glamour when research over the past 90 years reveals not only that students do not learn it and are hostile toward it, but that the study of grammar has no impact on writing quality? Many explanations have been adduced, some not so flattering: it is easy to teach by simply assigning page and exercise numbers; it is easy to grade; it provides security in having 'right' answers, a luxury not so readily available in teaching writing or literature . . .*
>
> *the grammar sections of a textbook should be treated as a reference tool that might provide some insight into conventions of mechanics and usage. [Grammar] should not be treated as a course of study to improve the quality of writing.*
>
> (Hillocks and Smith, 1991: 600)

In the conclusion to their article, Andrews and his colleagues write:

> *On the basis of the results of [our] two in-depth reviews, we can say, first, that the teaching of syntax . . . appears to have no influence on either the accuracy or quality of written language development for 5- to 16-year-olds. This does not mean to say that there could be no such influence. It simply means that there have been no significant studies to date that have proved such an effect.*
>
> (Andrews *et al.*, 2006: 51)

'The grammar question': government answers since 1984

English from 5 to 16

In 1984, Her Majesty's Inspectorate published a slim booklet called *English from 5 to 16*. Unexceptionably, the booklet proposed that teachers should be promoting pupils' development as speakers and listeners, readers and writers. It then said that teachers should:

teach pupils about language, so that they achieve a working knowledge of its structure and of the variety of ways in which meaning is made, so that they have a vocabulary for discussing it, so that they can use it with greater awareness and because it is interesting.

(Her Majesty's Inspectorate, 1984: 3)

From today's perspective, this proposal, quoted in isolation from the rest of the booklet, sounds eminently reasonable. Reading the booklet as a whole at the time, however, weighing up what its authors might really have in mind as the more important things to teach pupils about language, and putting these thoughts next to worries about other aspects of the booklet (the detail in its proposals for age-related objectives for pupils at 7, 11 and 16, and its narrow, muddled and often backward-looking collection of statements about what a language or English curriculum should contain), many teachers came to the conclusion that the booklet was once again proposing something which had been vigorously debated for the previous 20 years, and rejected: the tempting idea that learners, in order to get better at using an element of the language they are learning as mother tongue, need a set of rules, definitions and distinctions about that element in advance.

Decoded, the part of *English from 5 to 16* from which I have quoted was returning to a dispute over whether English teachers needed to reinstate old-fashioned grammar teaching as a major element of the curriculum. Overwhelmingly, those who wrote down their responses to the booklet and sent them in to HMI said 'No'. Their suspicion was that the distinction which, for example, Katharine Perera made in her book, published in the same year as *English 5 to 16*, between teachers' understanding of grammar and grammatical development and the use of grammatical categories in explicit teaching, was being blurred.

When HMI published *English from 5 to 16: The Responses to Curriculum Matters 1* in 1986, it acknowledged the degree of dissent from the original booklet on this and other topics. It suggested setting up an enquiry, 'with the ultimate object of drawing up recommendations as to what might be taught [about language] to intending teachers, to those in post and to pupils in schools' (Her Majesty's Inspectorate, 1986: 40).

The Kingman Report

The government accepted the idea of an enquiry and convened the Kingman Committee to discuss the matter. The Kingman Report was published in March 1988. On the particular question of grammar teaching, the report declared:

> *Nor do we see it as part of our task to plead for a return to old-fashioned grammar teaching and learning by rote. We have been impressed by the evidence we have received that this gave an inadequate account of the English language by treating it virtually as a branch of Latin, and constructing a rigid prescriptive code rather than a dynamic description of language in use. It was also ineffective as a means of developing a command of English in all its manifestations. Equally, at the other extreme, we reject the belief that any notion of correct or incorrect use of language is an affront to personal liberty. We also reject the belief that knowing how to use terminology in which to speak of language is undesirable.*
>
> (The Kingman Committee, 1988: paragraph 11)

This statement, quoted from Chapter 1 of the report, was greeted by a deep sigh of relief from the profession, although there was some puzzlement that the committee had apparently discovered groups of teachers who refused to accept that there was such a thing as an incorrect use of language and never used any terminology in their teaching, and had felt that this tendency was as dangerous as 'old-fashioned grammar teaching and learning by rote'.

The Cox Report

The government was less than delighted with the Kingman Report, because it had failed to provide what the government wanted, which was a ringing endorsement of the virtues of 'old-fashioned grammar teaching'. Persisting in its belief in these virtues, it produced the terms of reference for the Cox Committee, which was to propose the contents of a National Curriculum for English (to include pupils' knowledge about language). I quote:

> *The Kingman Committee . . . has made recommendations for attainment tar-*
> *gets for knowledge about language at the ages of 7, 11 and 16. The Working*
> *Group [i.e. the Cox Committee] should build on these to recommend attain-*
> *ment targets covering the grammatical structure of the English language.*
>
> (The Cox Committee, 1989: Appendix 2, paragraph 3)

Precariously, the terms of reference tried to link grammar teaching with great literature, as follows:

> *The Working Group's recommendations on learning about language [for*
> *which, in the government dictionary, read grammar] and its use should draw*
> *upon the English literary heritage.*
>
> (*ibid*.: Appendix 2, paragraph 3)

The Cox Committee's proposals for the National Curriculum for English deftly declined the government's invitation to produce attainment targets on grammar, and gathered together a much broader set of concerns under the title 'knowledge about language': accent, dialect and Standard English; some of the forms and functions of speech; the nature of literary language; historical change in English; some of the forms and functions of writing; characteristic differences between speech and writing. The committee, in giving reasons for the list that it had chosen, explained that it did not want to overload teachers with too much that was unfamiliar; it believed that teachers' own knowledge about language was not complete or sure enough to justify further recommendations. The Cox Report optimistically says:

> *substantial programmes of teacher training are required if teachers are*
> *themselves to know enough to enable them to design with confidence pro-*
> *grammes of study about language. Such training is now under way. It may*
> *be, when such training programmes have been followed for a few years, that*
> *it would be appropriate for knowledge about language to become a sepa-*
> *rate profile component.*
>
> (*ibid*: paragraph 6.3)

The first National Curriculum for English

There is much to admire in the original programmes of study for English (Department for Education and Science and the Welsh Office, 1990). As mentioned in the introduction to this book, they are over-detailed, and the attempt to corral the iterative nature of learning in English within ten attainment levels led to theoretical and pedagogical absurdities. But the vision of learning which the programmes of study embodied remains one which, a generation later, I broadly support.

However, as a result of Cox's concern about the limitations of teachers' knowledge about language, including grammar, the references to grammar in the original programmes of study are occasional and brief. The orders for speaking and listening and for writing, spelling and handwriting variously require that pupils should come in time to have a firm grasp of Standard English, spoken and written; this requirement is properly tempered by another, that at Key Stages 2 to 4 'Pupils should be encouraged to respect their own language(s) and dialect(s) and those of others'. The orders for writing, spelling and handwriting require that pupils 'should be taught, in the context of discussion about their own writing, grammatical terms such as sentence, verb, tense, noun, pronoun' (at Key Stage 1); and be taught about 'some common prefixes and suffixes' (at Key Stage 2).

The Language in the National Curriculum Project (LINC)

The training to which the Cox Report referred in 1989 was beginning to be provided at the time by the LINC Project. This is not the place to recount in detail the history of the LINC Project and the political strife it caused. (Readers wishing to know the full story could consult my article 'The Knowledge about Language Debate 1984–1993' [Richmond, 2012a] or Alastair West's article 'How We Live Now: LINC, Politics and the Language Police in Toytown LEA', in *Where We've Been: Articles from the English and Media Magazine* [1996].)

Suffice to say that the government wished the project to conduct a top-down programme of training in grammar, which would eventually touch every secondary English teacher and every teacher in primary schools in England and Wales, and that those who led the project prepared a set of training materials which, while including attention to grammar, embodied a much broader understanding of knowledge about language, something closer to Halliday's third aspect mentioned above – 'learning about the nature of language itself' – and indeed very close to the list of topics to do with knowledge about language proposed in the Cox Report. The government eventually refused to publish the training materials. Neither would it waive Crown Copyright so that a commercial publisher might publish them. Despite this act of blatant censorship, tens of thousands of copies of the materials have since been distributed in unofficial form by the University of Nottingham, where Professor Ronald Carter, the project's director, was and is based.

Grammar in the National Literacy Strategy

As we speed over the revisions and re-revisions of the National Curriculum for English which have taken place since it was introduced, we see an increasing emphasis on explicit grammar teaching. Given what I have said towards the beginning of the chapter, about the value of appropriately pitched grammar teaching in helping pupils as readers and as talkers about texts, I can only welcome this.

However, it appears that policy-makers simply decided to ignore the research evidence then available to them on grammar teaching and competence in writing, some of which I have summarised. (I accept that the research by Andrews *et al.* [2006] is relatively recent.) Probably frustrated by the failure of the LINC Project to deliver the goods they had ordered, they resolved to push on with their conviction that explicit grammar teaching will make better writers. (Such a position also makes good copy in some quarters of the press.) While there was general agreement not to return to what Kingman called 'old-fashioned grammar teaching and learning by rote', the direct connection between explicit grammar teaching and the quality and correctness of pupils' writing was asserted as truth.

The National Literacy Strategy, part of the government's National Strategies which ran from 1997 to 2011, saw such teaching as essential in the effort to raise standards of literacy generally, and proposed a three-part framework for teaching grammar at word, sentence and text level. For example, the introduction to *Grammar for Writing* (2000), a document published by the National Literacy Strategy and directed to schools teaching pupils at Key Stage 2, begins thus:

> *We all use language to think and communicate. Language is systematically organised by its grammar which is inextricably linked to meaning and communication – we cannot make sense without shaping grammatical and linguistic structures. All pupils have extensive grammatical knowledge. Much of this is implicit, but they are able to generalise and improvise from this knowledge . . .*
>
> (Department for Children, Schools and Families, 2000: 7)

All perfectly true.

Teaching which focuses on grammar helps to make this knowledge explicit, extend children's range and develop more confident and versatile language use . . .

(ibid.: 7)

True, in the senses we have discussed so far; that is, as providing a meta-language for the discussion of language.

Some would argue that the study of grammar is worth teaching in its own right because it is intrinsically interesting – and so it is. This is not the primary aim here; our aim is to improve children's writing. Grammar is fundamental to this, as a means to an end, but a means which involves investigation, problem-solving, language play and a growing awareness of and interest in how language works. This book focuses on the teaching of sentence level objectives in the Literacy Hour but, throughout, the emphasis is on how children's growing understanding and use of grammar helps them to write more effectively.

(ibid.: 7)

'[I]nvestigation, problem-solving, language play and a growing awareness of and interest in how language works': all excellent things. But the idea that the study of grammar improves learners' writing in a direct sense, that the 'understanding and use of grammar', as a result of conscious analytical teaching, helps them to write more effectively, is here an article of faith, a piece of dogma, not a statement based on evidence. The article of faith continues:

It should be clear from this that the purpose of teaching grammar is not simply the naming of parts of speech, nor is it to provide arbitrary rules for 'correct' English. It is about making children aware of key grammatical principles and their effects, to increase the range of choices open to them when they write.

(ibid.: 7)

Not the naming of parts: good. Not arbitrary rules for correctness: good. But the sentence that follows betrays the same illusion, the same false idea of causality. To have a theoretical understanding of what an adjective is and does grammatically does not directly lead to more effective use of adjectives in writing. To be shown a range of adverbial phrases – of place, of time, of manner, of concession – does not directly lead to the more apt selection of an adverbial phrase next time a writer needs one.

The relationship between competence and reflection

Is there any escape from the sterility of the disagreement described in the chapter so far? Earlier, I offered a pseudo-mathematical expression of a negative kind. Here is a diagram of a positive kind to express my view of the proper relationship between developing competence in language and the ability to reflect on aspects of language (Figure 6.2).

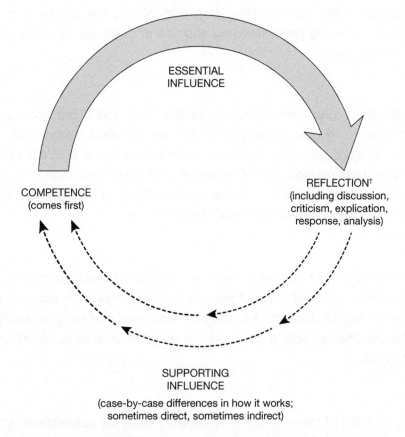

ESSENTIAL
INFLUENCE

COMPETENCE
(comes first)

REFLECTION[†]
(including discussion,
criticism, explication,
response, analysis)

SUPPORTING
INFLUENCE
(case-by-case differences in how it works;
sometimes direct, sometimes indirect)

[†]Reflection involves appropriate use of terminology; it might be described as 'turning round on your own (and others') practice'

Figure 6.2 The relationship between competence and reflection.

If we could get a right relationship between language competence and reflection on language (which would include analysis and the use of terminology), we would have solved our problem.

The 3-year-old child learning to talk is acquiring and demonstrating large amounts of implicit knowledge, but there would be no point in engaging the child in reflection on the psycholinguistic processes involved. To say to her or him 'Isn't it interesting that you were over-generalising from verbs with *–ed* endings in the simple past tense when you said "drived" just then?' would be absurd. There is an accumulation of competence which will much later feed into reflection, but there is no feedback from reflection to competence at this stage. The same child at five, however, reading a picture book, will enjoy the story in the book and also reflect on the arrangement of words and images there. There will be some feedback from reflection to competence when the child is asked to make her or his own picture book. A few years later still, the same child reading poetry as part of a class activity is likely to benefit as a future reader and writer of poetry if the teacher provides opportunities for reflection on the structure, content and background of the poems the class is studying, and on the particular characteristics of poetic language the poems demonstrate. Grammatical categories and terminology may well form part of that discussion. And in the upper years of Key Stage 2, a class studying the introduction to Charles Dickens' *A Christmas Carol* will certainly be helped to appreciate the power of that prose by having access to grammatical categories and terminology, appropriately introduced.

The use of terminology

The central principle that should guide teachers in their decisions as to the use with pupils of terminology, including grammatical terminology, is that its introduction must be based on some prior understanding of what the terminology refers to. At some point in their development, children have to encounter and understand the word *word* (a metalinguistic term describing a particular category within language) and *sentence* (though for the teacher to use the term *sentence* in purposeful discussions with pupils is a very different thing from defining in an abstract way that thing which comes between a capital letter and a full stop) and *noun* and *verb* and *adjective* and *adverb* and *subject* and *object* and *connective*. As long as these terms are introduced at an appropriate stage in learners' development as users of language (and I am well aware that teachers teach whole classes, not isolated individuals, and will have to make judgements sometimes based on their sense of what the majority of learners in a class are able to understand), there is a good chance that many in the class will be able to make sense of the terms. If the use of grammatical terminology is offered to learners who have no prior, implicit, conceptual understanding of what the terminology refers to, the offer will be meaningless.

All areas of the language and English curriculum carry terminology, of course; terminology is not confined to grammar, nor to writing conventions, nor to literary terms. We could set the terms we have used so far within a potentially endless list: *speech mark, metaphor, text, pronoun, play, character, rhyme, alliteration, chapter, genre, paragraph, intonation, accent, alphabet, fiction, database, script, caption, camera angle.* Here is an assortment of terms, some little and some large, all of which signify important concepts or refer to potentially valid activities in the language and English curriculum. If teachers ask themselves, when in doubt, 'Will this piece of terminology serve meaning?', that will help them in the fine judgements they have to make.

Experience is the main driver of competence in writing

Having willingly acknowledged the value of the right kind of reflection on language, including the discussion of grammar, I remain convinced that the principal driver of competence in writing is enjoyable reading and discussion of a diversity of worthwhile texts, plenty of practice in writing across a range of genres and styles, and interventions by teachers which pay attention first and foremost to what the learner has written and then to the effectiveness and correctness, or otherwise, of the manner in which it has been expressed.

The present situation in England

The requirements for grammar teaching at Key Stages 1 and 2 in the new English orders (Department for Education, 2014a) represent an unbalanced understanding of the relationship between competence and reflection, between use and analysis.

Appendix 2 of the new National Curriculum orders for English, on vocabulary, grammar and punctuation, which is statutory and which applies principally to Key Stages 1 and 2, begins thus:

The grammar of our first language is learnt naturally and implicitly through interactions with other speakers and from reading . . .

(*ibid.*: 75)

Perfectly true.

Explicit knowledge of grammar is, however, very important, as it gives us more conscious control and choice in our language. Building this knowledge is best achieved through a focus on grammar within the teaching of reading, writing and speaking. Once pupils are familiar with a grammatical concept [for example 'modal verb'], they should be encouraged to apply and explore this concept in the grammar of their own speech and writing and to note where it is used by others.

(*ibid.*: 75)

This is much more dubious. In particular, it is not the case that, once learners have been taught about modal verbs as a category, they will make more sophisticated and correct use of modals in their writing. Such an expectation demonstrates a simplistic view of how competence develops. To go back to the competence/ reflection model, this view wants to turn the arrow linking reflection back to competence into a straightforward road from cause to effect. It may be that at the end of an effective, appropriately pitched lesson on modal verbs, learners will be able to recognise and indeed generate examples of properly positioned modals in sentences. It is going too far to say that in the weeks and months to come they *will*, as a result of that lesson, also use modals better in their writing. Perhaps there will be an influence; if there is, it will be an aid to the major driver and developer of competence, which is positive experience of reading and writing.

Metalinguistic overload

In the new orders for Key Stages 1 and 2, there is an extraordinary overload of metalinguistic concepts and categories to be taught explicitly. At Year 1, children must learn about plural noun suffixes and that the prefix *un-* changes the meaning of verbs and adjectives. In Year 2, they must learn subordination and noun phrases. In Year 3, as well as learning about conjunctions, adverbs and prepositions, they must understand the use of the present perfect tense and take their understanding of subordination as far as the concept of the subordinate clause. Year 4 pupils must know about fronted adverbials and determiners. Relative clauses and cohesion are statutory for Year 5 pupils, while at Year 6 they must be introduced to the passive voice and to ellipsis. The subjunctive makes an entry in the upper years of Key Stage 2. In Appendix 2, it is there admittedly as a non-statutory example of the statutory requirement to study the difference between structures characteristic of informal and of formal language. In the 'Writing – vocabulary, grammar and punctuation' orders for Years 5 and 6, however, learning about the subjunctive is statutory: pupils must be taught to '[recognise] vocabulary and structures that are appropriate for formal speech and writing, including subjunctive forms'.

The above is a small selection from the statutory requirements for grammar; I say nothing here about punctuation or non-grammatical elements of vocabulary. This formidable set of new responsibilities for teachers is accompanied by a (non-statutory) glossary of terms (*ibid.*: 89–107) which, taken as a whole, could usefully serve as part of the syllabus of an A-level course in language and linguistics. I hasten to say that it is desirable that teachers, *at their level*, should know about the grammatical categories and terms listed in the glossary. The glossary announces itself 'as an aid for teachers, not as the body of knowledge that should be learnt by pupils'. Nonetheless, the grammatical terms as defined there are offered as supports for the explicit teaching to primary-school pupils of many of the concepts and categories they represent.

This will not work. Most teachers will do their best to meet statutory requirements, as they always have done, but a price will be paid. Too much time will be given up to separate grammar teaching at an unrealistically advanced level, at the expense of time given to the teaching of writing, which – I hope I have made sufficiently clear in the chapters on writing – will include attention to all the aspects of convention and control which developing writers need: to the manner as well as the matter of what they write.

Assessment in grammar, punctuation and spelling at Year 6

From summer 2013, Year 6 pupils have taken an annual, externally set test in grammar, punctuation and spelling. From summer 2016, Year 2 pupils have also taken a test in grammar, punctuation and spelling. These tests are separate from tests of reading and internal moderated assessments of writing.

There is a full discussion of assessment and testing arrangements 3 to 11 in Chapter 13. The discussion includes a particular criticism of the testing of grammar separately from the assessment of writing and the testing of reading. The chapter proposes alternative arrangements for the testing of reading and writing, which would include the testing of grammar.

Grammar in primary and in secondary: the wrong way round

This book is addressed to teachers of children up to the age of 11. But the topsy-turvy nature of the orders for grammar requires a mention of teaching in secondary schools. If there is a time when knowledge about language should become more explicit, when the use of terminology should advance, when analysis of texts, including grammatical analysis, should occupy more of the teacher's and the students' time and attention, it is at the secondary-school stage. This is when students come much more to 'know what they know', to reflect on their knowledge, to engage in acts of what psychologists and psycholinguists call 'metacognition': learning about learning, reflecting on learning. Metalinguistic knowledge is a part of metacognition. And yet all the government's new, explicit, detailed, statutory demands about the learning of grammar apply to primary-school pupils. The orders for grammar at Key Stages 3 and 4 merely require students, in a general way, to 'carry on the good work' on grammar which supposedly has been largely completed by age 11, applying that work to more demanding texts.

This is the wrong way round. By all means let there be more grammar teaching in secondary schools, as long as it respects the principles I have repeatedly proposed. Let there be some but less grammar teaching at Key Stage 2. Let there be a little grammar teaching at Key Stage 1, but let those pupils be overwhelmingly preoccupied with the essential task of becoming confident users of language.

A defective understanding of the relationship between competence and analysis, with the weight of grammar teaching imposed on the primary years, proceeds from a wrong conception of learning. It is the same tempting conception which has led to the follies in the area of early reading which I discuss in Chapter 2. 'Get the rules straight first,' it says 'and competence will follow.' Wrong. A right conception of learning says 'Enable, encourage, support developing competence first, and awareness and application of the rules – and an active interest in those rules – will follow.'

Readers will find a better-balanced, appropriately rigorous set of alternative proposals for the teaching of grammar in Chapter 11.

Grammar within knowledge about language

The teaching of grammar sits best within the overall study of language as a phenomenon (Halliday's third kind of language learning, as quoted in the section '"The grammar question"'). Here I summarise five categories of knowledge about language (which, as it happens, are quite close to the Cox Report's proposals for the teaching of knowledge about language [The Cox Committee, 1989], as described in the section '"The grammar question": government answers since 1984'). The categories are:

- variety in and between languages;
- history of languages;
- language and power in society;
- acquisition and development of language; and
- language as a system shared by its users.

We can expand each of these five sub-divisions.

Variety in and between languages: between speech and writing; of accents and dialects; of functions, registers and genres in speech and writing, including those of literature; differences and similarities between languages, including comparisons of words and scripts.

History of languages: historical change in English, and in some of the world's other languages, ancient and contemporary; ephemeral as well as long-term change; the emergence of Standard English and its importance in today's society.

Language and power in society: speaker/listener, reader/writer relationships, for both interpersonal and mass uses of language, with a particular concern for the ways in which social power is constructed and challenged through language.

Acquisition and development of language: babies learning to talk; children learning to read and write; a potentially lifelong expansion of language repertoires.

Language as a system shared by its users: vocabulary – connotations, definitions and origins of words; grammar – the functions and forms of words in groups; phonology – the sound systems of spoken language; graphology – the systems of marks that give us written language (including spelling, punctuation, layout and handwriting); the structure of longer pieces of spoken and written text (for example conversations, sports commentaries, speeches, stories, arguments, descriptions, poems, reports, campaign posters, online diaries and blogs).

Whether in the course of other activities or as specific investigations, pupils and teachers might look explicitly at language in ways which pay attention, variously or simultaneously, to some aspects of all five of these things. The individual topics are not, of course, offered as lesson keynotes; if we enter the explicit consideration of language through any one door, we are immediately walking about in a room which could have been entered through other doors. And we should remember that the magnificent, mysterious reality of language will always elude complete attempts at analysis: a warning which applies particularly aptly to the study of grammar.

In the alternative curriculum in Chapter 11, I sketch the broad lines of a teaching programme for knowledge about language at Key Stage 2.

Teachers' linguistic subject knowledge

Some teachers in primary schools do not know enough about grammar to be able to teach it effectively. This lack of knowledge remains a major obstacle to giving grammar its proper place within the language and English curriculum. Two excellent books on grammar for primary-school teachers are *Teaching Grammar Effectively in the Primary School* (Reedy and Bearne, 2013) and *Teaching Grammar Effectively at Key Stage 1* (Bearne *et al.*, 2016). The books offer lesson plans and resources for grammar teaching covering most of the new requirements, and exemplify the key principles of teaching in the context of worthwhile texts and involving pupils actively in investigating language in use. If teachers are to make any kind of success of implementing the new requirements, they will need resources like these.

One simple thing which the government or an agency commissioned by the government could do now would be to take the new non-statutory glossary of terms to which I have already referred (Department for Education, 2014a: 89–107) and adapt and expand it, making it a more enjoyable read, with a more learner-friendly mode of organisation than the alphabetical, and with the grammatical categories accompanied by full examples, embedded in real and interesting texts, rather than by the thin and decontextualised examples used at present.

To conclude . . .

At present, an agreement which would unite government and the profession on the teaching of grammar is a long way off. There are those in powerful positions who cling to the idea that pupils lack a grasp of 'proper grammar', a lack which profoundly disadvantages them as writers, that this has been the fault of teachers insufficiently concerned with correctness and over-indulgent of a loose and uncritical 'creativity' in the work of their pupils. Such people claim that large amounts of analytical grammar teaching early on will solve the problem.

This view is wrong; furthermore, it is often advanced for reasons of political advantage rather than as a result of sincere conviction arrived at after careful thought. However, grammar teaching, appropriately pitched and taught in the context of the study of actual, authentic, interesting texts, is to be welcomed. This chapter is not an 'anti-grammar' tract. It is 'pro-grammar', as long as the understanding of the place of grammar in the English, language and literacy curriculum as a whole is properly judged. There is a key difference between the teaching of grammar as a set of decontextualised drills and exercises and its teaching as part of the study of real, continuous, pleasure-giving texts. The first will fail, as has been shown by repeated research over many years; the second has a good chance of success.

The new orders on grammar teaching are unbalanced in terms of the excessive expectations they place on primary-school pupils and teachers, and the insufficiently demanding expectations they place on secondary-school students and teachers. Chapter 11 contains a rigorous but much more realistic alternative curriculum for grammar at Key Stage 1, and grammar and knowledge about language at Key Stage 2.

Some teachers' own linguistic subject knowledge is inadequate to the task of teaching grammar in the way recommended in this chapter. I have recommended two excellent resources which help to meet the need. Meanwhile, the government, or an agency commissioned by the government, could also help by adapting and expanding the existing non-statutory glossary of grammatical terms, accompanying the terms with full examples, embedded in real and interesting texts.

7 Drama

John Richmond

Summary of main points

Drama's potential contribution to learning and to the life of schools is diverse and enriching. It is a means of enhancing learning in a range of curriculum subjects and areas. It has the potential to develop qualities of empathy and respect for difference in children and young people. It enables active and collaborative learning.

Drama has close links with literature and with narrative generally, and therefore has a special significance within English teaching.

Drama is an art form.

Drama is a prominent feature of a school's extra-curricular cultural life.

Like all other forms of learning, drama is affected by and may be realised via digital and electronic technologies and media. These new technologies and media can extend the realistic possibilities of what may be achieved in the classroom and drama studio. For example, a few years ago, the idea that drama could be filmed, played back and instantly commented on would have seemed ambitious. Today, tablet computers and smartphones mean that such a practice is easily achievable.

There is a weakness at the heart of drama's official relationship with the statutory curriculum in England. This stems from the failure of the UK government, when the National Curriculum for England and Wales was introduced in 1989 and 1990, to grant drama the same status as was accorded to art and music: that of foundation subject. The situation today remains as it was then, despite strenuous efforts by organisations and individuals representing drama teaching to persuade successive governments to grant drama foundation-subject status.

Statutorily, drama sits within English. The references to drama within successive versions of the National Curriculum for English since 1989 have never amounted to a coherent and rigorous description of the subject. They offer no sense of progression and development. The references in the new National Curriculum for English are no more adequate than those in previous versions. Chapter 11 offers an alternative.

Educational drama has a long theoretical history. During the second half of the twentieth century, expert thinkers extended our understanding of drama as a mode of learning and showed how this understanding can bear fruit in effective classroom work. A debate (and sometimes a dispute) developed between those who preferred to emphasise learning *through* drama and those who preferred to emphasise learning *about* drama. The former were less concerned with drama as product than with the multiple benefits of drama as process. The latter, while not denying the value of drama as process, wished to assert that drama is an art form which can be taught, and that drama activity will and should often have an outcome in performance. There is no need to decide in favour of drama as process or as product. It is both.

Theorists of drama teaching

This section owes a great debt to Nicholas McGuinn, the first half of whose *The English Teacher's Drama Handbook* (McGuinn, 2014) offers a superb selective summary of the evolution of an understanding of what drama in education is or could be. McGuinn's contribution to the section amounts to a form of co-authorship.

Rousseau and Froebel

Two famous figures from past centuries established the idea that a child's play is a centrally important element in her or his education: Jean-Jacques Rousseau, in *Émile* (Rousseau, 1979 [1762]), and Friedrich Froebel, in *The Education of Man* (Froebel, 2005 [1826]). Linked to this thought is another, equally profound: that the teacher and the learner should not be fixed in asymmetrical power relationships, with the learner always subservient to and dependent on the wisdom and benevolence of the teacher.

> *From a drama teacher's perspective, one of the most significant points on which Rousseau and Froebel are particularly united is their insistence that, from birth, children are actively engaged in the construction of meanings. A child's play, Froebel argues, 'is not trivial, it is highly serious and of deep significance' (Froebel, 2005: 55). If adults cannot understand this, it is because they do not know how to interpret what they see.*
>
> (McGuinn, 2014: 6)

It may easily be imagined how ideas of this kind did not chime with the utilitarian purpose of universal state education as introduced in the UK in 1870. Indeed, the conflict between those who see education as the taxpayer's investment in a future economically productive workforce, and those who – while recognising the necessity for young people to emerge from schooling literate and numerate – see education as a broader, more human process, as something to do with culture, is with us today.

Piaget and Vygotsky

Two great psychologists of the twentieth century also saw, in different ways, the central importance of play in the child's development, and were interested in the relationship between play and drama. They were Lev Vygotsky, some of whose thinking is touched on in other chapters in the book, and Jean Piaget.

> *Piaget acknowledges that there are similarities between drama and symbolic play . . . For [him], the key distinction between play and drama is that the participants in the latter . . . are consciously aware of and reflective upon the fiction with which they are engaged.*
>
> (Piaget, 1976 [1951]: 569, in McGuinn, 2014: 14)

> *Vygotsky sets particular store on the aesthetic qualities of drama. It is, he argues, the most 'syncretic [that is, the most combining] mode of creation', because it affords children access to so many of the arts . . . 'Drama, more than any other form of creation . . . is closely and directly linked to play . . . The staging of drama provides the pretext and material for the most diverse forms of creativity on the part of the children.'*
>
> (Vygotsky, 2004: 71 [1967], in McGuinn, 2014: 15)

Three English pioneers

In summarising the work of the most influential twentieth-century writers on drama in education in an English context, McGuinn finds two unifying themes and one fault line. The unifying themes are inherited from the four writers I have just named: that the teacher is a co-learner along with the child, though one with particular rights, responsibilities and knowledge; and that drama is a development of play. The fault line is in the differing emphases given to process and product in drama, as between drama as a form of learning, engaged in for the benefit of the learners, and drama as performed art, engaged in for the benefit of performers and audience.

Three early twentieth-century writers on drama seem to straddle this fault line without difficulty. Harriet Finlay-Johnson (author of *The Dramatic Method of Teaching*, 1912), Henry Caldwell Cook (author of *The Play Way: An Essay in Educational Method*, 1917) and Marjorie Lovegrove Hourd (author of *The Education of the Poetic Spirit: A Study of Children's Expression in the English Lesson*, 1949) all share 'Froebel's enthusiasm for play as a powerful learning medium'; 'all three practitioners are implacably opposed to systems of rote-learning – and the examination systems that necessarily accompany them' (McGuinn, 2014: 17–18). Finlay-Johnson gives examples of her use of drama as a learning medium which still sound exciting, if perhaps a little imperialistic:

> *inkwells are transformed into 'breathing holes' for seals in a geographical simulation of a voyage to Newfoundland . . . or a chalk pit outside the school is commandeered as the setting for a re-enactment of General Wolfe's scaling of the Heights of Abraham in 1759, or a 'roll-call' is improvised to lend poignancy to a reading of Tennyson's poem 'The Charge of the Light Brigade'.*
>
> (Finlay-Johnson, 1912: 136, 118, in McGuinn, 2014: 23)

At the same time, the students of all three writers rehearse and perform plays, including those by Shakespeare.

Peter Slade

Peter Slade's book *Child Drama* was published in 1954. Slade became 'world-famous as a pioneer of drama therapy, as a champion of children's theatre and as an educator of drama teachers' (McGuinn, 2014: 28). He advocated and practised an extreme version of child-centredness in pedagogy.

> *it is we who must learn. The Children [Slade always writes 'Child' or 'Children' with an initial capital] teach us . . . all that is wanted is a place where Children go to the Land [of Child Drama – capital D] with the help of an understanding adult.*
>
> (Slade, 1954: 278, 296, in McGuinn, 2014: 28–29)

Slade's contribution is enormous.

> *He went far beyond his predecessors by boldly declaring . . . 'Child Drama is an Art in itself, and would stand by that alone as being of importance' . . . [He] took up the challenge of thinking through just what exactly the 'domain'. . . of Child Drama might contain . . . [He] attempts, in his first book, to create a conceptual map of what [child] development might look like in terms of a young person's staged, incremental encounter with drama . . . [He attempts] to provide a metalanguage for the domain of Child Drama . . . Where Finlay-Johnson and Caldwell Cook offer consistently enthusiastic but ultimately rather nebulous endorsements of [play's] qualities, Slade attempts a more sustained scrutiny of what he, just as much as his predecessors, believes 'may be the correct approach to all forms of education'.*
> (Slade, 1954: 105, 12, 75, 12–14, 42, in McGuinn, 2014: 34–35)

Slade was strongly opposed to the artifice of conventional theatre. He considered it a danger to children's well-being.

> *'the proscenium form of theatre has disastrous effects on the genuine Drama of the Child . . .' The 'showing off' encouraged by acting for an audience might be bad enough; but for a child to be a member of an audience is to signal something close to spiritual and moral capitulation: 'Nothing is more cruel than to force Children to sit as audience when others are playing. If they want to, then things have gone very far wrong – we have suppressed them.'*
> (Slade, 1954: 44, 58, in McGuinn, 2014: 31–32)

On the other hand, Slade was 'not averse to young people being taught theatre skills when they have reached the requisite stage of maturity and development' (McGuinn, 2014: 34–35).

Teachers who have taken children (lower-case c) to the theatre (proscenium or otherwise), and drawn pleasure and satisfaction from their enjoyment of the experience, may well find Slade's warnings about the dangers lurking there absurd. McGuinn, while paying due credit to Slade's contribution and influence, is aware of another contradiction in his legacy. His insistence that drama is an art form, and his romantic conception of the wisdom of the child, sit uncomfortably with his declaration that 'some of the best work with Children is done by experienced teachers *who really understand what they are doing* [original italics], and yet, strangely enough, have very little knowledge of Drama' (Slade, 1954: 271, in McGuinn, 2014: 37). As McGuinn says, 'where does that leave the key elements of effective pedagogy: content knowledge and application, planned progression, differentiation, classroom management, formative and summative assessment?' (McGuinn, 2014: 37).

Brian Way

Brian Way's *Development through Drama* (1967) was a major advance, in that it linked theoretical understandings of drama's value with practical, detailed advice on how to bring that value to bear in the reality of classrooms which were often physically less than ideal for drama, and which contained 30 or more young people not all of whom were naturally wise or desperately keen to engage in dramatic activity.

(In 1974, having been appointed, as I thought, to teach English in a secondary school in south London, having a degree in English literature but no post-graduate training of any kind, I arrived to start work two days after my appointment. I was handed my timetable. It did indeed include two English classes which I would teach for five lessons a week. It also included nine drama classes which I would teach for one lesson a week each, in a small hall surrounded by rooms where academic subjects were being taught to children sitting quietly in rows. After a few days of something close to chaos, I found *Development through Drama* in Dillon's bookshop, and the quality of my teaching improved a notch or two.)

> More than any specialist described so far, Way provides such detailed descriptions of drama exercises, improvisations and extended role plays that it would still be possible today for a teacher to deliver a lesson or sequence of lessons from the instructions provided in the book. In the section on Speaking, for example, Way offers forty scenarios for improvised dialogue . . . which, with a little updating, could still be employed to good effect in an English classroom focused on the language of persuasion and argument.
>
> (McGuinn, 2014: 54)

> Perhaps most innovative of all from an English perspective is Way's enthusiasm for media conventions and strategies . . . Arguing that students must learn to look 'with the selectivity of the lens of a sensitive camera'

(Way, 1967: 59), he devotes a section of the book's chapter on Improvisation to an exploration of potential links between drama and film – considering, for example, how a photographic image might afford the starting point for improvisation, or a freeze frame might be 'shot' from different camera angles; or thinking about how a musical score might enhance mood and atmosphere.

(McGuinn, 2014: 55)

Gavin Bolton and Dorothy Heathcote

Gavin Bolton and Dorothy Heathcote, two more hugely influential figures in the evolution of teachers' understanding and practice of drama, share Brian Way's more practical approach, recognising the great skill required of a teacher, whether specialist in drama or not, if he or she is to bring about pupils' successful and satisfying learning. Two of their most important publications are *Drama as Education: An Argument for Placing Drama at the Centre of the Curriculum* (Bolton, 1984) and *Drama for Learning: Dorothy Heathcote's Mantle of the Expert Approach to Education* (Heathcote and Bolton, 1995).

Like Way, Bolton and Heathcote are scornful of lax, optimistic approaches to drama teaching which assume that any kind of free expression must be good. All three reject Slade's romantic idealisation of the child.

Two phrases in particular have come to be associated with Bolton's and Heathcote's work: Heathcote's *mantle of the expert*; and the idea and practice of *teacher in role*.

Mantle of the expert means that learners in a drama lesson, as long as they are in possession of or supplied with the necessary information, understanding or skill, can exercise an authority role in the drama by deploying that power. Sometimes a learner will already have the necessary information, understanding or skill. Sometimes the teacher will need to provide it or show the learner how to get hold of it. The benefits of the combination of the deployment of information, understanding or skill with the realisation of the effect of that deployment on others in the drama lie in the gaining of a profounder grasp of whichever area of knowledge or experience is under consideration than could be achieved by other means.

Teacher in role self-evidently means that the teacher no longer simply sets up a drama, watches it unfold and brings it to a conclusion or accepts the conclusion which the learners offer. He or she intervenes in the drama, taking a role of some kind. The role may range from one of fictional authority to one of fictional subservience.

In giving the mantle of the expert to children, and/or in taking on a fictional role, the teacher casts off for fictional purposes a conventional authority role, of which in one sense the learners are nonetheless still aware, and provokes a dynamic in the drama lesson of trust and suspension of disbelief which is of rare value. The relationship between teacher and learners is, for the moment, changed.

Peter Abbs and David Hornbrook

Whatever differences there were between the approaches and beliefs of Slade, Way, Bolton and Heathcote, whatever the distance travelled over the years during which they worked, it would be fair to say that their principal concern is for drama as process and as an instrument of learning. They are proponents of learning *through* drama. Peter Abbs and David Hornbrook shift the emphasis from learning *through* drama to learning *about* drama. Their key books are *Living Powers: The Arts in Education* (Abbs [ed.], 1987a), which Abbs edited and to which he contributed the essay 'Towards a Coherent Arts Aesthetic' (Abbs, 1987b), Hornbrook's *Education and Dramatic Art* (Hornbrook, 1989) and his *On the Subject of Drama* (Hornbrook, 1998).

It is important, however, to stress the word 'emphasis' in the previous paragraph. Learning through and learning about drama are dualisms which, taken literally, could suggest that one group is only interested in, let us say, trust games or the empathetic taking of roles in the re-creation of historical events; and the other group is only interested in voice projection and stage lighting. These are parodies. Slade, despite his objection to proscenium theatre, believed, as we have seen, that young people could be taught theatre skills 'when they have reached the requisite stage of maturity and development'. Neither Abbs nor Hornbrook would say that the practices promoted by Way, Bolton and Heathcote are without value. Like these three figures, Abbs and Hornbrook are critical of loose, free-wheeling approaches to dramatic expression. They call for 'an appropriate balance between a knowledge of drama and the mastery of its practices' (Hornbrook, 1998: 9, in McGuinn, 2014: 68).

That said, the difference in emphasis between Abbs and Hornbrook and what went before is clear. Abbs and Hornbrook believe that there is a body of knowledge which can be identified as the territory of drama, and that it can be taught.

Abbs clearly sees drama's future within the arts. He proposes:

> that drama shares with the performing arts a conceptual terrain that can
> be defined by four present participles: 'making', 'presenting', 'responding'
> and 'evaluating' (Abbs, 1987a: 63, 54) . . . Writing a decade later, Hornbrook
> endorses this position, though, in order to cement the relationship further,
> he conflates 'evaluating' with 'responding' (Hornbrook, 1998: 63).
>
> (both quotations in McGuinn, 2014: 68)

Both writers wish to reinstate (or possibly establish for the first time) the teaching of conventions and techniques within drama. And there is an unmistakable
shift in the direction of theatre in their work, however broadly that word may
be defined. (It *is* broadly defined; Hornbrook's vision of theatrical culture worth
teaching is global.) He writes:

> Students will not simply intuit how to light a performance, any more than
> they are likely to perform well without being taught at least the rudiments
> of acting or direct without studying the way in which stage pictures are
> organised.
>
> (Hornbrook, 1998: 56, in McGuinn, 2014: 69)

Hornbrook admires the master/apprentice relationship of the medieval guild
or craft. This emphasis is different from that implied by the giving of the
mantle of the expert to the learner, or by the taking of a fictional role by
the teacher.

Process or product?

McGuinn sums up well the dilemma produced if the Abbs and Hornbrook position is regarded as the kind of alternative to the Bolton and Heathcote position
which forces the practitioner to choose.

> Introducing curriculum rigour in terms of content and critical method not only
> gives the lie to those who would regard drama as academically 'soft' and inex-
> tricably linked to the vagaries of 'self-expression'. It can also . . . empower
> learners with real expertise . . . Choosing this route, however, brings signifi-
> cant consequences for English pedagogy. First, it requires the construction

of a coherent and progressive drama curriculum. Second, it implies, in some measure at least, that the dais be returned to the classroom [a reference to Frank Whitehead's famous publication, The Disappearing Dais: A Study of the Principles and Practice of English Teaching *(Whitehead, 1966)] and that the teacher move from co-learner to transmitter of knowledge – a drama-specific knowledge that might lie beyond the ambit of traditional training in English pedagogy. Third – and perhaps most important of all – it threatens to weaken the commitment to democracy, inclusivity and personal growth that makes drama so appealing to English teachers in the first place. If skills are to be taught and applied, then, inevitably, some students will learn to apply those skills more effectively than others . . . Subject-specific discourse might empower, but it might also intimidate and exclude. What drama might gain in terms of aesthetic crafting, it might lose in terms of 'spontaneity and camaraderie'.*

(McGuinn, 2014: 75–76)

So, as we survey the situation now, is there such a dilemma?

Jonothan Neelands

Jonothan Neelands' paper, 'Drama: The Subject that Dare Not Speak its Name' (2008), was written principally 'for student teachers of English in England . . . to introduce them to the main issues informing drama pedagogy in contemporary classrooms' (McGuinn, 2014: 77). The paper has reached far wider audiences since its publication. Its polemical title drops a heavy hint that the author knows all is not well in drama's relationship with the official curriculum. The hint is confirmed in the text.

In theory [the current position of drama in the official curriculum] presents schools in the English system with the opportunity to design and implement their own ideas and values of what drama means in terms of curriculum, pedagogy and assessment. In practice, the lack of a national consensus about what drama is and where it might be best positioned, taught and assessed leads to a degree of professional insecurity amongst teachers employed as drama specialists and has also led to a long and sometimes fierce contest to define what is legitimate drama in schools.

(Neelands, 2008: 2)

Neelands is frank about the process/product debate, or division, which has preoccupied drama for so long.

> *In the literature of drama in schools in anglophone countries, battle lines are often drawn between so called 'product' and 'process' approaches to teaching drama . . . The product approach is often associated with 'theatre' as a subject of study and the 'process' approach with improvised forms of drama used as a method of teaching and learning across the curriculum. A 'product' approach tends to assume that drama is properly concerned with the study of the western traditions of playwriting and performance and focuses on the development of the performance skills needed to realise an 'established' canon of plays and authors and also the critical and cognitive skills and understandings needed to understand and appreciate drama in both its literary and dominant performance modes. This approach tends to be uncritical of the class and culturally restricted paradigm of theatre, which underpins it, a paradigm of theatre and theatrical production that closely reflects the history and tastes and preferences of the English middle class theatre audience.*
>
> *(ibid.: 4–5)*

If the latter part of this quotation is an oblique criticism of Abbs and Hornbrook, it is unfair in the sense that their understanding of theatre goes far beyond 'the western traditions of playwriting and performance' and 'the tastes and preferences of the English middle class theatre audience'. However, the first two sentences are crisp and accurate. Meanwhile:

> *In its extreme forms, process drama approaches may eschew any attempt to 'perform' or to engage students with the literary tradition of theatre. Instead, students are engaged in creating drama experiences through improvisation and spontaneous forms of role-play . . . Process drama is often considered to be a method or means of learning for use across the curriculum, rather than as a subject. It is often closely associated with 'liberal' or 'progressive' models of teaching and it claims to develop a wide range of social, personal, critical, cognitive, communication and imaginative/creative skills and understandings. At its heart is the idea that students learn through the direct experience of working within a fictional drama context, which is not observed by an audience.*
>
> *(ibid.: 5)*

Process or product: no need to choose

Neelands offers a table of genres of work in drama, ranging from those at the more theatrical, product-focused end of the continuum to those more focused on process and on pupils' learning (*ibid*.: 3–4). He says, clearly enough:

> *Increasingly, good drama practice at all levels is characterised by a more holistic approach that seeks to capture the strengths of both the process and the product traditions.*

> (*ibid*.: 6)

In other words, Neelands proposes that we should have our cake and eat it when it comes to the theory and practice of drama. There is no need to sign up to membership of the process or the product 'club'. All the approaches which have been proposed by the major theorists of drama have their validity. Only extremes are excluded: that is, the positions of those who would condemn performance as irrelevant to or even dangerous for learners' emotional and cognitive development and well-being; and of those on the other hand who would insist that 'an actor (or stage manager or director or lighting technician) prepares' is the only motto for educational drama worth bothering with.

The present situation in England

My understanding of educational drama follows Neelands' in seeking 'to capture the strengths of both the process and the product traditions'. Drama can be many things, drawing on both traditions and a mixture of them. And an enormous amount of excellent, diverse drama work is being done in schools.

However, the official status of drama in the statutory curriculum is a story of missed opportunities. The fact that drama *can* be many things does not mean that it *is* or *has been* all or – in some schools – any of those. The failure of legislators to make up their minds about where drama sits in the curriculum has led to long-term uncertainty about the subject and, in some schools, to a hopefulness that drama is being done somewhere and somehow, because the clear responsibility for doing it does not lie unequivocally with anyone.

An opportunity lost

The greatest loss of opportunity, in terms of drama's status in the school curriculum in England, occurred when those who legislated for the National Curriculum which took effect in 1989 and 1990 decided not to give drama the status of a foundation subject, along with art and music. English was given the guardianship of drama. Although in the first English orders for speaking and listening (Department of Education and Science and the Welsh Office, 1990) the occasional mention of imaginative play, improvised drama, role-play, simulations and group drama encouraged, indeed required, teachers in primary schools and secondary English teachers to use drama in their teaching, the lop-sided, half-in, half-out legal status of drama was taken as a signal that schools did not need to provide for it in the way that they needed to provide for art and music.

Mitigating the effects of the government's failure

Numerous worthwhile efforts have been made since 1989 to deal with the problem of drama's Cinderella status in the National Curriculum. The government itself, via its National Literacy Strategy (later National Strategy), published detailed advice on teaching and assessing drama (Department for Education and Employment, 1998; Department for Education and Skills, 2001, 2003). The Office for Standards in Education offered guidance to school inspectors and teaching staff on evaluating the quality of teaching and learning in drama (for example, Office for Standards in Education, 2002). There was much to commend in these publications. However, they could not overcome the structural problem which schools had inherited as a result of the failure described in the previous section.

Other organisations weighed in to help. For example:

In 2003, the Arts Council published the second edition of Drama in Schools *[Arts Council England, 2003] which was intended to fill the gap left by drama's exclusion from the National Curriculum as a subject in its own right. In the absence of any national agreement on drama, many schools [were] left without the levels of support and guidance offered in National Curriculum subjects.*

(Dickinson, Neelands and Shenton Primary School, 2006)

The document to which these authors refer is excellent. Amongst other things, it offers brief statements of what good drama looks like at Foundation Stage, at the four compulsory Key Stages, at post-16 and in special schools. Here is the statement for the Foundation Stage:

Pretending to be others in imagined situations and acting out situations or stories are important activities in the dramatic curriculum for the Foundation Stage . . . The imaginative role-play area and other play situations provide many opportunities for very young children to experience and develop their early drama skills and knowledge, and to learn about the world . . .

Children can suggest their own ideas for planning and creating a role-play area. Then, as they play, the teacher or other adult can intervene sensitively as an active participant. This validates and extends the narrative of the play, supports appropriate language and allows the children to explore the power of their roles. Creative drama develops alongside imagination, confidence and language. As children engage in these drama activities they become increasingly aware of the use of space and the way body language communicates meaning.

(Arts Council England, 2003: 9)

Here are extracts from the statement for Key Stages 1 and 2:

A flourishing arts curriculum in a primary school enables pupils to enjoy drama as a subject in its own right, and as a learning medium across the curriculum. Drama is a vital element of primary pupils' entitlement to a balanced arts education . . . Pupils at this age unselfconsciously mix drama, dance, music, visual art and aspects of media in assemblies, concerts and less formal events . . .

Exploring a story imaginatively in drama can include what may happen before the story begins or at the end, as well as beyond the events of the story. The opportunity to act out a story to others can be a highlight of the school experience for some pupils, particularly if they find other means of expression more difficult. Primary school pupils benefit from visits to and from theatre companies. This may help them to understand the process of making, performing and responding to plays and provide insights into a range of cross-curricular themes and issues, enhancing the teaching of other subjects, such as history and citizenship.

(*ibid.*: 11–12)

The statements are accompanied by case studies of successful drama lessons at each age group.

An important chapter in the book is 'Structuring Drama in Schools', which is a kind of manifesto for drama, proposing a framework within which it should be taught, practised and assessed.

Drama should be taught progressively through and across each key stage, building upon previous learning. The three interrelated activities of making, performing and responding provide a useful framework for identifying and assessing progression and achievement, and match similar categories in music: composing, performing and appraising, and in dance: creating, performing and evaluating. For the purposes of planning and assessment, making, performing and responding are treated separately, although they are frequently integrated in practice. Pupils improvising, for example, are simultaneously making, performing and responding. Similarly, the emphasis placed on each can change across the key stages. However, the principle of balance is important and teachers should aim to include aspects of each activity in their schemes of work.

Making encompasses the many processes and activities employed when exploring, devising, shaping and interpreting drama.

Performing covers the skills and knowledge displayed when enacting, presenting and producing dramas, including the use of theatre technology.

Responding incorporates reflecting on both emotional and intellectual reactions to the drama. This reflection is deepened as pupils gain a knowledge and understanding of how drama is created.

To ensure breadth of study during each key stage, pupils should be taught the skills, knowledge and understanding required to make, perform and respond to drama through:

- *a broad range of stimuli, including artefacts, literature, non-fiction and non-literary texts such as photographs and video clips;*
- *working in groups of varying size and as a class;*
- *performing to a range of audiences;*
- *a range of genres, styles and different media;*
- *seeing a variety of live and recorded performances from different times and cultures;*
- *using ICT to explore and record ideas, research themes and enhance their production work.*

(ibid.: 29)

The making, performing (or presenting), responding trilogy is familiar now. The manifesto is followed by a detailed set of level descriptions for pupils' achievement in making, performing and responding at each level of the (now abandoned) National Curriculum eight-level scale plus 'exceptional performance'. I make use both of the trilogy and of the descriptions of achievement in the alternative curriculum for drama 3 to 11 in Chapter 11.

Drama in the new National Curriculum

While other organisations and individuals have been trying to bring clarity to an unclear situation, successive governments since 1989 have been responsible for numerous revisions and re-revisions of the National Curriculum for English. None of these has significantly enhanced the value given to drama in official terms. It has continued to shelter awkwardly in English. We will skip over these superficial changes and come to the present day. In the new National Curriculum orders for English, the following requirement appears in an introductory general section on spoken language:

> All pupils should be enabled to participate in and gain knowledge, skills and understanding associated with the artistic practice of drama. Pupils should be able to adopt, create and sustain a range of roles, responding appropriately to others in role. They should have opportunities to improvise, devise and script drama for one another and a range of audiences, as well as to rehearse, refine, share and respond thoughtfully to drama and theatre performances.
>
> (Department for Education, 2014a: 15)

Below is every reference in the new orders to drama at Key Stages 1 and 2 and to activities connected with it, however tangentially.

The brief, undifferentiated set of orders for spoken language for the whole of Key Stages 1 and 2 contains the requirement that pupils should be taught to 'participate in discussions, presentations, performances, role play, improvisations and debates' (*ibid*.: 18).

The requirement that 'pupils should become more familiar with and confident in using language in a greater variety of situations, for a variety of audiences and purposes, including through drama, formal presentations and debate' appears in the introduction to the section on Years 3 and 4 (*ibid.*: 35).

The reading comprehension orders for Years 3 and 4 include the requirement that pupils should '[listen] to and [discuss] a wide range of fiction, poetry, plays, non-fiction and reference books or textbooks'. They should '[prepare] poems and play scripts to read aloud and to perform, showing understanding through intonation, tone, volume and action' (*ibid.*: 36–37).

At Years 5 and 6, 'Pupils' knowledge of language, gained from stories, plays, poetry, non-fiction and textbooks, will support their increasing fluency as readers, their facility as writers, and their comprehension'. '[P]upils' confidence, enjoyment and mastery of language should be extended through public speaking, performance and debate' (*ibid.*: 42–43).

In the reading comprehension orders for Years 5 and 6, pupils should '[continue] to read and discuss an increasingly wide range of fiction, poetry, plays, non-fiction and reference books or textbooks'. They should '[prepare] poems and plays to read aloud and to perform, showing understanding through intonation, tone and volume so that the meaning is clear to an audience' (*ibid.*: 44–45).

The writing composition orders for Years 5 and 6 include the requirement that pupils should 'perform their own compositions, using appropriate intonation, volume, and movement so that meaning is clear' (*ibid.*: 49).

Several of these quotations focus on the perfectly valid, indeed important activity of the reading and writing of scripted literary drama. However, this activity is well away from the centre of the idea of drama as summarised or quoted in this and previous sections of the chapter. There is no point in finding detailed fault with individual requirements. Many of them are admirable in themselves. The problem resides in the fact that, put all together, they do not add up to a substantial, coherent, rigorous, iterative, developmental account of a subject in the school curriculum.

This is an unsatisfactory situation.

Drama in the school curriculum: another way

While drama in England continues to shelter within English, other educational legislatures have taken a different decision. In his 2008 paper quoted earlier, Jonothan Neelands offers a list.

Drama is included as a discrete subject and as a strand in the Arts in the National Curricula of a growing number of other national education systems. These include certain provinces and states within the USA, Canada and Australia; Cyprus, Taiwan, Hungary, Czech Republic, Norway, New Zealand, France, Malta amongst others. Drama is part of a statutory entitlement to the Arts in Scotland, Northern Ireland and the Republic of Ireland.

(Neelands, 2008: 1)

Let us take one English-speaking country from Neelands' list. The Australian Curriculum, Assessment and Reporting Authority (ACARA) is responsible for a recently introduced curriculum in Australia's schools. Here are three quotations from ACARA's website, drilling down from the curriculum as a whole, to The Arts, to Drama:

The Foundation – Year 10 Australian Curriculum is described as a three-dimensional curriculum that recognises the central importance of disciplinary knowledge, skills and understanding; general capabilities; and cross-curriculum priorities.

Disciplinary knowledge is found in the eight learning areas of the Australian Curriculum: English, Mathematics, Science, Health and Physical Education, Humanities and Social Sciences, The Arts, Technologies and Languages. The latter four learning areas have been written to include multiple subjects, reflecting custom and practice in the discipline . . .

In the Australian Curriculum, The Arts is a learning area that draws together related but distinct art forms. While these art forms have close relationships and are often used in interrelated ways, each involves different approaches to arts practices and critical and creative thinking that reflect distinct bodies of knowledge, understanding and skills. The curriculum examines past, current and emerging arts practices in each art form across a range of cultures and places.

The Australian Curriculum: The Arts comprises five subjects: Dance, Drama, Media Arts, Music, Visual Arts . . .

Drama is the expression and exploration of personal, cultural and social worlds through role and situation that engages, entertains and challenges. Students create meaning as drama makers, performers and audiences as they enjoy and analyse their own and others' stories and points of view. Like all art forms, drama has the capacity to engage, inspire and enrich all students, excite the imagination and encourage students to reach their creative and expressive potential.

(ACARA, 2016)

ACARA offers clear guidelines for the teaching of Drama from the foundation year up to Year 10: the entire school age-range. There is also guidance as to how Drama is to be configured or combined with the other four subjects in The Arts.

England embarrassed

The comparison between Australia's and England's approach to drama embarrasses the latter. The two countries are in different leagues in terms of substance, coherence, rigour and the understanding of iteration and development. It is too soon to say how successful will be Australia's attempt at giving full status to drama within the curriculum. However, the arrangements summarised here, which have been subject to extensive consultation between the Australian federal government and its agencies and the states and territories of Australia, and have been prepared with the active involvement of schools and teachers' organisations, have a good chance of doing what England has failed to do with its half measures and hopeful compromises: put drama firmly on the map.

An alternative

The proposals for drama 3 to 11 in the alternative curriculum in Chapter 11 owe much to the Australian model. The proposals could be adopted and adapted for various purposes: as an alternative to the collection of references to drama in the new National Curriculum for English; as an aide-memoire for the use of drama across all areas of the curriculum; or as the basis of a future curriculum for drama as a foundation subject of the National Curriculum.

To conclude . . .

Across England, drama continues to be taught effectively and imaginatively by thousands of teachers, specialists or not, in a diversity of curriculum settings. Through the work of these teachers, drama makes its essential contribution to the education of children and young people as whole, social beings. Drama is a fundamental part of education for culture.

Learning *through* drama and learning *about* drama are equally valid approaches. There will be occasions when the one or the other approach predominates. There will be occasions when both are in play.

All areas of the curriculum are potentially capable of supplying content whose learning will benefit from the use of drama. For the teacher of language, literacy and literature, the range of possibilities for the enrichment of learning through drama is wide.

Learning about drama will draw on a diversity of theatrical traditions, styles and techniques. It should also draw on traditions, styles and techniques which have developed in drama on film and television and which are developing in drama on recently invented digital platforms.

Drama's official status in the National Curriculum in England is a matter of unfinished business. At some point in the not too distant future, England's Department for Education should complete the business by according drama the status of a full National Curriculum subject. If this were to occur, it would not of course mean that drama ceases to be a key activity, an essential mode of learning, in any area of the curriculum. It would simply mean that an activity which, along with music, image-making and dance, is as old as human civilisation itself, would finally have been accorded proper official recognition in England's schools.

8 Media

Andrew Burn

Summary of main points

In the past, media education has often been seen as a form of 'inoculation': of protection against the cultural, moral and ideological ill effects of the mass media. More recently, media education has struck a more positive note. Its emphasis is on the value of popular culture and on the importance of media forms such as cinema, television, comic books, video games, animation, advertising, news media and social media in representing our world.

Media education in the National Curriculum in England has been contained within English. This has provided positive opportunities for teachers and learners, raising the profile of moving-image texts, introducing the idea of multimodal texts, and emphasising the importance of digital media. However, media education's place within English has also caused problems: emphasising factual media at the expense of fiction; suggesting a 'suspicious' mode of reading media texts (in contrast to the 'appreciative' mode expected for literary texts); and restricting media education to the reading section of the curriculum, thus making it mandatory to 'read' media texts, but not to 'write' them.

In the most recent version of the National Curriculum for English, media education has effectively been expunged. It should be fully reinstated. Any adequate media curriculum should equally emphasise 'reading' (analysis of media) and 'writing' (production of media).

Media education 3 to 11 is best located within language, literacy and literature work. This arrangement allows for a coherent approach to the study and making of texts and meanings across all media, which can extend and strengthen pupils' understanding of textual structures, contexts and functions. It is the arrangement most likely to provide entitlement to media education for all children in the Early Years and in primary schools.

The study of media, drama and literature together allows teachers and pupils to explore the spectrum of cultural taste, from elite canonical texts through to popular cultural forms, and the increasing tendency for these to collapse into one another. The contrasting modes of engagement with texts characteristic of media and literary studies in schools, 'rhetorical' and 'poetic' stances respectively, are stronger if united.

A media education curriculum from 3 to 11, involving 'reading' the media, 'writing' the media and engaging with the contexts in which media practices occur, must be recursive. It cannot artificially distribute certain kinds of work across 'ages and stages', but should suggest how the same work (for example, editing a film) might change, expand, become more challenging and diverse, as pupils get older, gain more experience and become more autonomous.

Media education: four patterns

A glance at the construction of media education in the English curriculum reveals four patterns which make useful starting points for a consideration of what is happening in media education now, and what might develop in the future.

The first pattern: media education as suspicious reading

The four patterns follow a common theme, set by the first pattern, in which media education has been constructed as a kind of suspicious reading, pushing teachers and pupils towards the scrutiny of newspapers and television programmes to detect bias, misrepresentation and other distortions of some imagined 'truth'.

Behind this suspicious reading lies a tangled history of protectionist impulses, clearly identified by David Buckingham in his *Media Education: Literacy, Learning and Contemporary Culture* (2003), and further explored below: impulses to protect children from what are seen as the various debilitating effects of the mass media, whether such effects be cultural, ideological or moral. While these impulses may be considerably stronger in the US than in the UK (or indeed in European media education in general), they are nevertheless a factor in the institutional regulation of media texts for children and in the value systems sometimes applied to schools' choice of texts.

The second pattern: media education's fact/fiction divide

The second pattern discernible in curricular constructions of media in English is that media have often been imagined as a genre of factual representation and communication: essentially, news media. It's as if the entire function of narrative texts and imaginative fiction is reserved for literature. Two histories are noteworthy here. One features F. R. Leavis, whose critical readings of media texts for school pupils never embraced the narrative structures of comic strips or the poetics of film, but rather made advertising their object of attack. Leavis notoriously invented many of the advertising texts he used, the better to exemplify their debased nature (Leavis and Thompson, 1977 [1933]).

The other history in this second pattern helps to explain how, regrettably, media literacy is now once again only being seen as a matter of how citizens retrieve and critically appraise factual information. This is the history of the computer. As Lev Manovich has memorably described, the computer, from its inception in the form of Babbage's Analytical Engine in the 1830s, has developed as a processor of information, in contrast to the history of photography (also beginning in the 1830s with Daguerre's daguerrotype), which is a history of cultural representations (Manovich, 1998).

As these two technologies have become fused in the multimedia computer, ICT educators are having difficulty understanding how the number-cruncher has become a tool of cultural production; while teachers of language and literacy struggle with the implications of the cultural representations which have been their traditional stock-in-trade – films, poems, stories – becoming computable. It is partly for this reason that computer games, a cultural form which has always by definition been a set of computable representations, pose such interesting and challenging questions for teachers as they consider how to teach such a form in the classroom.

In the wider world of policy, some politicians and officials have continued to be trapped by this division of media into, effectively, fictions on the one hand and factual information on the other. In Europe, at least, the fictions have been largely the interest of film educators, who have considered how cinema narratives can be critically explored in schools in much the same appreciative way that literature teachers deploy in their approach to literary fictions. Meanwhile, the policy-makers have been largely preoccupied with how factual information is conveyed to citizens through electronic media, particularly online.

So, the general effect of this fact/fiction divide in the educational and policy arenas is to overemphasise both the importance and the risks of factual information in children's lives, and to almost completely neglect the most important uses children actually make of the media: the music, dreams, fantasies, play, dramatic narratives, whimsical performances, album-making, aspirational self-representation, parodic invention and casual communication which make up most of their online lives.

The third pattern: media education as reading not writing

The third pattern in the construction of media in the official English curriculum is that it represents, essentially, an act of critical *reading*. Media within the National Curriculum for English has been located within its reading section, with no equivalent provision made in the writing section. In England, it has been mandatory since the inception of the National Curriculum for English to teach children to *read* the media (that is, critically interrogate it), but not to *write* it (that is, produce their own media texts) (Qualifications and Curriculum Authority, 2007). (But, as the section 'The present situation in England' below relates, even this requirement has been abandoned in the new National Curriculum for English.) There is a doubly suspicious stance here: a suspicion, again, of media texts, positioning them as objects of a critical gaze quite different from that envisaged for literature; but also a suspicion of children's own media production work, implicitly devalued by comparison with creative writing.

The fourth pattern: media texts as poor relations of literature

Finally, successive versions of the English curriculum have demonstrated a suspicion of semiotic modes beyond language. The argument takes curious turns. In 2004– 2005, a 'conversation' was initiated with stakeholders by the Qualifications and Curriculum Authority (QCA), the government agency then responsible for curriculum development, about the future of the English curriculum. In its response document, the QCA argued, in reply to a number of submissions making the case for a version of the curriculum incorporating contemporary media texts, that:

Alongside views that media and screen-based texts [can] have their place in English 21 there is the caveat that these should never be at the expense of our rich book-based literary heritage – a point more fully elaborated in terms of the purpose and value of engaging with verbal language: the study of literature has one conspicuous advantage over the study of film and television media, in that it develops the skills of analysis, argument and discourse alongside language skills.

(QCA, 2005; my emphasis)

The authors of the document here display a softened stance on the teaching of texts such as comics, films and television, allowing them a place as part of a wider cultural landscape; but there remains the firm belief that they need to be treated suspiciously, and to be seen as somehow thinner, more insubstantial, less nourishing than literature.

This chapter opposes the 'poor relation' view of media texts. There is no logical reason why the study of comic strip and animated film, for example, should not develop 'the skills of analysis, argument and discourse alongside language skills' just as effectively as the study of classic literature.

A model for media education

This section offers a model for media education, illustrated by examples.

Media and English have been kissing cousins ever since Leavis' launch of the 'inoculation' approach to media, as mentioned in the previous section: the development of critical close reading skills in pupils to protect them from the ill effects of the mass media. We have seen the three kinds of protectionism in the history of media education which Buckingham (2003) has identified: Leavis' cultural protectionism; the attempt of radical pedagogy in the 1970s and 1980s to protect children from the ideological effects of the media; and the moral protectionism which Buckingham associates more with media education in America.

Let the cousins continue to kiss

Most primary-school teachers in the UK who teach about the media would not now subscribe to any form of protectionism, taking instead a positive view of children's media cultures and practices, not least because of a general shift towards forms of creative production enabled by the increasing availability of digital authoring tools. However, they would see themselves as teaching forms of critical awareness. In this section, I will focus on three aspects of media education which can inform teaching. It's important not to produce neat models of media education which emphasise difference from, even incompatibility with, language, literacy, drama and literature. Such models lead to media as a tacked-on appendage to the English curriculum, at best. More productive, maybe, is to muddle the boundaries, find common ground and use tensions to challenge each field of study to move beyond its limitations and prejudices.

The three areas I will focus on are *cultural distinction*, *rhetoric and poetics* and *creative production*. They roughly correspond to key concepts in the English curriculum as identified by the QCA (2007): cultural understanding, critical understanding, and creativity. However, my emphasis here will be on the development of media literacy, which is also often understood in terms of this '3Cs' model (Bazalgette, 2008; Burn and Durran, 2007). In my model, a 'CRC' model, the concepts are rather differently understood, in ways which can usefully inform teaching.

Cultural distinction

The simple way to state the problem here is to say that the official English curriculum has traditionally been concerned with 'high' culture (though those teachers who come under the category identified in the Cox Report [The Cox Committee, 1989] as 'cultural analysts' have always contested the literary canon and the values associated with it); and that, meanwhile, media education has been committed to popular culture (though those who emphasise the importance of film sometimes observe their own kind of canon).

However, the official curriculum, oddly, renders the question of culture, high or popular, pretty well invisible. A search through versions of the National Curriculum for English for references to 'culture' or 'cultural' reveals only rather tokenistic references to multiculturalism, as if culture only becomes visible through contrast between ethnic groups. Contrasts between the cultures of different social classes, which might be expected to reveal something of the tension between popular and elite cultural forms and preferences, are not available as a mode of inquiry in the English curriculum. Nevertheless, it is important to acknowledge that these kinds of cultural distinction still exist and to consider how to approach them in the classroom. In any case, my argument is that we don't need to choose. We can, and should, have both extremes of the cultural spectrum, and anything in between that suits our purpose and our pupils' interests.

Rhetoric and poetics

Literature teaching and media education have quite different approaches to the characteristics of texts. Approaches to literary texts have often focused on their aesthetic form and have been characterised by what we might call a mode of appreciation, a *poetical* mode. By contrast, media texts have been approached in what we might call a *rhetorical* mode, exploring the politics of representation and interrogating the motivations of producers and audiences.

These two modes have long histories which can be traced back to Aristotle: we can detect the legacy of his *Poetics* in the traditional approach to literature, and the legacy of his *Rhetoric* in the approach to media texts. I simplify here for the sake of contrast; but, in the habits of mind that have constructed literature as an object of reverence and media texts as objects of suspicion, something like this contrast seems stubbornly resistant to change. We need both rhetoric and poetics if we are to attend to the politics of representation in both media and literary texts, as well as to the aesthetic forms in which such representations are framed. Indeed, these should not be alternative, incompatible ways of looking at culture, but indivisible: two sides of the same coin. All rhetoric operates through aesthetic form and claims aesthetic value; all aesthetic form has a rhetorical, even political, purpose.

The rhetorical stance of media education could be considered under the headings *institutions*, *texts* and *audiences*.

Institutions

The idea of media institutions is a staple of media education. It is rarely considered in the teaching of literature, though much of Dickens' work was structured by the contingencies of magazine publication, though the careers of the women writers of the nineteenth century were at the mercy of male publishers, and though the literary creations of modern novelists are commonly franchised by multinational media organisations. To move beyond the immediate pleasures of engagement with media texts in order to consider the shadowy regimes of production and distribution that lie behind them can seem dry, remote and hard to pin down. There are also uncertainties: what institutions are we talking about exactly? What do we need to know about them? Why do we need to know it?

Here is one primary-school example of the study of media institutions. A colleague explored the cross-media *Harry Potter* franchise by looking at logos on the covers of the book, the DVD box and the game box. The media institutions involved included Bloomsbury, Sony, Knowwonder games, Electronic Arts, the *Times Educational Supplement*, Dolby sound and several more. The complexity of function speaks for itself. Some institutional functions are familiar, yet opaque. The age-rating of both films and games, for example, was familiar to the pupils; but they had little knowledge of the institutions that create these regulatory constraints which affect their viewing and play. The logos of the BBFC (British Board of Film Classification) and PEGI (Pan-European Game Information), which determine age-rating for films and games respectively, prompted the pupils to explore these institutions and their different motivations: one is a public body, the other an industry-created system.

Another example comes from a Year 4 primary classroom where the activity involved researching the BBC. When the teacher asked 'Does anybody know how the BBC gets its money?', some children began to use previously acquired knowledge to help them speculate. 'There are no adverts on the BBC so it's not like Sky.' Jamie speculated that the audiences have to pay for the channels they watch and seemed to be drawing from experience of subscription channels. The children were beginning to generalise from their own experience of the media, even if this produced the wrong conclusion. The teacher asked, 'Do you have to pay to get the BBC?' Odette said, 'No, it's always been there.' She was surprised when the teacher provided information about the licence fee. This evidence of partial understanding of media economics shows how children theorise from their experience and how they amend their ideas with new information.

Texts

A rhetorical approach to texts will centre on the question of *representation*. At one level, representation means any semiotic act: any utterance, written word, image, dramatic gesture is a representation of some aspect of a multiple and shifting 'reality'. The question to explore with pupils is the nature of the relationship between the representation and that 'reality'.

The example here comes from a Year 3 classroom, where the class is studying newspapers and making their own. The children have analysed a series of front-page headlines, looking at how they condense the narrative into a few words, how they give clues to the reader about the importance and meaning of the story, and how they use language in memorable and unusual ways. When they move on to making their own front pages, they put this new knowledge to good use. One child uses a pun for his headline about recent bad weather in the school's local area: 'Snow Way!' The children had recently learned about the efficiency and humour of puns, and the use of punctuation in headlines for emphasis, and Jamie was putting his newly acquired knowledge to work in a different context.

This example demonstrates the importance of keeping the rhetoric and poetics of the media closely linked; two sides of the same coin. The analysis and production of news media inevitably foregrounds rhetorical functions – exploring texts which persuade, inform, entertain – but they can accomplish this through the study and use of linguistic features which are essentially the ones which poets also deploy.

Audience

Teachers often encourage pupils to create texts for a particular audience. But who that audience might be, or how we might get a concrete idea of her, him or them, is a slippery business. We can imagine, for instance, a series of concentric circles, the innermost of which is the pupils themselves. What are their reading/viewing/playing preferences? How do they make particular cultural choices? What kinds of pleasure do they derive from the texts they choose? In what social groups do they engage with these texts? What cultural practices do they engage in as audiences? The next circle outward might be a specific other audience, involving making texts for a partner primary-school class, for a parents' evening, for a local council meeting, for a visiting VIP.

This kind of differentiation of audiences can be seen in a project in which Year 4 children devised their own media campaign to promote health awareness for a (fictional) virus. To research their own health advertising campaign, the class watched a range of public health advertisements and speculated about audience responses. 'Too much information bores people, too much scary stuff puts them off', one group decided. The children were differentiating between audience reactions. Watching flu adverts, the class became aware of their own visceral reactions to the ads: the groans, moans and 'yuks'. They sang along with the catchy refrain from a swine flu advert, 'Catch it, bin it, kill it', punching their arms in the air. They had begun their audience research with themselves, recognising that audience pleasure is as important as the factual message of the advert.

As a further part of the research, going outwards, two children interviewed dinner ladies, who were emphatic about the importance of health measures in schools and families. A group of three interviewed the school secretary. They were surprised when she said she had no TV.

The children realised that audiences different from themselves may have different interests, which they would need to address in their campaign. They considered the value of different media, including radio and the internet. They had learned something about the importance of audience media preferences.

Creative production

Creativity in education is a highly contested idea, appearing in a bewildering variety of forms (Banaji and Burn with Buckingham, 2007). Here, I draw on the work of the Russian psychologist Lev Vygotsky, for whom the creativity of children and adolescents was closely related to play (Vygotsky, 1998 [1931]). In playful activity, children learn the meaning of symbolic substitution through the manipulation of physical objects: Vygotsky's well-known example is a child using a broomstick as an imaginary horse. These symbolic understandings become internalised and develop into the mental processes which generate creative work. For Vygotsky, true creativity only develops, however, when the imaginative transformations of play are connected with thinking in concepts: in other words, with rational intellectual processes.

What might creative production look like in the primary media classroom?

Scary films

In one example, from a Year 2 classroom, 6-year-olds are devising their own 'scary films'. They have looked at a range of picture books and films which exemplify such stories, involving monsters, aliens and things that go bump in the night. They have discussed the oddness of creating stories which frighten people and the appeal this holds for audiences. They move on to storyboard, film and edit their own stories. A much-debated point in the discussion is how to convey the sense of fear, and in particular how to show the monsters in their stories.

One group decides to show 'the monster in the library' in its full glory, with two children dressing up in a green cloak with a monster mask. Another group decides, with encouragement from the teacher, that they won't show the monster at all, but will create the sense of the frightening phenomenon entirely through showing the reaction of the victim. In one frame of the children's storyboard, a character has been drawn especially small to communicate vulnerability. The teacher asks how this might be filmed. The children tell him to stand on one of the desks so that he can film the character from a high angle, again representing vulnerability.

These two approaches exemplify aspects of Vygotsky's model of creativity. In the former case, material resources are collected and repurposed to create the visual effect of the monster, much as Vygotsky's broomstick horse is created by children at play. The monster is, however, elaborated through dramatic movement (the children wriggle convincingly across the library floor), and vocal articulation (grunts), so that a more developed narrative is created. This narrative is, in turn, developed further by the filming of the monster and the victim, and the editing which alternately cuts between them, showing the victim's deliciously terrified reactions. The playful imaginative creation of a fantasy figure is subordinated to the logic of narrative structure and meaning.

The second group's decision is rather more complex. To appreciate that an entity in film can be represented by its absence is a step forward, and to imagine a monster only evident through the emotional effects it creates is obviously a step further on from imagining a broomstick to be a horse. Here, the resources involve the dramatic work of the victim and the use of what Vygotsky calls 'tools', which can be both material and conceptual. In this case, the high-angle filming is the material tool, while the concept of the power imbalance it represents is the conceptual tool. The use of these tools creates the sense of fear visible in the victim and also creates an implied monster rather than a visible one, which in turn shows the children's understanding of the inferential work of the audience.

Creativity here, then, is by no means a vague, romantic affair, but a specific set of imaginative processes organised by a mixture of signifying systems. The meanings of dramatic action, the grammar of film, the significance of costume and mask, and the emotional (and narrative) meanings of music are all integrated in the children's work.

Machinima

Another example is drawn from a project in which a group of 30 11-year-olds make a machinima film. Machinima is perhaps the most recent cultural form in the world of animation. The word itself is a portmanteau combining 'machine' and 'cinema', with a substitution of the 'e' by an 'i', implying 'animation' and 'animé'. Machinima is defined by Kelland *et al.* (2005: 10) as 'the art of making animated films within a real-time 3-D environment'. It can be thought of as animation made from the 3-D environments and animated characters of computer games or virtual immersive worlds.

The children's film tells the story of a computer geek called Jeff, who meets an alien character, Dr T, in a videogame, travels with him to Cleopatra's palace, and eventually prevents his evil plan for world domination.

Martha and Rosa are editing the scene in which two characters, Jeff and Dr T, have arrived at Cleopatra's palace and have to convince her guard to let them in. They are editing to a printed script, which is a transcript of the improvised dialogue of the voice-acting group in the class. They tell me how they will edit a conversation sequence:

AB: If you were filming two people talking, how would you do it?
R: You'd put the camera there, and one of them would be there, and one would be there [indicating 'side by side' with hands].
AB: What's your other option?
R: You could put the camera on the person talking . . .
M: And then switch it round.

Here, Martha and Rosa first suggest a two-shot for a conversation and move towards the idea of shot-reverse-shot in response to my question. Elsewhere in my conversation with them, they show that they are quite confident about the idea of shot distance and its function of emphasis. They describe kinds of camera movement and the function of low- and high-angle shots to signify power, although these have not been explicitly taught at this stage. When asked how these ideas could apply to their scene, they suggest that Cleopatra and the guard might be filmed from a low angle. When they move on to insert

Figure 8.1 Martha's and Rosa's shot-reverse-shot sequence, with the music track composed by another group.

camera angles, they do exactly this. Figure 8.1 shows the two shots in which Dr T and Jeff meet Cleopatra's guard.

As with the 6-year-olds in the previous example, the imaginative processes here which create the characters, the story and the setting are articulated through the grammar of the moving image. The girls editing the sequence in Figure 8.1 are having to work out how to create the narrative tension in the encounter between Dr T, Jeff and Cleopatra's guard. To do this, they need to employ the familiar shot-reverse-shot sequence of film grammar. However, although in a sense this is 'old news', since it is a formula they view and understand on TV and film most days of their lives, in another sense they are having to create it from new.

It is often argued that the continuity editing conventions of film are designed to be invisible, to produce an apparently seamless representation of reality which 'sutures' the viewer into its view. If this is true, it partly explains why, although children read the shot-reverse-shot convention repeatedly in their daily lives, when it comes to making their own films, it's as if they need to repeat a chapter of film-making history and discover it for themselves. This is creative work: a purposeful planning of how to represent a conversation through multiple points of view.

Recursive processes

These examples indicate that creativity, rather than being a kind of mystical divine gift, is something we can be specific about, nurture in particular ways and evaluate. The examples also give some sense of how learning progression works in media education: it is recursive rather than linear, as the outline curriculum for media in Chapter 11 will propose. In one sense, the 6-year-olds in the examples above are doing the same thing as the 11-year-olds: planning, filming and editing. Yet the examples also make it clear that these processes are becoming increasingly sophisticated, complex and diverse in their forms of representation, in ways teachers can recognise and build on. They are also multimodal: the example in Figure 8.1 shows how the girls have incorporated the music track composed and performed by another group. This raises the question of how media teaching might collaborate more broadly across the arts.

To sum up, then, we can say that creativity in media production builds on playful experiment, and involves:

- imaginative work, bringing images, ideas, stories, sounds into being in ways that are new, innovative, valuable;
- the use of and transformation of existing cultural resources – visual, auditory, material;
- the use of physical and conceptual tools, many of which are exactly those explored in the rhetorical and poetic work described earlier.

The present situation in England

Media education has existed in various versions of the National Curriculum as a sub-set of English, where, significantly, it has been located within the reading component. We saw earlier that it has been mandatory for schools in England (other than academies and free schools) to teach pupils how to 'read', or analyse, media texts, but not to 'write', or make them. Apart from anything else, this position has been inconsistent with the Office of Communication's statutory responsibility to promote the creation of media texts alongside the critical understanding of them. In the primary curriculum, media education has been even more weakly represented than in the secondary curriculum.

The disappearance of media from the new National Curriculum for English

In the new version of the National Curriculum for English in England (Department for Education, 2014a), media has been erased from all four Key Stages. This can only be seen as a politically motivated act by the government. Its inclinations can be deduced from the report it commissioned into Cultural Education (Department for Culture, Media and Sport, 2012), which rehearsed the case for the arts in education, with a heavy emphasis on the existing National Curriculum foundation subjects, art and music, a brief consideration of the merits of drama and dance as independent subjects (subsequently ignored by the government), and a lengthy set of proposals for extra-mural activities to cover the other art forms. These activities included film education; but the word 'media' and the phrases 'media studies' and 'media education' were conspicuously absent from the report.

There exists, then, no core entitlement in England for media education for all children, and no provision at all below Key Stage 4 and GCSE, where there are specialist courses. This is a woeful state of affairs. An education system supposedly preparing future citizens to take part in a society whose media, in all its manifestations, will profoundly affect their professional, social and personal lives has opted to ignore that fact; and, as other chapters have noted, has opted to ignore virtually all forms of digital and electronic expression and communication.

Chapter 11 proposes a comprehensive provision for media education from 3 to 11.

To conclude . . .

Language, literacy, literature, drama and media education belong together. They need and support each other; they stimulate and enliven each other; they also serve as correctives to each other's prejudices, restrictions of scope and intellectual limitations.

We need to move beyond the opposed stances of suspicion and reverence applied respectively to media texts and literary texts. So literature is out of its jacket, marked with the signs of its economic and material production, bleeding into other media, subject to the online transformations of fans able to rewrite the hallowed word with no respect for textual boundaries. Conversely, films, television drama, comic books and computer games have grown their own respectable histories, canons and heroic author-figures. They are collected, revered, curated, acknowledged by the institutions of high art which once reserved their attention for the traditional elite arts.

In this world of cultural reversals, teachers owe it to their pupils to make common cause across language, literacy, literature and media teaching: to embrace models of literacy which collapse the boundaries between elite and popular culture, between today's and yesterday's cultural moment, between the meaning and the structure of texts, between texts' use of language and of other modes. Nothing will be lost, and there is much to gain.

At present, these intentions are impeded by the abandonment of any reference to media education in the National Curriculum for English.

9 Learners of English as an additional language

John Richmond

The numbers

The Distinctiveness of English as an Additional Language: A Cross-Curriculum Discipline (*Working Paper 5*), edited by Hugh South, was published in 1999 by the National Association for Language Development in the Curriculum (NALDIC). NALDIC is the principal professional association for teachers concerned with English as an additional language (EAL). The paper correctly states that in the year of its publication there were 'more than 500,000 bilingual pupils in the school population'. Much more recent figures compiled by NALDIC show that in 2015:

> There are more than a million children between 5 and 16 years old in UK schools who speak in excess of 360 languages between them in addition to English. Currently there are 1,061,010 bilingual 5–16 year olds in English schools, 29,532 in Scotland, 10,357 'newcomer' pupils in Northern Ireland and 31,132 EAL learners in Wales. So the number of EAL learners in UK schools doubled between 1999 and 2014, and is likely to continue to grow.
>
> (NALDIC, 2015)

This is a significant group: approximately one in six of the total. It is important that teachers understand both what these EAL learners have in common with learners for whom English is a mother tongue (EMT), and what is distinctive about their situation and their needs.

The common ground

To state what EAL and EMT learners have in common is the easier task. Both groups need an experience of learning in which the learner's prior knowledge, skill and understanding are creatively challenged and extended by the learning tasks and contexts the teacher provides, so that the new knowledge, skill or understanding which the teacher wishes the learner to acquire are accessible.

The principles and the practices set out in all the preceding chapters in this book apply with equal force to EAL as to EMT learners.

The differences between EAL and EMT learners

Even a brief attempt to describe the difference between the positions of EAL and EMT learners will take a little longer. And there is no such thing as a 'typical' EAL learner. EAL learners differ from one another in their home languages, in the extent to which they are literate in those languages, and in their proficiency in oral and written English. Full and early bilingualism is increasingly common, and fluent literacy in both English and another language (or two) increasingly widespread.

However, here are five teaching principles which recognise the likely distinctive needs of the EAL learner as he or she strives to understand what is going on in the classroom and to meet the demands of the curriculum. They are drawn from a section in South (1999), the publication cited earlier.

How much does the learner know already?

First, teachers (which might mean classroom teachers, teaching assistants or teachers specifically assigned to support EAL learners) need a more precise understanding of EAL learners' prior knowledge of the content to be addressed, and of the degree of competence in English, with specific regard to that content, which the learner has. How much does he or she know already? What new aspect of competence in English, for example recognition of items of technical vocabulary, grasp of structure in laying out a piece of factual prose, understanding of the frequent use of the passive voice in scientific reports or the past tense in narrative, does he or she need to be introduced to in order to make sense of the new knowledge?

The need for greater explicitness in presentation

Second, the context for the introduction of new knowledge, skill or understanding needs to be presented with greater explicitness for EAL than for EMT learners. As children progress through the school system, the curriculum typically becomes more independent of context, more abstract. Teachers need to work against this tendency with their EAL learners. Visual and graphic supports – for example, sets of pictures, diagrams, maps or timelines – can help here. So can the teacher's more frequent and deliberate use of concrete examples and comparisons.

Production should be encouraged early

Third, while it is true that EAL learners engage in a great deal of what might be described as 'quiet learning' – learning which, while certainly not passive, is receptive and involves much listening and inference, they should also be encouraged to produce English, spoken, read or written, at whatever level of competence they can manage, from an early stage. It goes without saying that their efforts should be accorded generous praise.

The value of cross-language comparison

Fourth, and connected to the third principle, EAL learners (like learners of English as a foreign language and learners of a foreign language in school) are in an excellent position to develop metalinguistic awareness as their bi- or multilingual competence develops. If one can say more or less the same thing in more than one language, it is likely that one will sometimes want to describe how the two languages do a certain job similarly or differently. Similarity or difference may be in grammar or vocabulary or shades of meaning or direction of script. Teachers should draw EAL learners' attention to these similarities and differences, and encourage the use of linguistic terminology as appropriate to the learners' stage of development. This use can include terminology from the first language, especially if there is a teacher or another pupil who shares that language. It is easier to transfer a skill or a conceptual understanding from the stronger to the weaker language than to acquire it wholly through the weaker language. This is a good practical way to enhance pride in bi- and multilingualism, and to engage EMT learners in the discussion of these things too.

The need to keep a close check on progress

Fifth, teachers need to be aware of the progress EAL learners are making (or not making) from greater dependence (on contextual supports, on additional preparatory information, on adult help) towards independence in their learning. It may be argued that teachers need to be aware of this progress or lack of it with EMT learners too. They do. But because, typically, EAL learners need more support in the early stages, the gradual removal of that support, the gradual assumption that the EAL learner can cope without it, needs careful monitoring.

While it is true that most EAL learners can move quickly (within about two years) to a degree of fluency and comprehension enabling them to communicate with their EMT peers and to operate reasonably successfully in the classroom (the answers they give to a teacher's question, for example, show that they have some understanding of the topic being discussed), they are still a long way from having what Cummins (1984) describes as 'cognitive academic language proficiency' – the capacity to access and grasp the academic curriculum with the same likelihood of success as their EMT peers. It may take seven years, or longer, for them to achieve this proficiency. Hence the need for the teacher to maintain a close check on EAL learners' progress, so as to be sure that their rate of progress is not being held back by language issues where a specific intervention would clear an obstacle.

EAL learners and talk

Chapter 1 emphasised the fundamental role of the spoken language in all aspects of cognition and learning. It is *the* indispensable means of access to new knowledge, skill or understanding. And talk is the ground from which competence in literacy grows. Huge amounts of learning, much of it unconscious, occur as EAL learners listen to and absorb the English all around them, in school and in their world at large. This learning includes a developing grasp of the vocabulary, grammar and sound system of English, and all the paralinguistic and sociolinguistic customs and patterns (intonation, nodding and shaking of the head, turn-taking, polite ways of asking questions or of disagreeing, constructive ways of contributing to conversations) which EMT learners have usually acquired from early childhood.

It is vital that EAL learners are allowed the time and exposure for the essential receptive learning of all these things to take place. Teachers should not mistake silence for inattention. However, as the third of the teaching principles above says, EAL learners should 'also be encouraged to produce English, spoken, read or written, at whatever level of competence they can manage, from an early stage' and 'their efforts should be accorded generous praise'.

EAL learners and literacy

EAL learners with some experience of literacy in a language other than English are engaged in the complex process of simultaneously learning – as readers and writers – the writing systems of their first language and of English, and are making comparisons between them.

Nationally, EAL learners lagged behind first-language English speakers by a couple of percentage points in the 2014 Year 6 reading and writing tests in England, although there was large variation within and between language groups and within and between the local authorities and regions of England. In inner London, the same percentage of EAL and first-language English speakers (90 per cent) achieved level 4 in the reading and writing tests. Nationally, the two groups performed similarly on the grammar, punctuation and spelling test. Chinese girls consistently outperform everyone else, both EAL learners and first-language English speakers, although their advantage is narrowing (see Department for Education, 2015b).

Progress by EAL learners towards high levels of achievement in the reading and writing of English is increasingly notable in many schools. But there is still much to be done.

Reading

The reading classroom should contain books written in the first languages of EAL learners and in bilingual editions.

The left-to-right and top-to-bottom convention in English writing is just that, of course: a convention. Teachers should point it out as such to all the learners in a class. This understanding will be enhanced when there are EAL learners in the class who have some degree of literacy in writing systems which use other conventions.

Whereas first-language English readers can often infer the meanings of unfamiliar words from context, this has been shown to be a less reliable strategy for EAL learners (see, for example, Laufer, 2003). Bilingual books can help EAL learners check their understanding of the English. Encouraging young readers to read and talk about material written in their first language can have a positive consequence in terms of confidence and interest in reading books in English, as well as an immediate pay-off in terms of the experience of pleasure in reading and learning about specialist topics. There's also a significant body of research that shows EAL learners develop their command of vocabulary in the additional language through extensive reading in that language, so they should not be confined to a diet of shortened and simplified texts (see, for example, Coady, 1997, and Day and Mamford, 1998).

Writing

The EAL writer is trying to make meaning in English writing as best he or she can, and trying to meet all the demands on a writer discussed in Chapters 4 and 5. It is likely that some features of her or his first language will appear in English writing. These first-language features are markers of the fact that the first language uses a particular form (usually a grammatical construction) to make meaning differently from the way the thing is done in English. What the EAL learner does *not* need at this point is more abstract, less experience-based instruction. It is very useful if the teacher (or, more likely, a bilingual teaching assistant) knows enough about the child's first language to recognise the fact that the intervening feature has come from the first language, is able to point out why it is there in the English writing, and what its English equivalent is. In every other respect, the EAL learner needs the same balance of concern for content and support in the gradual acquisition of control of the writing system as the first-language English writer needs.

10 Speakers of non-standard varieties of English

John Richmond

A linguistically complex competence

Many children grow up in communities where the language of the home and the immediate community is a non-standard dialect of English or an English-based Creole, some of whose grammatical, lexical and sound features differ from their equivalents in Standard English. The linguistic situation of these children is often complex. Some of them, for example those with a background in the Caribbean who also use the indigenous non-standard dialect of the place in the UK where they live, have access to more than one non-standard variety of English. (Multilingual children use non-standard varieties of their languages too. Many of the Bengali-speaking children in schools in England, for instance, speak a form of the language significantly different from that of printed books.) These speakers may move between varieties of English or use mixtures of them as a result of often unconscious decisions made in context.

It is almost never the case nowadays that these children *only* speak a non-standard variety or varieties of the language. They are simultaneously aware of and influenced by Standard English. They come into contact with it through the media, through reading, in schooling: through their multiple contacts with the world beyond the home. And the language of the home is itself likely to use both standard and non-standard forms at different times.

The common ground which all varieties of English, including Standard English, share is vastly greater than the areas of difference.

Respect for difference

Schools and teachers have a responsibility to respect the language of a pupil's community and culture, whatever it is. In the past, some teachers have seen it as their responsibility to encourage or even force children to speak in the dialect associated with success as they, the teachers, perceive it, and as other powerful forces, such as employers, are said to perceive it. At its crudest, this approach equates Standard English with correct English. Under the apparent – and usually sincere – benevolence of a desire for their pupils to do well, some teachers have been the transmitters of the message that, to the extent that their pupils' language differs from Standard English pronounced in the accent of a white middle-class southerner, it is inadequate, inappropriate or incorrect. And it has come as a shock to be told that a form or a sound that a teacher thought of as wrong or rough is simply somebody else's. Engendering enormous heat in the argument, underlying it really, have been the facts about class in Britain. It has been difficult not to make instant and persistent judgements about the quality or intelligence of a person on the basis of the way he or she speaks, rather than on the basis of what he or she says, because class divisions and suspicions have been, and to a great extent still are, deeply rooted in British society.

A dilemma

The worst examples of teachers' rejection or belittling of pupils' non-standard speech are probably behind us. However, today's teachers still face a dilemma: they wish to respect the language of their pupils' communities and cultures; they also acknowledge that Standard English, in its spoken as well as its written form, has a currency unlike that of any other variety of the language in many of the social contexts for which they are supposed to be preparing their pupils. How may this dilemma be resolved?

There is no value in the attempt by teachers in Early Years settings or primary schools to standardise non-standard features in a child's speech. However kindly the attempt, it is likely to be taken by children as a critical comment on their language and therefore on them. There are so many more important things to work on in the development of children's language and literacy up to the age of 11, and children during the primary years often come unconsciously to understand the choices to be made in those cases where the grammar of a non-standard variety is different from that of Standard English.

Language diversity as a part of knowledge about language

Although the principal audience for this book is teachers of children up to age 11, I will briefly say how I think the dilemma just stated should be resolved in the secondary years. This will require a digression. Chapter 6 of this book, on grammar and knowledge about language, says that a characteristic of development in learners is the ability more and more to reflect consciously, abstractly, on language – their own and other people's – in use. This is why the government's new orders on the teaching of grammar have a wrong emphasis: primary-school pupils are to be taught an unrealistically large body of grammatical concepts and terminology, while secondary students are required merely to 'carry on the good work' – which, it is presumed, will have been done by the age of 11 – by applying these concepts and terminology to more advanced texts. The emphasis should be the opposite. Because secondary-school students are better able to reflect consciously and abstractly on language, there should be *more* analytical grammar teaching in the secondary than the primary years, not less.

Grammar teaching is best done as part of the teaching of a wider programme of knowledge about language, including teaching about language variety. In the context of such a programme, young people in secondary schools who have access to one or more non-standard varieties of English should be shown the standard equivalents of the non-standard forms in their speech, so that they are enabled to use oral Standard English for the purposes for which and in the contexts in which it is appropriate. In this way, young people come to understand that there are historical reasons for variety in English (and every other language): a 'double negative' or a non-standard verb inflection or an item of dialect vocabulary are not intellectual lapses. Older students have a good chance of seeing the value of the confident control of a wider speech repertoire, including Standard English, without that widening seeming to be a negative judgement on the language of their home background or of their peer group, and therefore a judgement on themselves.

Non-standard forms in writing

Some non-standard features find their way into the school writing of speakers of non-standard varieties of English. This writing, unless pupils are consciously using a non-standard variety as part of a story or playscript or poem, is in Standard English. Features of this kind are small in number, but they tend to be highly noticeable. Different ways of marking the past tense and the use of 'double negatives' are two common examples.

In working with pupils who have access to non-standard dialects or Creoles, it is useful if the teacher knows enough about a pupil's language background to recognise a non-standard feature when he or she sees one in the child's writing, to explain why it is there and what its Standard English equivalent is. The teacher needs to be able to distinguish between errors that any developing writer might make and examples of non-standard forms. The nature of the teacher's intervention, however, should be similar in the two cases: it should appeal to the pupil's developing knowledge of Standard English, derived from multiple encounters with it in speech and writing, while reassuring her or him that progress towards competence in written Standard English will not be impaired by this extra complexity. The worst thing a teacher could do, of course, would be to communicate in some way that non-standard forms are 'bad' or 'wrong' or 'illogical'. There are cases ('hisself' versus 'himself' and 'amn't I?' versus 'aren't I?', for example) where non-standard forms are more 'logical' than their standard equivalents.

Meanwhile, it is important to remember, as already stated in the section 'A linguistically complex competence', that the similarities which unite all forms of English – Standard and non-standard – greatly outnumber the differences between them. The fundamental principles about the teaching of writing apply with equal importance to children who have non-standard forms of English in their language repertoire as to children who only have access to Standard English.

11 An alternative curriculum for English 3 to 11

John Richmond

Andrew Burn has written the proposals on media.

General principles

The book so far has contained 'the argument': a statement or restatement of fundamental truths about how children acquire competence and confidence as users of language, and how teachers can best help them to do so. In the course of the argument, there has been careful and sometimes stringent criticism of the requirements of the statutory framework for the Early Years Foundation Stage and of the requirements for Key Stages 1 and 2 in the new version of the National Curriculum for English in England. This chapter contains a complete alternative curriculum for English 3 to 11, addressing the shortcomings of the Early Years Foundation Stage statutory framework and the new English orders, while incorporating material from those documents which can be welcomed.

Continuity

It will be seen that, as far as possible, the categories into which the alternative curriculum is divided are aligned horizontally (that is, across the modes of language) and vertically (that is, from one age group to another). Learning English and learning through English are essentially recursive processes in which common fundamental abilities and experiences are repeated in ever more demanding contexts as children move through the school system.

It will also be seen that the age categories here are simpler than those in the statutory orders. Key Stage 1 is not divided into two separate years, or Key Stage 2 into two two-year periods, as in the government's requirements. While seeking to justify the sub-divisions which it has introduced within Key Stages 1 and 2 of the new National Curriculum, the government itself acknowledges the practical difficulties which these sub-divisions bring:

The programmes of study for English are set out year-by-year for key stage 1 and two-yearly for key stage 2. The single year blocks at key stage 1 reflect the rapid pace of development in word reading during these two years. Schools are, however, only required to teach the relevant programme of study by the end of the key stage. Within each key stage, schools therefore have the flexibility to introduce content earlier or later than set out in the programme of study. In addition, schools can introduce key stage content during an earlier key stage if appropriate.

(Department for Education, 2014a: 17)

Teachers are always dealing with learners at varying stages of development, even when they are in the same year group, and it is teachers who are in a position to judge when best to introduce new knowledge, understanding and skill to individuals or to the class as a whole. Key Stages are administratively useful but educationally arbitrary divisions.

Malleable material

This alternative curriculum is offered as malleable material rather than as a set of tablets of stone. To change the metaphor, there are likely to be equally good or better ways of 'cutting up the cake' of the curriculum than those proposed here. I offer one warning only: any attempt to cut up the cake which fails to spot that similar ingredients run all the way through it will lead only to incoherence.

In its wording, the alternative curriculum attempts descriptions of the kinds of classroom learning that effective teachers continually strive for. It will be noticed that the modal verb 'should' appears nowhere. Teachers are not helped by that kind of prodding. However, I would be insincere not to admit that, implicitly, these descriptions are desiderata, not plain statements of what is already happening everywhere.

This book has already acknowledged that not all of the requirements of the Early Years Foundation Stage statutory framework and the new National Curriculum for English are ill-judged; some we can actively welcome. With that partial welcome freely conceded, it may nonetheless be that primary schools not bound by the National Curriculum – academies and free schools – would prefer to base their English teaching on the proposals here rather than on the government's offering. I hope that even those schools still bound by law to follow the new National Curriculum might find practical encouragement in the realisation that, in those areas where the government's requirements are inadequate or misguided, there is an alternative.

And let me return to the 'purest of ironies' mentioned in the book's introduction. The government has an 'aspiration' that more and more state schools in England shall become academies. As we say in the introduction, in May 2016 it hastily backtracked from its intention, announced only two months previously, to *force* all schools to become academies by 2022. Nonetheless, its March 2016 White Paper retains the promise that academies can choose to treat the National Curriculum 'as an ambitious benchmark which autonomous academies can use and improve upon' (Department for Education, 2016a: paragraph 1.55a). This alternative *is* such an improvement.

Sources

Most of what follows is my or Andrew Burn's own devising. However, I acknowledge the following sources for wording in some of the sections of the alternative curriculum.

Talk

The Early Years proposal for talk is simply a slight reworking of the government's existing statutory guidance (Department for Education, 2014c), which is perfectly acceptable. (In the cases of early reading and writing, however, where the government's Early Years statutory guidance on reading and writing is inadequate, there are clear alternatives.)

Writing

The proposals for writing occasionally draw on forms of words which have been used at earlier stages of the preparation, introduction and continual revision of the National Curriculum for English, for example in the Cox Report (The Cox Committee, 1989). Some of the wording in the sections on spelling and handwriting at the Early Years Foundation Stage and at Key Stages 1 and 2 is taken from *Understanding Spelling* (O'Sullivan and Thomas, 2000).[1]

Drama

The alternative curriculum for drama is indebted to three sources in particular for much of its wording: the objectives at 7 and 11 in *Drama from 5 to 16* (Her Majesty's Inspectorate, 1989: 3–5); the level descriptions for drama in *Drama in Schools* (Arts Council England, 2003: 35–40), which have been turned 'inside out' to create curriculum rather than assessment guidelines; and the guidelines for Drama in the Australian curriculum (ACARA, 2016).

The drama proposals could be regarded as a replacement for the collection of references to drama within the new National Curriculum for English, as an aide-memoire for the use of drama across the curriculum, or as the basis of a future curriculum for drama as a foundation subject of the National Curriculum.

Age-spreads

The alternative curriculum for talk, reading, writing, drama and media goes all the way from 3 to 11. The alternative curriculum for grammar starts at age five, and for knowledge about language at age seven.

Overlaps

The sections of the alternative curriculum are not watertight categories. Readers will quickly spot that there are overlaps between them. Those for talk, reading and writing have sub-categories linking each with the other two modes, and with drama. There are references to media elsewhere than in its own section. There are aspects of talk, reading and writing which point towards grammar and knowledge about language. These overlaps are deliberate; they are necessary characteristics of the whole reality that is language learning, however necessary it may be to divide the whole in order better to comprehend it.

Talk

Early Years Foundation Stage

- Communication and language development involve giving children opportunities to experience a rich language environment; to develop their confidence and skills in expressing themselves; and to speak and listen in a range of situations.

- Children express themselves effectively, showing awareness of listeners' needs. They talk about events that have happened, are happening or are about to happen in the future. They develop their own narratives and explanations by connecting ideas or events.
- Children listen attentively in a range of situations. They listen to stories, accurately anticipating key events and respond to what they hear with relevant comments, questions or actions. They give their attention to what others say and respond appropriately, while engaged in another activity.
- Children follow instructions involving several ideas or actions. They answer 'how' and 'why' questions about their experiences and in response to stories or events.

Key Stage 1

Play

- Pupils engage in collaborative, exploratory and imaginative play.

Links with other modes

- Pupils listen and respond orally and dramatically to stories, rhymes, poems, songs and information texts, printed and electronic, told, recited and read. They are helped to discuss their written work with other pupils and the teacher. They engage in drama, whether improvised on the basis of simple frameworks provided by the teacher, or using simple scripts.

Discussion

- Pupils discuss events in their own lives and in the life of the school, being encouraged to offer information and opinions in groups and to the class as a whole. The teacher takes every opportunity to show pupils how to extend initially simple or tentative utterances, for example by asking pupils to justify opinions they have offered.

Good listening

- Pupils learn how to pay proper attention to the speech of others, whether that of the teacher or of other pupils. They respond appropriately to instructions and suggestions. This attention begins to be demonstrated in the quality of their responses to the speech of others, whether in their own speech or in appropriate actions.

Media

- Pupils are given opportunities to respond orally to visual and electronic media.

Instrumental language

- Pupils are shown how to give and receive simple explanations, information and instructions, and how to ask and answer questions clearly. Within a structure provided by the teacher, they are shown how to plan learning activities requiring oral collaboration.

Oral performance

- Pupils tell stories and explore narratives, invented or based on models which they have read or heard.
- Pupils are helped to recite short poems which they have learned by heart.
- Pupils perform for others in the class, and sometimes – as in school assemblies – beyond the class. They learn the importance of being a responsive audience for others' performances.

Groupings for talk

- Pupils work in pairs, small groups and as a whole class.

Key Stage 2

Links with other modes

- The stories, poems, songs and information texts which pupils read and hear make increasing demands on their powers of comprehension and oral response. Pupils are helped to recount orally the essential matter of texts they have read and heard, and comment on those elements of the texts which they found particularly effective.
- Pupils' use of drama and role-play, both improvised and scripted, involves longer and more complex planning and preparation.
- When discussing their written work with the teacher, and when reading written work to a group or to the class as a whole, pupils are encouraged to reflect orally on the decisions they made in producing the writing as they did.

Discussion and argument

- When expressing opinions, or giving information in groups or to the class as a whole, pupils justify and support their statements.
- Pupils are introduced to the idea of argument: that the exchange of opinion and information will involve complexity and challenge. They are shown the difference between information and opinion in oral exchanges.
- The subject matter which the teacher introduces for discussion begins to range outside the lives of individuals, their families and the school, to take in topics in the wider world which are of concern to pupils.
- Drama and improvisation are used to provide opportunities for discussion and argument.

Summary

- Pupils learn how to summarise a group's collective opinion on a particular topic and how to report that summary to the class as a whole.

Good listening

- The teacher places increasing stress on the importance of good listening, praising those pupils who show, by their response to the contributions of others, that they have paid proper and sometimes critical attention to those contributions.

Media

- The visual and electronic media with which pupils engage gradually become more sophisticated and information-heavy, making greater demands on pupils' powers of inference and memory, so that their oral responses to those media are accordingly fuller, more nuanced and more complex.
- Pupils begin actively to produce media of their own, using whatever range of electronic technology is available to the school.

Instrumental language

- Pupils have opportunities to give and receive increasingly complex oral instructions in the course of engaging in collaborative activities. The planning of group activities makes greater demands on pupils' ability to co-operate and to arrive at consensus.

Oral performance

- The opportunities for performed oral work become more demanding. As well as telling stories and reciting poems individually, pupils engage in group performances of longer and more complex pieces which require planning, the assignment of parts, and some dramatic sense. These pieces are likely to involve prose and playscript as well as poetry.
- Pupils become more confident in performing for others in the class and for audiences beyond the class. They learn to be an appreciative audience for adult performers – for example, actors, poets, musicians and storytellers – working in or outside the school.

Groupings for talk

- Pupils work in pairs, small groups and as a whole class.

Reading

Early Years Foundation Stage

- Children are introduced to picture books, which the teacher or other adult reads to and with them individually, in small groups or as a whole class. The picture books contain stories, poems, songs and rhymes, and simple information texts. The teacher makes particular use of picture books with repetitive language structures.
- Children are encouraged to pay attention to meaningful print in the immediate setting in which they are learning, and on visits beyond the setting.
- Children are encouraged to discuss, with the teacher and amongst themselves, the books and other meaningful print they encounter. The teacher encourages children to take over and join in with the reading of those parts of books and other print that they recognise.
- In the course of the reading they undertake with children, the teacher takes the opportunity to point out grapho-phonic regularities in pairs or larger groups of words. The word displays in the settings in which children are learning also feature some of these regularities.
- Children are shown the written forms of their names and are helped to read them.
- Children learn the letters of the alphabet and are introduced to some of the speech sounds the letters represent.

Key Stage 1

The content of reading

- Pupils continue to read picture books, collections of poems, songs and rhymes, folk tales, myths, legends, historical and contemporary stories, and information texts.
- Pupils' own writing forms part of the resources which the teacher uses to promote reading.
- Especially in classrooms where there are pupils learning English as an additional language, books are available in the pupils' first language(s) and in bilingual editions.
- Pupils are surrounded by meaningful print in the classroom, in addition to that in books. This print is present in and on labels, captions, notices, sets of instructions, plans, maps, diagrams, and word and sentence displays. Pupils often listen to and watch audio and audio-visual resources which combine sound, picture and text.
- Pupils are introduced to texts as sources of reference. They are shown how to use dictionaries and encyclopaedias, printed and electronic, appropriate to their age group. They are shown the purpose of contents lists and indexes in books.

The clues to successful reading

- As a result of frequent and pleasurable encounters with books, pupils build up a vocabulary of whole words that they recognise on sight.
- Pupils are helped to use all the clues or cues which readers need to make successful sense of print and other writing. These clues or cues are: semantic, syntactic, grapho-phonic, pictorial, textual and bibliographic.
- Pupils are helped to an understanding of the grapho-phonic regularities which exist in written English words. Letter-to-phoneme regularities and regularities in onsets and rimes are pointed out in the course of reading, and examples of such regularities are in evidence in classroom displays. It is made clear to pupils that such regularities are partial, not complete; there are many words, especially amongst those that pupils encounter most commonly, which do not observe such regularities.
- Building on their knowledge of the letters of the alphabet, pupils learn more of the diversity of speech sounds which letters, especially vowels, commonly make in the context of different words.

Links with other modes

- Pupils have opportunities to relate their reading to their spoken language. In addition to talking to the teacher and to each other about their reading, they recite, retell and dramatise texts they have read.
- In their own writing, pupils have opportunities to retell or adapt texts they have read.

Groupings for reading

- The teacher arranges for a variety of groupings for reading. He or she regularly shares books with the whole class, inviting pupils' participation in the reading and discussion of the text. The teacher also organises the class into small groups in which, regularly, the same text is being read and discussed by pupils, with the support of the adults working in the room.
- The teacher often listens to the reading of individual pupils.
- Pupils discover the pleasure of independent reading.

Key Stage 2

The content of reading

- Pupils have continual opportunities to read high-quality, pleasure-giving texts. These texts cover a wide range of genres: realistic contemporary and historical fiction, traditional stories such as fairy stories, myths and legends, plays, poetry, information texts and discursive writing.
- Pupils become confident in the use of reference sources such as encyclopaedias, dictionaries and thesauruses, printed and electronic.
- Pupils are shown how meaningful continuous text often combines with other modes, such as illustrations, diagrams, maps and captions, to communicate narratives, ideas and information in both printed and electronic resources.
- In studying poetry, pupils are shown something of the range of forms, terms and techniques which poets and poems use.
- Pupils' own writing forms part of the resources for reading.
- Pupils encounter texts which extend their existing competence as readers and have opportunities to read fast and easily texts well within their existing competence.
- Especially in classrooms where there are pupils learning English as an additional language, books are available in the pupils' first language(s) and in bilingual editions.

- Pupils listen to and view readings on DVD, radio, television and the internet. They watch filmed versions of books and discuss the differences between the film and the book.

The skills of successful reading

- Those pupils who have not by Year 3 achieved fluency as decoders of text are offered more intensive help in learning to use all the clues or cues which readers need to make successful sense of print and other writing. These clues or cues are: semantic, syntactic, grapho-phonic, pictorial, textual and bibliographic.
- Pupils are shown some of the more advanced skills which successful readers employ in order to construct meaning from texts. These include:

  - following the narrative of a piece of writing (whether imaginative or factual), inferring what is happening and speculating about what may come next;
  - interpreting ideas and themes in a text, and forming questions and comments during and after reading;
  - skimming, scanning and selecting in order to locate and record information;
  - comparing and combining information from different sources;
  - describing the features, fabric and fun of language in literary and other texts;
  - learning and making use of appropriate terminology in discussion of texts.

Links with other modes

- Pupils have regular opportunities to discuss their reading with other pupils and with the teacher, articulating their responses to what they have read and listening carefully to the responses of others. They respond to their reading in drama and role-play.
- Pupils' increasing familiarity with a range of kinds of text leads them to try out for themselves some of this range in their own writing.

Groupings for reading

- The teacher arranges for a variety of groupings for reading. He or she frequently reads aloud to the whole class, often inviting pupils' participation in the reading and discussion of a text. He or she also organises the class into small groups in which the same text is being read and discussed by pupils. There are also regular opportunities for individual, independent reading of books chosen by the pupil, with guidance from the teacher.

- Pupils recommend books they have read to other pupils, giving reasons for their choices.
- The teacher sometimes listens to the reading of individual pupils.

Writing

Early Years Foundation Stage

- Children are encouraged to draw pictures and to accompany the pictures with 'writing' explaining what the pictures represent. This 'writing' may be emergent writing, in that the marks do not correspond at all to conventional letters and words, or a mixture of emergent writing and conventional letters and words.
- Children are encouraged to include writing, for example notices and signs, in their dramatic play. They are provided with materials enabling them to do so. Children write about the imaginative content of their play.
- Role-play offers starting points for later writing.
- The teacher provides models of writing in the books shared with the children: story books; books of poems, rhymes and songs; the simplest information books. The writing the teacher asks children to do often emerges from this shared reading.
- The teacher models writing herself or himself by writing publicly for and with the children, asking them for contributions to the writing.
- The classroom is rich in meaningful print. The teacher continually draws children's attention to the print, reading it and explaining what it means.
- Children have some early handwriting practice. The teacher begins to teach handwriting by manual demonstrations of how letters are formed. Children practise the forming of letters by movement of their hands and arms, tracing the letters in the air before practising them on paper; by tracing letters in sand; by making letters from play dough; and using templates. The teacher scribes groups of words for children who are not confident enough to write at all, and shows them how to write underneath a group of words that he or she has written, or to trace over the words using tracing paper.
- Children are shown how to write their own names and are introduced to the alphabet and to the names of the letters.
- When children make use of phonetic or idiosyncratic spellings, the teacher praises the boldness of their efforts, while sometimes also saying 'This is how we see it written down'.

Key Stage 1

The content of writing

- Pupils continue to produce short texts, often descriptive captions for their drawings.
- The range of pupils' writing widens, to include: imaginative stories, accounts of real-life experiences, poems, letters, responses to artistic experiences, simple playscripts, diaries, writing in role as historical or mythical figures, reports of science experiments, recipes. All these kinds of writing may be produced using digital and electronic equipment as well as with pen and paper.

The distribution of writing

- Pupils are shown that most writing is to be read and enjoyed by a readership wider than the teacher, though the teacher is a vitally important reader. Writing is regularly read aloud to the class; it is displayed on the classroom walls; it is combined into books or booklets to form part of the class's library; it is read aloud at events beyond the classroom, such as school assemblies. Writing on computers, or writing transferred from paper to computer, is shared electronically with classes in other schools.

Links with other modes

- Pupils are introduced to a wide range of longer texts, which the teacher reads to the class as a whole, and which pupils read in groups and individually. Oral work, such as storytelling, the recounting by pupils of recent experiences, and improvised drama, is a starting point for writing. On the basis of this range of reading and oral work, pupils are shown how to write longer texts themselves.

The modelling of writing

- Teachers engage in shared writing with pupils, using a flip chart or blank big books or the whiteboard. In the course of this shared writing, they teach about the content and structure of texts and about conventions of the writing system.

Groupings for writing

- As well as taking part in writing as a collective activity involving the teacher and the whole class, pupils write in pairs and small groups. They are encouraged to offer each other ideas, comment on each other's work and help each other with conventions, for example spellings.
- There are also occasions when pupils write quietly and individually.

The writing system

SPELLING

- The classroom contains a wide range of resources for spelling, including alphabet cards and strips, alphabet books and early dictionaries, name cards showing pupils' names in upper and lower case, word banks relating to work currently being done in the class, displays of groups of words which exhibit spelling patterns, and displays of common, high-frequency words which need to be learned individually.
- Through shared reading and writing, the teacher teaches the spellings of some of the many common words which do not conform to regular spelling patterns and shows pupils that there are regular spelling patterns by which other words may be grouped.
- Although always willing to give spellings, the teacher encourages pupils to be independent in their efforts to spell conventionally: to 'have a go' first; to consult a word bank or dictionary, classroom-made or published; to ask a friend; to write out the word in different ways before looking it up. Pupils have personal spelling journals. Once new correct spellings are in the spelling journal, pupils are shown how to practise them using the Look–Say–Cover–Write–Check routine.
- Once pupils begin to produce continuous texts, the teacher introduces them to simple proofreading habits.

PUNCTUATION

- Through shared reading and writing, pupils are taught about conventions of punctuation appropriate for this age group, including the correct use of capital letters, full stops, commas, question marks, exclamation marks, apostrophes and speech marks.
- Examples of the correct punctuation of phrases and sentences are displayed around the classroom.

LAYOUT

- Pupils are shown a variety of ways of laying out their writing, for example how to combine writing with illustration in engaging ways. They are introduced to the use of paragraphs and chapters in prose and verses in poetry.
- Teachers show pupils how to explore the more flexible possibilities of layout on computers.

Handwriting

- Work on pupils' handwriting, begun at the Early Years Foundation Stage, continues. (See the teaching methods suggested in the alternative curriculum for the Early Years Foundation Stage.)
- The teacher teaches letter formation either by grouping letters which are similarly formed, or according to the frequency of their usage, beginning with the most frequently used letters. He or she points out the value of the fluent handwriting of frequently used groups of letters in internalising common spelling patterns.
- While they are writing, pupils are able to see alphabet strips (lower and upper case) using correct letter formation.
- Familiar songs, rhymes, poems and phrases such as proverbs can be used for handwriting practice.

Key Stage 2

The content of writing

- The range of forms of writing to which pupils are introduced and which they attempt includes: chronological accounts, descriptions, discursive essays, poems, prose stories, playscripts, diaries, letters, writing for formal or public purposes such as a speech, sets of instructions, writing in response to direct experience and to stimuli such as stories, poetry, films on television, DVD or online.
- These forms of writing are employed to achieve a range of purposes, including: to recount, to re-present, to remember, to explain, to instruct, to advocate, to discuss, to narrate, to distil a thought or idea in concise terms, to respond to an aesthetic experience.

The distribution of writing

- The media by which forms of and purposes for writing are communicated includes: handwritten scripts on paper, word-processing on screen, physical book-making, wall displays, poster campaigns, blogs, web publishing, emails, reading aloud, staged and filmed presentations.
- Pupils write for a variety of audiences, in addition to the teacher, in and beyond the classroom, including: other pupils in the class, pupils in other classes in the school and in neighbouring schools, other groups in the local community, groups around the UK and internationally reached through the internet.

The composition of writing

- Pupils have the opportunity to fashion and change their work, redrafting and polishing it until it brings satisfaction and pleasure both to the writer and to the reader.

Links with other modes

- Pupils have opportunities for the copious reading of high-quality texts – factual, instructional, persuasive and imaginative – which help them to develop competence and confidence in handling forms of and purposes for writing. They are shown how writers craft texts to achieve particular meanings and effects.
- Oral work often precedes writing. Sometimes writing emerges from improvised drama.
- Pupils' writing often combines with the other modes of language, for example in oral presentations which include performed, quoted or displayed writing, or in part-scripted, part-improvised drama.

The modelling of writing

- As at Key Stage 1, teachers engage in shared writing with pupils, in the course of which they teach about the content and structure of different kinds of text and about conventions of the writing system.

Groupings for writing

- As well as taking part in writing as a collective activity involving the teacher and the whole class, pupils write in pairs and small groups. They offer each other ideas, comment on each other's work and help each other with conventions of the writing system. Digital media such as class blogs provide good opportunities for this kind of collaboration.
- There are also occasions when pupils write quietly and individually.

The writing system

SPELLING

- Teachers draw pupils' attention to common spelling patterns in English. Some of the many English spellings which have to be learned as a whole are displayed on the classroom walls, appearing in the context of meaningful sentences.
- Pupils are shown the use of dictionaries, printed and electronic, appropriate for their age group, and of appropriate spelling apps on tablet computers and other digital equipment.
- Pupils are encouraged to be independent in their efforts to spell conventionally, although the teacher should always be prepared to give spellings if pupils' independent strategies have failed.
- Pupils have personal spelling journals in which to note new correct spellings. They are shown how to practise them using the Look–Say–Cover–Write–Check routine.
- When pupils write on computers, they use the spellchecker (set to UK English spelling conventions), while being warned that spellcheckers are not infallible; they cannot detect homonyms or homophones.
- Pupils become familiar with the habit of proofreading the drafts of their texts.

PUNCTUATION

- Teaching of the most common features of punctuation (capital letters, full stops, commas, question marks, exclamation marks, apostrophes and speech marks) continues as at Key Stage 1, in the context of the study of meaningful sentences and texts, including texts produced by pupils. Other punctuation marks (semi-colons, colons, brackets) are introduced in the same way.

LAYOUT

- Pupils are shown how writing is laid out in handwritten and word-processed prose and in printed books, including the use of paragraphs, chapters and sections within chapters. They learn about the layout of different kinds of poetry, of playscript and of writing used in conjunction with illustrations, as in comic books.
- Pupils are shown how print is laid out on the internet and how writing using different font styles and sizes can combine with other modes, for example images, sounds and colour, to maximise its effect. Pupils try out the more flexible possibilities of layout which computers offer.

Handwriting and typing

- Employing the same approaches as are recommended for use at Key Stage 1, teachers help those pupils who have not developed a clear, relaxed and individual handwriting style by Year 3 to do so.
- From Year 3 onwards, pupils are taught to use a computer keyboard, with the aim that they are able to type at least as fast as they can handwrite.

Standard English

- When features of non-standard English or features deriving from the first language of an EAL learner are inadvertently used in pupils' Standard English writing, the teacher points out those features and says what their standard equivalents are. Pupils may sometimes consciously use non-standard forms in their writing, for example in some poetry and in the dialogue of stories and plays.

Grammar and knowledge about language

Key Stage 1 – grammar

- In the course of their reading of texts presented by the teacher, pupils are shown examples of *nouns*, *verbs*, *adjectives*, *adverbs*, *pronouns* and *connectives*, and are introduced to these terms. Pupils are asked to identify examples of these *classes* of word in their own and in others' writing. The classroom has displays of such examples.

- Pupils are introduced to the idea of a *sentence* (a group of words which expresses a complete, finished thought or idea). They are shown how a sentence can be constructed (during which they are shown the purpose of simple *connectives*) and how sentences, placed one after the other, can build towards an effective continuous text.

Key Stage 2 – grammar

- Pupils are introduced to different kinds of noun (*common*, *proper*, *collective*, *abstract*); to the idea that verbs can express states and feelings as well as actions; to the diversity of kinds of adjective, adverb and pronoun. They are introduced to the word classes *article*, *preposition*, *exclamation*.
- Pupils are introduced to the idea of *phrase* (a group of words which does not contain a verb) and to the idea of *clause* (a group of words containing a verb, which can also be a sentence but does not have to be).
- Pupils are introduced to the idea of *noun*, *verb*, *adjectival* and *adverbial phrases*.
- The idea of clause is linked to the introduction of three kinds of sentence: *simple*, *compound* and *complex*. Teaching about *complex sentences* leads to the introduction of the idea of the *subordinate clause*.
- Pupils learn about another distinction in sentences: that between *statement*, *question*, *command* and *exclamation*.
- Pupils are shown examples of deliberately *incomplete sentences*: sentences with no verb, which may contain no more than one word, which writers have used to achieve special effects.
- Pupils are introduced to the idea of the *subject* of a sentence. Complete sentences (except some commands and exclamations) must have a subject and a verb. Some sentences also have an *object*. The object can be *direct* or *indirect*.
- Pupils are shown the difference between *simple present*, *simple future* and *simple past tenses* in verbs.

Key Stage 2 – knowledge about language

- Pupils are shown that many words operate in *word families*. Often, individual words within families are distinguished by *prefixes* and/or *suffixes*. At the heart of a family of words is a *root word*.

- Pupils are introduced to simple *etymology*, so that they have some understanding of the historical and linguistic origins of some common words.
- Pupils are shown examples of *synonyms* and *antonyms* and are introduced to these terms.
- Pupils are shown examples of texts from different periods, so that they have some understanding of how writers' use of vocabulary has changed over time.
- Pupils are taught about some aspects of variety in contemporary English, for example the use of different accents, dialects and word usages in Britain, Ireland and across the English-speaking world.
- Pupils are introduced to the beginnings of *text grammar*: that is, they are shown how sentences, paragraphs and longer chunks of text relate to each other in different ways, depending on the kind of writing being studied.

Drama

Early Years Foundation Stage

Making

- Children play inventively and with concentration, both alone and with others. They take on roles and engage in action in their play.
- Children use role-play areas provided by the teacher and suggest ideas of their own for planning and creating role-play areas.

Presenting

- Children take part in simple dramatic presentations to the class, based on stories which the teacher has told or read, or on situations which the teacher has suggested.
- Children use voice, facial expression, gesture, movement and space in their presentations.
- Children use simple aids to performance, such as the dressing-up box.

Responding

- Children respond to the intervention of the teacher as a participant in role-play.
- Children respond to the simple dramatic presentations they watch, both as audience and as commentators on what they have seen.

Key Stage 1

Making

- Pupils engage in drama games introduced by the teacher.
- Pupils move beyond play towards an awareness of the aesthetic nature of drama.
- Pupils discover the disciplines and pleasures of working with other pupils in role-play, improvisation and the preparation of presentations.
- Pupils begin to recognise the need to practise presentations to make them better.
- Pupils have opportunities to play a character or put across a particular point of view in drama, through speech, gesture or action.
- Pupils prepare and learn by heart a few lines in scripted performances.
- Pupils are introduced to some of the techniques of improvised drama.
- Pupils are introduced to some of the techniques of theatre.

Presenting

- Pupils participate in group and whole-class dramas.
- Pupils are introduced to simple scripted dramas of one or more scenes.
- Pupils learn to take turns in speaking parts, whether in improvised or scripted presentations.
- Pupils use their voices and bodies to create characters and atmospheres, employing language appropriate to those characters and atmospheres.

Responding

- Pupils come to understand and take pleasure in the difference between 'real' and 'pretend'; in adult terms, they are helped to reflect on the symbolic nature of drama.
- Pupils are able to explain the key differences between a play and a story in prose or poetry.
- Pupils are able to comment on a presentation with the beginnings of critical judgement: what were the 'good' and 'not so good' things about the presentation? What would make it better? What was their favourite moment as spectators?

Key Stage 2

Making

- Pupils become confident in the dramatic portrayal, individually or in groups, of characters and situations taken from literature, oral storytelling, factual sources or situations introduced by the teacher, derived from elements of any subject or area of the curriculum.
- Pupils become familiar with several of the techniques of process drama.
- Pupils learn how to take material from existing sources and express it in dramatic form.
- Pupils learn by heart longer parts in scripted dramas.
- Pupils learn how to structure longer and more complex dramatic sequences.
- With the help of models of written drama provided by the teacher, pupils begin to write play scripts, initially of single scenes, later moving on to multi-scene scripts.
- Pupils develop their skill as collaborators, negotiating the content of the drama, roles to be taken and responsibility for making or acquiring necessary equipment, in drama work done for its own sake or in preparation for a presentation.

Presenting

- Pupils show increasing control of and subtlety in portrayal of character, development of tension, use of humour, comedy, poignancy and surprise, in presentations, scripted, semi-scripted or wholly improvised.
- Pupils carry out dramatic intentions with clear but unforced control over movement and voice.
- Pupils explore the use of elements of theatre such as staging, dramatic structure, props, costumes, sound and lighting to increase the impact of presentations.
- Pupils begin to use modern media and electronic technology to enhance and support their work in drama.
- Pupils have opportunities to perform presentations for audiences in addition to other members of the class (for example to other classes in the school, including classes of younger pupils, to school assemblies and in performances to which parents and the wider community are invited).

Responding

- Pupils develop an understanding of generic repertoire in drama, for example by seeing and comparing: television and film dramas of various kinds, including animation; theatrical genres such as puppetry and mime, as well as conventionally staged presentations by human players using language and action; scripted, semi-scripted and wholly improvised dramas; realistic, mythic and fantasy dramas; comedy and tragedy.
- Pupils advance their understanding of some of the techniques of theatre and of drama on film and television.
- Pupils have the experience of being taken to theatrical productions outside school, and of watching and participating in theatrical events in school provided by outsiders.
- Pupils recognise strengths and weaknesses in their own and others' dramas through critical observation of and comment on the characters created, the issues involved and the processes employed.

Media

Early Years Foundation Stage

Reading media

- Children view children's TV programmes and films together in class. They talk about these experiences, expressing their own likes and dislikes.

Writing media

- Children role-play favourite characters from TV and film.
- Children re-present their favourite films, programmes and other media (for example, by making posters of them).

Setting the media in their context

- Children discuss friends' and family's media preferences.
- Children discuss rules about media use in the family and school; they invent their own rules.

Key Stage 1

Reading media

- Pupils experience, enjoy and discuss different media, especially film, TV and games, as a whole class.
- Pupils explore early understandings of who makes the media.
- Pupils explore early understandings of how media texts are put together to make meaning.
- Pupils explore early understandings of media audiences, moving from themselves and their families to others.

Writing media

- Pupils make short print-media texts, including comics and magazines.
- Pupils make, act for and edit short films.

Setting the media in their context

- Pupils explore how texts are connected (for example, how the *Harry Potter* stories exist as books, films, games and merchandise).
- Pupils explore media histories (for example, how adverts from the 1950s are different from today's).
- Pupils explore media regulation further (for example, by being taught about and discussing the TV watershed).

Key Stage 2

Reading media

- Pupils experience and enjoy class viewings of TV and film, including full-length movies, and discuss these.
- Pupils collectively play and discuss age-appropriate electronic games.
- Pupils organise media texts in categories such as genre.
- Pupils compare their own media preferences with those of others.
- Pupils explore media institutions and audiences through practical research projects.

Writing media

- Pupils make more complex media texts, such as news broadcasts, longer edited films, simple video games and websites/blogs. They re-present their own experiences of film, TV, print media, games and social media in these productions.
- Pupils make media texts to represent ideas, social groups and individuals.
- Pupils make media texts for identified audiences.

Setting the media in their context

- Pupils explore more complex links between texts, such as remakes and adaptations over time.
- Pupils explore links between texts and narratives in English, drama and media (for example, book, stage adaptation, film and video games of Pullman's *Northern Lights*).
- Pupils explore more detailed regulatory practices, such as age-labelling systems on films and games, and who produces them.

Note

1 Reproduced by permission of the Centre for Literacy in Primary Education, www. clpe.org.uk.

12 Assessment 3 to 11

John Richmond

General principles

Curriculum and assessment have an interactive and mutual influence on one another. A central principle ought to be: decide on your curriculum first; then decide how to assess progress within that curriculum effectively. Too often, the order of priority of attention to the two things has been the opposite. But even within a right understanding of the relationship, modes of assessment have a profound effect on what is taught and learned in the curriculum, and how it is taught and learned.

The introduction to this book noted the irony of the government's intention that the National Curriculum, currently a statutory document and one which has been laboured over in its many versions for many years, becomes merely an advisory document when state schools in England become academies. However, as also remarked in the introduction, and as the government is well aware, it is through the system of tests and examinations that a government can exert closer control over classrooms than through the requirements or advice of a curriculum statement.

In the book so far, there have been occasional references to current and planned tests and other assessment arrangements affecting children up to age 11. This chapter assembles in one place a critique of these tests and other assessment arrangements, and offers practical, educationally prefer-able alternatives in every case where current or planned arrangements are unsatisfactory.

Early Years Foundation Stage

Early Years Foundation Stage profile

One tool for formal assessment at the Early Years Foundation Stage is the Early Years Foundation Stage profile, which has been in operation in one form or another since 2003, and which accumulates findings about a child's achievements throughout the reception year, leading to the completion of the profile as a written document during the last term of that year.

The Early Years Foundation Stage profile (Standards and Testing Agency, 2015a) is a broadly enlightened instrument. The principles on which it is based are admirable:

> *Reliable and accurate assessment at the end of the EYFS is underpinned by the following principles:*
>
> - *Assessment is based primarily on the practitioner's knowledge of the pupil. Knowledge is gained predominantly from observation and interaction in a range of daily activities and events.*
> - *Responsible pedagogy must be in place so that the provision enables each pupil to demonstrate their learning and development fully.*
> - *Embedded learning is identified by assessing what a pupil can do consistently and independently in a range of everyday situations.*
> - *An effective assessment presents a holistic view of a pupil's learning and development.*
> - *Accurate assessments take account of contributions from a range of perspectives including the pupil, their parents and other relevant adults.*
>
> *(ibid.: 7)*

A section of the guidance entitled 'Responsible pedagogy' contains an eloquent statement of the right relationship between teaching and assessment:

> *Responsible pedagogy enables each pupil to demonstrate learning in the fullest sense. It depends on the use of assessment information to plan relevant and motivating learning experiences for each pupil. Effective assessment can only take place when children have the opportunity to demonstrate their understanding, learning and development in a range of contexts.*
>
> *Pupils must have access to a rich learning environment which provides them with the opportunities and conditions in which to flourish in all aspects of their development. The learning environment should provide balance across the areas of learning. Integral to this is an ethos which*
>
> - *respects each child as an individual;*
> - *values pupils' efforts, interests and purposes as instrumental to successful learning.*
>
> *(ibid.: 8)*

The formal profile document requires teachers to judge, at the end of a child's reception year, whether he or she is meeting or exceeding a level expected at the end of the Early Years Foundation Stage in each of 17 'early learning goals descriptors', or is best described as being at an 'emerging level' in each of the goals.

The goals are grouped within three 'prime areas of learning': communication and language; physical development; personal, social and emotional development; and within four 'specific areas of learning': literacy, mathematics, understanding the world, expressive arts and design.

These are combined with 'a short narrative describing the pupil's 3 characteristics of effective learning' (*ibid.*: 4), which are 'playing and exploring', 'active learning' and 'creating and thinking critically' (*ibid.*: 19).

There is a discussion to be had about whether 17 goals and 3 key characteristics of learning amount to an over-complex description of a child's achievement at the end of the reception year. I would favour a simplification, leading to the reduction of the number of goals to seven, making them coterminous with the three prime and the four specific areas of learning.

The overall excellence of the intention of the profile is spoiled, so far as the judgements on literacy are concerned, by the intrusion into the learning goals for reading and writing of the government's overriding obsession with phonics. Those two learning goals (or, in my simpler model, a single goal for literacy development) could be rewritten so as represent a broader understanding of how young children's powers of literacy develop. However, to stick to the bigger picture, the Early Years Foundation Stage profile gives teachers at Key Stage 1 ample information as to the achievements and needs of pupils beginning Year 1.

Baseline assessment: a bad idea abandoned

The other tool for formal assessment at the Early Years Foundation Stage, intended to come into full effect from September 2016, was to have been 'baseline assessment'.

Baseline assessment would have made a judgement on children's attainment in English and mathematics at the beginning of their reception year. The government approved three providers (a number reduced from six) as designers of the assessments. Schools could choose the provider they preferred. They could also choose a provider other than one approved by the government, but in that case 'we won't reimburse any costs and or report your progress' (Standards and Testing Agency, 2016). Baseline assessment was not compulsory; the original guidance, issued in February 2015 was as follows:

> *Government-funded schools that wish to use the reception baseline assessment from September 2015 should sign up with an approved provider before the start of the academic year. In 2022 we'll then use whichever measure shows the most progress: either your reception baseline to key stage 2 results, or your key stage 1 results to key stage 2 results.*
>
> *From September 2016 primary schools will only be able to use reception baseline to key stage 2 results to measure progress. If you choose not to use the reception baseline, from 2023 we'll only hold you to account by your pupils' attainment at the end of key stage 2.*
>
> (*ibid.*)

As may be seen, baseline assessment was to become the only measure officially recognised by the government as the starting point for assessment of children's achievement from reception year onwards. The status of the Early Years Foundation Stage profile would inevitably have been downgraded.

It's clear that the government's preoccupation, in attempting to introduce baseline assessment, was with primary schools' overall accountability over a seven-year period. This preoccupation conflicts with the kind of enlightened understanding of the relationship between assessment and actual progress, a statement of which I quoted earlier: 'Responsible pedagogy . . . depends on the use of assessment information to plan relevant and motivating learning experiences for each child'.

It was obvious to any thoughtful observer that the plans for baseline assessment were flawed. Why allow schools to choose between three providers? How could comparability thus be assured? In contrast, there is only one provider for the Early Years Foundation Stage profile and the tests at Key Stages 1 and 2. Why make baseline assessment voluntary, but then say that the forthcoming Key Stage 1 tests of reading (compulsory) and of grammar, punctuation and spelling (optional) and the teacher assessment of writing would not, from September 2016, be regarded as an accountability marker in judging schools' performance four years later, at the end of Key Stage 2? Was there a veiled threat in the government's guidance on this: 'If you choose not to use the reception baseline, from 2023 we'll only hold you to account by your pupils' attainment at the end of key stage 2'?

It is remarkable that these profound shortcomings were not evident to the government long before its last-minute announcement in April 2016 (Department for Education, 2016b) that baseline assessment would not after all be used for accountability purposes. Schools would still have the option to use an assessment tool from one or other of the three providers in the 2016–2017 academic year and would be funded by the Department for Education to do so. But the attempt to use baseline assessment, in its planned form, as the starting point of a system of accountability over seven years was abandoned.

> *Key stage 1 (KS1) will continue to be used as the starting point from which to measure this year's reception pupils' progress to KS2. We remain committed to measuring the progress of pupils through primary school and will continue to look at the best way to assess pupils in the early years.*
>
> (*ibid.*)

At the time of writing, there is no indication as to the government's progress in continuing 'to look at the best way to assess pupils in the early years'. My suggestion for doing this follows.

Early Years Foundation Stage: an alternative proposal for assessment

To provide a 'floor level' of children's achievement in spoken language, literacy and mathematics, I propose that reception-class teachers use the tripartite system of 'emerging', 'meeting' and 'exceeding' levels already built into the Early Years Foundation Stage profile arrangements. The teachers could make these brief assessments a few weeks after meeting the children, once they have got to know them well.

A simpler form of the existing Early Years Foundation Stage profile, with 7 learning goals rather than 17, and retaining the short descriptions of the 3 key characteristics of effective learning, could then be used as the fuller account of children's achievements and needs at the end of the reception year, to be handed on to the children's teachers at Year 1. These assessments would be externally moderated.

Key Stages 1 and 2

The position until summer 2015

Key Stage 1

Until summer 2015, pupils at the end of Year 2 were assessed by their teachers in reading, writing, and speaking and listening. For reading and writing, teachers used tasks designed in 2007 or 2009 to make their assessments.

A selection of teacher assessments of reading and writing in a minimum of 25 per cent of schools in each local authority was externally moderated.

Teachers' judgements of pupils' achievement in the spoken language were not externally moderated.

These assessments led to the assignment of a National Curriculum level in the three modes.

In addition, since 2012, Year 1 pupils have undergone a 'phonics check', intended to test their grasp of synthetic phonics in reading. As discussed in Chapter 2, the check utterly fails to represent everything we know about how a successful 5- and 6-year-old reader should be operating. It also utterly fails to detect a failing 5- and 6-year-old reader, because to be able to pronounce isolated, phonically regular words, half of them non-existent, is no guarantee of being able to read in the sense of being able to understand meaningful print.

Key Stage 2

Until summer 2015, pupils at the end of Year 6 took externally set, externally marked tests in reading and in grammar, punctuation and spelling. They were assessed internally in writing and in speaking and listening. Writing was moderated in the same way as at Key Stage 1; the minimum percentage of schools in a local authority a selection of whose teacher assessments were moderated was 25 per cent. As at Key Stage 1, pupils' achievements in the spoken language were not externally moderated.

The texts on which pupils' powers of comprehension were tested in the two reading tests (one test for pupils likely to gain levels 3, 4 or 5 and one for pupils who might gain level 6) were carefully chosen and interesting. However, the tests focused on far too narrow a range of the competences which pupils at Year 6 should be bringing to bear on texts. A description of the desirable range of these competences appears in the Key Stage 2 section of the proposals for reading in the alternative curriculum in Chapter 11.

Similarly, the level of demand which the two Year 6 grammar, punctuation and spelling tests (as with reading, one for pupils likely to gain levels 3, 4 or 5 and one for pupils who might gain level 6) made on pupils at Year 6 was not unreasonable.

The fundamental objection to the grammar, punctuation and spelling tests, however, was and is (see the next sub-section) that the splitting-up of the holistic and interconnected activities which constitute writing has implicitly sent a malign message to pupils and teachers. To require Year 6 pupils to attend in Papers 1 and 2 at the lower level and in Papers 2 and 3 at the upper level to isolated sentences in which they can have had no great interest, which bore no relation to the real work in literacy which they were (or should have been) doing, sent exactly the wrong signal. The signal was, in effect, 'The books you have been reading and the writing you have been doing are all well and good. But this is something else. This is grammar, punctuation and spelling'. Meanwhile, higher-attaining pupils were told, in effect, that spelling does not matter when it comes to an important, externally marked piece of extended writing (their Paper 1).

There was a significant symbolism in the fact that both sets of tests were set and marked externally, while writing was assessed internally by the pupils' teachers. With regard to the activity of writing understood as a whole, teachers were not trusted to see and judge manner (grammar, punctuation, spelling) as well as matter (content). Manner is clearly what counts to those in charge, so it needed to be externally controlled. There was probably also an economic calculation: while it was possible to mark these tests quickly, since many of the questions had right or wrong answers, it was not possible to do so when pieces of writing had to be judged as wholes.

The government's plans from summer 2016

That was the past. Unfortunately, the government's requirements for testing at Key Stages 1 and 2 from summer 2016 are no improvement on the past, and in some respects make matters worse.

Key Stage 1

Beginning in summer 2016, there are compulsory tests for Year 2 pupils in reading and optional tests in grammar, punctuation and spelling. These tests are externally set, but marked by teachers in school. (An absurdity, in passing: the 2016 Year 2 grammar, punctuation and spelling test had to be abandoned, because it had already appeared online as a practice paper. The Standards and Testing Agency seems to have been responsible for the blunder.)

Writing is assessed by teachers on the basis of pupils' work throughout the year.

Teachers' marking of the tests of reading and of grammar, punctuation and spelling, and their assessments of pupils' writing, are moderated by local authorities. At least 25 per cent of schools in a local authority are moderated each year.

The Year 1 phonics check continues.

On 3 November 2015, the then Secretary of State for Education gave a speech entitled 'One Nation Education' at the Policy Exchange think tank in London. Amongst other proposals, she announced a further review of assessment at the end of Key Stage 1, with the possibility that, after consultation, the arrangements in place for summer 2016 might be replaced by tests which, in addition to being externally set, would also be externally marked (as has happened from summer 2016 at Key Stage 2 – see below). Her precise words were:

> to be really confident that students are progressing well through primary school, we will be looking at the assessment of pupils at age seven to make sure it is as robust and rigorous as it needs to be.
>
> We'll be working with headteachers in the coming months on how we get this right, holding schools to account and giving them full credit for the progress they achieve.
>
> (Department for Education, 2015c)

It remains to be seen whether, if Key Stage 1 does go the way of Key Stage 2, the tests will still be of reading and of grammar, spelling and punctuation, or will be organised differently.

Key Stage 2

Beginning in summer 2016, Year 6 pupils continue to take tests in reading and in grammar, spelling and punctuation. These new tests will have only one version each, but will include questions designed to test higher-achieving pupils. The tests will be externally set and marked. Writing – understood as being somehow separate from grammar, punctuation and spelling – continues to be internally assessed, with moderation at 25 per cent.

Reading and writing dismembered

This is not the place for a detailed critique of the individual questions and tasks in the four tests, and of the assumptions behind them. The important thing to note is that the objections I registered to the Key Stage 2 tests in use up to summer 2015 remain at this Key Stage, and have been extended to Key Stage 1 (in the latter case adding to the incoherence already in existence in the assessment of reading brought about by the Year 1 phonics check).

The grammar, punctuation and spelling tests divorce those three aspects of language from the contexts in which they should be considered: actual, whole, authentic pieces of writing, read or written. And there is no justification – only, perhaps, an argument to do with cost – for the continuing decision to test reading externally but to allow teacher assessment for writing.

Assessment of speaking and listening abandoned

The assessment of speaking and listening at both Key Stages, even in the unmoderated form which applied until 2015, has been abandoned completely.

The end of levels

National Curriculum levels have been abolished with the introduction of the new National Curriculum. Beginning in summer 2016, government and schools use another measurement system, known as scaled scores. In September 2015, the Commission on Assessment without Levels, which the government had set up, issued its final report. The report offers this rationale for the removal of levels:

> *Despite being intended only for use in statutory national assessments, too frequently levels also came to be used for in-school assessment between key stages in order to monitor whether pupils were on track to achieve expected*

levels at the end of key stages. This distorted the purpose of in-school assessment, particularly day-to-day formative assessment. The Commission believes that this has had a profoundly negative impact on teaching.

Too often levels became viewed as thresholds and teaching became focused on getting pupils across the next threshold instead of ensuring they were secure in the knowledge and understanding defined in the programmes of study. Depth and breadth of understanding were sometimes sacrificed in favour of pace. Levels also used a 'best fit' model, which meant that a pupil could have serious gaps in their knowledge and understanding, but still be placed within the level. This meant it wasn't always clear exactly which areas of the curriculum the child was secure in and where the gaps were.

(Department for Education, 2015a: 5)

The report makes clear and useful distinctions between in-school formative assessment, in-school summative assessment and nationally standardised summative assessment. It emphasises the essential link between curriculum, pedagogy and assessment in terms very similar to those with which I began this chapter. It advises schools to be wary about purchasing one of the commercial assessment systems being promoted to them in the post-levels world:

Schools should . . . ensure that any system that they buy into fully meets the needs of their school curriculum and assessment policy. It is very important that these systems do not reinvent levels, or inappropriately jump to summary descriptions of pupils' attainments. Nor should they overburden teachers with recording duties or data management.

(*ibid.*: 32)

The government responded to the commission's report, agreeing with all its recommendations. It supports the commission's view that in-school assessment (both formative and summative) should be left to schools:

It is right that the Commission has not prescribed a specific model for in-school assessment. We believe that schools are best placed to determine what type of system will work for them. They have detailed knowledge of their pupils and the expertise to apply it. We encourage schools to make the most of the freedoms offered by the removal of levels and to use the Commission's advice to think carefully about the kind of system that would best meet the needs of their pupils, curriculum and staff when developing or reviewing their approach.

(Standards and Testing Agency, 2015b: 4)

I welcome the freedom being offered to schools with regard to their own assessment systems. In fact, that freedom was always there, theoretically. There was never any obligation on schools to use levels except for end-of-Key-Stage tests and teacher assessments. It was just that levels crept more and more into assessments – and into pedagogy – throughout Key Stages 1 and 2.

An effective and manageable approach to in-school assessment

Continuous formative assessment throughout the years of schooling is more important than brief summations at the ends of Key Stages, necessary as these are, because good formative assessment actually affects future progress, rather than merely offering a snapshot of a moment in that progress.

The commission's report gives the following as examples of day-to-day in-school formative assessment:

- *question and answer during class;*
- *marking of pupils' work;*
- *observational assessment;*
- *regular short re-cap quizzes; and*
- *scanning work for pupil attainment and development.*

(Department for Education, 2015a: 18)

The report offers the following as the primary purposes of day-to-day in-school formative assessment:

For pupils:

In-school formative assessment helps pupils to measure their knowledge and understanding against learning objectives and wider outcomes and to identify where they need to target their efforts to improve.

For parents:

When effectively communicated by teachers, in-school formative assessments provide parents with a broad picture of where their children's strengths and weaknesses lie and what they need to do to improve. This reinforces the partnership between parents and schools in supporting children's education.

For teachers:

In-school formative assessment should be an integral part of teaching and learning. It allows teachers to understand pupil performance on a continuing basis. It enables teachers to identify when pupils are struggling, when they have consolidated learning and when they are ready to progress. In this way, it supports teachers to provide appropriate support or extension as necessary. It also enables teachers to evaluate their own teaching of particular topics or concepts and to plan future lessons accordingly.

For school leaders:

In-school formative assessment provides a level of assurance for school leaders. If school leaders are confident their staff are carrying out effective formative assessment, they can be assured that problems will be identified at the individual level and that every child will be appropriately supported to make progress and meet expectations.

For the Government:

The Commission believes that the Government should not intervene at the level of formative assessment, which should serve the needs of pupils and teachers.

For Ofsted:

Ofsted will want to be assured that teachers are making effective use of formative assessment to support teaching and learning. It forms part of Ofsted's wider judgements about the quality of teaching in schools.

(*ibid.*: 19)

I support this understanding of the types and purposes of day-to-day formative assessment. A straightforward approach to in-school summative assessment of pupils' talk, reading and writing would be for teachers to take each of the points in the relevant Key Stage in each of the sections of the alternative curriculum in Chapter 11. They could make a judgement at regular intervals (termly, perhaps; half-termly at the most frequent), involving a few brief notes on the particular achievements or shortcomings of each learner within each point. How much progress, if any, has he or she made on the point in question since the last assessment occasion? What are the most likely means of extending that progress further?

One of the benefits of a good assessment system is that it feeds back into the curriculum. A system of the kind proposed here is both summative and formative. It suggests to the teacher the kind of help the pupil needs next. It also sometimes reminds the teacher that there has not been enough activity within a particular aspect of the curriculum to enable a meaningful assessment to be made, and that this shortcoming needs to be rectified.

Scaled scores to replace levels

Levels will be replaced by scaled scores. The government's guidance on scaled scores describes them thus:

> Scaled scores are used all over the world. They help test results to be reported consistently from one year to the next. We design national curriculum tests to be as similar as possible year on year, but slight differences in difficulty will occur between years. Scaled scores maintain their meaning over time so that two pupils achieving the same scaled score on two different tests will have demonstrated the same attainment. For example, on our scale 100 will always represent the 'national standard'. However, due to the small differences in difficulty between tests, the 'raw score' (i.e. the total number of correct responses) that equates to 100 might be different (though similar) each year . . .
>
> A pupil's scaled score will be based on their raw score. The raw score is the total number of marks a pupil receives in a test, based on the number of questions they answered correctly. The pupil's raw score will be translated into a scaled score using a conversion table. A pupil who achieves the national standard will have demonstrated sufficient knowledge in the areas assessed by the tests. This will mean that they are well placed to succeed in the next phase of their education.
>
> (Standards and Testing Agency, 2015e)

The guidance elsewhere refers to a performance descriptor for each of the tests, intended to demonstrate whether or not a pupil has achieved the national standard. Performance descriptors appear in the Standards and Testing Agency's test framework documents. (The performance descriptor for the Key Stage 1 reading test, for example, appears in Standards and Testing Agency, 2015c; that for the Key Stage 2 grammar, punctuation and spelling test appears in Standards and Testing Agency 2015d.)

The government obviously expects that its new system of scaled scores, combined with performance descriptors, will achieve better degrees of reliability and comparability across schools and from year to year than were achieved by levels. So far as teachers, pupils and parents are concerned, however, the move to scaled scores will simply replace one set of numbers with another set of numbers. In a later paragraph in its guidance, the Standards and Testing Agency acknowledges that we are still in the game of reducing a complex profile of achievement to a simple number, albeit one which it believes will be more valid and more reliable:

> *The old national curriculum levels are not relevant to the new national cur-riculum. However, in order to provide schools with some indication of the new standards, we have tried to indicate equivalence in a broad sense. At KS1 the national standard will roughly equate to an old level 2b. At KS2 this will roughly equate to an old level 4b. Otherwise levels and scaled scores will not be comparable.*
>
> (Standards and Testing Agency, 2015e)

An alternative proposal for end-of-Key-Stage assessment at Years 2 and 6

My alternative proposal for end-of-Key-Stage assessment at Years 2 and 6 takes into account the objections I have offered to the structure and format both of the arrangements in existence until summer 2015 and of those which have taken effect from summer 2016.

Two tests at the end of each Key Stage

It is perfectly possible to test reading and writing, in all the aspects appropri-ate for a given age group, using tasks involving the reading and writing of an appropriate selection of authentic texts.

I envisage two tests for each of Years 2 and 6: one for reading and one for writing. The four tests would be externally set and internally assessed, with moderation. The tasks the tests contain would be included in large online banks of resources, updated regularly, from which teachers could choose.

The tests would represent the broad range of possibilities for pupils' com-prehension of and responses to texts (in reading) and their competence and control as producers of texts (in writing), as represented by the requirements for reading and writing at Key Stages 1 and 2 in the alternative curriculum in Chapter 11.

A reading test of this kind would assess pupils' overall understanding of and response to the meaning and structure of three texts in different genres, as well as their recognition of words, their understanding of grammatical concepts and terminology, their grasp of conventions of punctuation, their apprehension of spelling patterns and families.

Similarly, a writing test requiring pupils to write three pieces of continuous prose in different genres, with a suggested word limit for each, would assess the extent of a writer's competence, not just as a communicator of meaning and a handler of different genres, but as a user of the conventions of punctuation and spelling, and as a controller of the grammar of English.

No need for separate tests on grammar, punctuation, spelling and phonics

The separate tests of grammar, punctuation and spelling and the Year 1 phonics check could then be abolished. Reading would be seen as what it is: an activity in which the decoding of words and the comprehension of meanings are complementary, interactive aspects of the same, complex process. Writing would recover its wholeness too. Grammar, punctuation and spelling would be put back where they best belong: as integral parts of the construction of meaning in the written language by producers (in the writing tests) and by receivers (in the reading tests).

Performance descriptors linked to the alternative curriculum

I would have online performance descriptors of competence in reading and writing, as the government intends at present. My descriptors would be accompanied by examples. Their purpose would simply be to help teachers and moderators decide whether a pupil had *not yet achieved*, had *achieved* or had *exceeded* an expected standard in reading and writing at the end of Key Stages 1 and 2; so there would be two performance descriptors, accompanied by examples, for each test at each level, one for achieving and one for exceeding the expected standard. The descriptors would be linked to the requirements for reading and writing in the alternative curriculum in Chapter 11.

Value talk as highly as reading and writing

I would value pupils' achievements in the spoken language as of equal importance with those in reading and writing. Recognising the difficulty, however, of setting effective tests for talk externally, I would supply schools with online performance descriptors of competence in the spoken language, supported by audio-visual examples. As with the performance descriptors for reading and writing, there would be two for Year 2 and two for Year 6, demonstrating the characteristics which a pupil must show in order to achieve and to exceed the expected standard in the spoken language. The purpose of the descriptors, as with those for reading and writing, would be to help teachers and moderators decide whether a pupil had *not yet achieved*, had *achieved* or had *exceeded* an expected standard in the use of the spoken language. Assessment of spoken language would be internal, with moderation, like that of reading and writing, but on the basis of pupils' achievements over the whole of Year 2 or Year 6.

Moderation of 25 per cent of schools in a local authority is normally sufficient

In 2014, the government proposed to double from summer 2015 the percentage of infant schools in a local authority a selection of whose teacher assessments at Key Stage 1 was moderated:

> To help increase confidence and consistency in our moderation of infant schools, we will be increasing the proportion of schools where KS1 assessments are moderated externally. From summer 2015, half of all infant schools will have their KS1 assessments externally moderated.
>
> (Department for Education, 2014b)

The government later abandoned this proposal. The default position should be a percentage of 25 per cent of schools for all occasions of external moderation, unless there are particular reasons for more extensive scrutiny.

In the longer term: trust teachers more

At some point in the future, once teachers have become familiar with these arrangements, the government might feel secure in relying on teachers' professional judgements in making accurate assessments of their pupils' achievement in reading and writing at Years 2 and 6 without the compulsory use of externally set tasks. From that point on, the online banks of tasks would remain and be refreshed regularly, but it would be for schools and teachers to choose whether or not to use them. (The tasks might be helpful, for example, to newly qualified teachers teaching Year 2 or Year 6 pupils for the first time.) Whatever happens, local moderation will always be needed.

To conclude . . .

Early Years Foundation Stage

The Early Years Foundation Stage profile is, overall, an excellent document, demonstrating an enlightened understanding of learning and of the relationship between learning and assessment. It is a little spoiled by the government's obsession with phonics as the only effective means of teaching early reading and is perhaps over-complex. But it remains the only instrument teachers need in order to assess children's achievements in the Early Years Foundation Stage.

The new baseline assessment was always unnecessary and a waste of teachers' time. Its abandonment (at least for the time being) is welcome.

Key Stages 1 and 2

The government's arrangements for testing at the end of Key Stages 1 and 2 from 2016 are no improvement on those which operated until 2015, and in some respects are even less satisfactory.

The Year 1 phonics check has no valve as an instrument for detecting failing readers. It bears no relation to what we know about how successful readers operate. It should be abolished.

The ending of levels is in itself welcome. It may well be that scaled scores will be more accurate and reliable than levels have been. However, so far as schools, teachers, pupils and parents are concerned, one set of numbers will have replaced another set of numbers.

The re-emphasis on the importance of in-school assessment, formative and summative, in the *Final Report of the Commission on Assessment without Levels* and in the government's response to the report, is welcome. I have suggested an approach to in-school assessment which accords with the spirit of these two documents.

The testing of reading and writing should treat these two complex activities as wholes. At present, the testing arrangements dismember them. The tasks on which pupils are tested should be available in an online bank, updated regularly, from which teachers can choose.

The spoken language should be assessed with the same rigour as reading and writing, using teachers' moderated judgements of pupils' spoken language throughout Year 2 or Year 6.

The outcome of testing or teacher assessment should be a judgement as to whether a pupil *has not yet achieved*, *has achieved* or *has exceeded* an expected standard in reading, writing and the spoken language. Online performance descriptors, with examples, would help teachers to make judgements. It is the accumulation of these judgements across a cohort of pupils which will provide schools, parents, the local authority and Ofsted with the information as to how effective is a school's teaching of English.

References

The combined reference list for this book and its sister volume, *Curriculum and Assessment in English 11 to 19: A Better Plan*, is available online at www.routledge.com/9780415784528.

Index

'e' denotes pages from the online section of Chapter 2 of this text, downloadable at www.routledge.com/9780415784528